Praise for *The Human Edge Advantage*

"*The Human Edge Advantage* is a must-read for leaders navigating our complex and fast-changing world. It helps leaders to be self-aware and authentic and provides practical advice for building resilience and fostering a sense of belonging and collaboration."

—*Gary Passman,* *CHRO, NeoGenomics Laboratories*

"*The Human Edge Advantage* is a wonderful read that addresses head-on how leaders can balance humanity with organizational and technological change. A much-needed resource for modern executives and team members!"

—*Eric Sydell,* *CEO, Vero AI, and co-author of* Decoding Talent

"*The Human Edge Advantage* is for leaders to tap into their true selves, build resilience, and foster a sense of belonging. Lisa Danels transforms leadership with all facets of authenticity, power, trust, connectedness, and co-creation. It is a must-read compendium with brilliant examples and stories for leaders of all kinds."

—*Ekaterina Herzig,* *EVP North America Duty*
Free & Managing Director Canada

"A practical manual that every leader should read. Danels shows how to cultivate an authentic leadership style that brings out the best in themselves and their teams."

—*Fabrice Chouraqui,* *CEO-Partner, Flagship*
Pioneering, and CEO, Cellarity

"*The Human Edge Advantage* arrives at the right time when leaders need a roadmap to help them navigate a complex and fast-changing world. It gives practical tools and tips to engage teams and ensure everyone is all in. It is a must-read for anyone who realizes that building success requires strengthening self-responsibility and compassionately building team collaboration."

—*Peter De Meester,* *Global COO Health*
Nutrition & Care, DSM

"Achieve self-mastery with *The Human Edge Advantage*—a new guide for leaders everywhere to become more self-aware and authentic. With an extensive selection of exercises and life stories, it's a must-read in today's complex organizational world."

— ***Marina Udier***, *CEO, Nouscom*

"*The Human Edge Advantage: Mastering the Art of Being All In* is a comprehensive guidebook that provides invaluable insights and practical tools for anyone seeking to enhance their ability to connect, engage, lead, and create meaningful change in their personal and professional lives. Lisa Danels has masterfully woven together her perspectives and practice-based knowledge of psychology, leadership, and human connection. She offers a unique perspective on the art of connection and collaboration for enhanced creativity and innovation—things that are much-needed in the modern world. Throughout, Danels sets the stage for harmonizing one's cognitive, emotional, and intuitive faculties, unlocking the potential for greater self-awareness and resiliencies and guiding readers to discover their purpose, values, strengths, and weaknesses—thereby enhancing authentic presence and orientation. The book provides thoughtful exercises and practical tools to tap into one's inner resources, overcome inner obstacles, while skillfully mapping out the necessary transformative journey for modern, empowered leaders. I highly recommend this book to all practicing managers and leaders, as well as HR professionals and coaches."

— ***Professor Kurt April, PhD***, *FRSA, Allan Gray Chair,*
University of Cape Town, South Africa

THE HUMAN EDGE
ADVANTAGE

MASTERING THE ART OF BEING *ALL IN*

LISA DANELS

Foreword by David Epstein, CEO Seagen,
and former CEO of Novartis Pharmaceuticals

Published by Human Edge Insights

Produced by GMK Writing and Editing, Inc.
Managing Editor: Katie Benoit
Copyedited by Amy Paradysz
Proofread by Kelly Nutter Clody
Indexed by Phyllis Manner
Text design and composition by Libby Kingsbury
Cover design by Libby Kingsbury
Printed by IngramSpark

Print ISBN: 979-8-9883417-1-0
Ebook ISBN: 979-8-9883417-2-7

Visit Human Edge at: human-edge.com

To learn more about Human Edge's services and products, such as the Core Fusion Assessment, please turn to the last page of this book.

Do not accept half a solution
Do not believe half-truths
Do not dream half a dream...
You are a whole that exists to live a life
not half a life

—Khalil Gibran

Dedicated to all leaders who walk the path of courage
to know themselves, who are humble enough to share power,
and who co-create possibilities.

ACKNOWLEDGMENTS

This book has not been written by me alone as so many people have touched me along the way and shaped my thinking and way of being, most importantly, my late father, Solomon Danels, who taught me excellence and taking risks; my mother, Sheila Danels, who taught me to care for others; and my husband, Christian Neubert, who continually teaches me the power of partnership and love.

To my spiritual teachers: Don Miguel Ruiz, Wayne Dyer, Marianne Williamson, Shakti Gawain, Alan Cohen, Cheri Huber, Joseph Marc Cohen, Esther Hicks, Byron Katie, Eckart Tolle, Gabrielle Roth, Neal Donald Walsh, M. Scott Peck, MD, and Paulo Coelho, who taught me how to walk my spiritual path, be true to myself, remove all the barriers to love, and live my divine purpose: Thank you for having the courage to share your wisdom with the world.

In the early days of my career while studying for my master's program at New York University, I was introduced to the work of Lee G. Bolman and Terrence E. Deal, who wrote a leadership fable called *Leading with Soul.* This shaped my thinking, taught me to lead with heart, and planted the seeds for a new frontier of leadership development. They first introduced me to the power of integrating the whole self into everything I do.

Thank you to the former CEB (Corporate Executive Board) Corporate Leadership Council, who provided best practices research and benchmarks and first introduced the gold books back in the '90s that commenced my love for research in the human resources field.

This book has been a true co-creative process and could not have been possible without the partnership of my colleague Jo Tincey. She ignited my imagination, opened my mind to think in a new way, and helped craft key messages in the book. I will be forever grateful for her beneficial contributions and ability to tap into her intuition. She taught me the power of authentic connection and co-creation in all the work we do at Human

Edge. A heartfelt thanks to Sara Asady, who helped prepare the tables in the book and created a companion assessment tool, CORE™ Fusion, that brings the authentic connection model to life. A special thanks to Davide Cannata, who read the manuscript and checked all the research to make sure it was sound and correctly interpreted.

A very special thank you to Gary M. Krebs, who gave me the structure and courage to write my first book. He guided me along the way and enabled the words to come to life on each page. His years of publishing experience proved invaluable and made my dream of being an author come true. A special thanks to managing editor Katie Benoit and copyeditor Amy Paradysz for their insights and enabling the co-creation of this book.

I owe a great debt to our Human Edge team, who supported and encouraged me to write this book while carrying a full workload. Every day you inspire me and push me to be a better leader. I couldn't be prouder to be part of such an amazing team.

Finally, thank you to the many leaders, HR colleagues, and organizations that I've worked with throughout my career. My learnings from you throughout my journey have helped shaped my thinking. I feel blessed that I get to do what I love every day, which is to enable others to wake up and be their most authentic selves.

CONTENTS

BY DAVID EPSTEIN, CEO SEAGEN, AND FORMER CEO OF NOVARTIS PHARMACEUTICALS

In today's complicated and challenging work environments, leaders find themselves caught in a dilemma of unprecedented expectations. They are under enormous pressure to be transparent and open, demonstrate vulnerability, and encourage creativity while empathizing with the needs of their employees. This is already a formidable task, especially when you consider that they are also being tasked with focusing on critical thinking, relying upon data to make critical decisions, getting things done at a faster pace, and meeting a bar that is constantly being raised by competitors and shareholders.

How do leaders get everyone fully engaged to deliver results when they can't balance their own hearts and minds and the workforce feels that it has already reached its limit? A new way of thinking is required. Leaders must go beyond traditional goals that are disconnected from the *why* and *how* and establish a space for co-creation that inspires new possibilities for people of all generations and backgrounds.

The Human Edge Advantage: Mastering the Art of Being All In guides leaders through how to access and orchestrate the most treasured aspects of their head, heart, and gut to adapt to the seismic, overwhelming changes organizations face. This unique approach—when combined with an aspirational vision for a company's offerings—leverages the full potential of humans and serves as a journey to where *all in* is no longer about giving everything we have but discovering limitless possibility wherever we look.

You will be touched by Lisa Danels's holistic approach and thoughtful provocation. It will change the way you think about leadership and instill you with the courage to be your most authentic self.

THE LEADERSHIP PARADOX

You've likely chosen this book because you feel the impact of managing in the digital and high-tech age requires a different approach. You want to be able to lead in a more meaningful way and know how to better navigate through it. The outside pressure is mounting, and you are being challenged to do more with less. You recognize that what made you successful in the past just isn't going to work today.

The harder and faster we work, the more challenging it becomes to keep up with increasing workloads and have time to tend to our relationships. We're all feeling this, but we don't openly acknowledge it; instead, we hunker down, push harder, and repeat the mantra "I have so much to do" or "I am so stressed out."

If you feel like the world is picking up speed, you aren't imagining it. Scientific studies indicate that data and technology are changing so rapidly that our brains can't keep up with them. Professors Roger Bohn and James Short from the University of California have measured the amount of data that enters the brain and found that an average person living today processes as much as 74 GB of information per day—the equivalent of watching sixteen films—through television, computers, cell phones, tablets, and many other gadgets. This is increasing at a rate of 5 percent a year. When there is such a high volume of information to process, our brains go into overdrive, and we spread ourselves too thin. We move into a state of feeling overwhelmed, which leads to disconnection. The paradigm shift is that we must go from setting goals and being achievement-oriented to authenticity and establishing a space for co-creation that inspires new possibilities for people of all generations, backgrounds, and points of view. To enable this shift and bring everyone *all in*, leaders will need to understand and dive into the world of human-centered leadership and *connection*.

New Ways of Leading Are Emerging— Human Centered

The old way of leading people can best be described by the acronym POLICE, which stands for: *planning, organizing, leading, implementing, controlling, and evaluating*. In today's workplace, this methodology no longer makes sense. A new generation of workers has emerged, and they want and expect more. Empathy is the new currency. Workers believe they already have the skills to POLICE their own work. They look for organizational leaders to care, create meaning, and drive outcomes at the societal level: According to a 2020 Mercer Global Talent Trends Report, "Win with Empathy," "37 percent of workers are motivated by strong corporate values, mission, and purpose, while 36 percent favor companies that focus on social equity." Thriving employees are twice as likely to work for an organization that effectively balances emotional intelligence (EQ) and IQ in decision-making—something fewer than half of companies typically get right.

These findings indicate the necessity of developing a new type of leader: one who uses empathy as a key ingredient and views interactive processes and co-creation as the new employee experience. According to Gartner, *human-centered leadership*, as it is known, is comprised of three key areas:

1. *Authentic:* act with purpose and enable true-self-expression, for themselves and their teams.
2. *Empathetic:* show genuine care, respect, and concern for employees' well-being.
3. *Adaptive:* enable flexibility and support that fit team members' unique needs.

Connection Is Everywhere We Look (When We Look)

We cannot access this new type of human-centered leadership without the capacity for connection. Our world economy and society are now interconnected by supply chains, communications technology, world events, and travel. We only need to look at the rapid and global impact of the COVID-19 pandemic for evidence of our interconnection. We're all part of a natural and social web of life that supports and sustains us, and we depend on it in ways we may not be aware of until we can no longer access them.

Outwardly, human connection is the one we seek the most; indeed, research shows that, when we experience disconnection from others, we also feel pain and loss. Professor Matthew Lieberman from UCLA's Department of Psychology and Biobehavioral Sciences uncovers the neuroscience of human connection and the broad implications for how we live our lives. His data suggest that when we describe emotional pain as physical pain—such as "she broke my heart" or "he hurt my feelings"—this is more than just metaphor; the experience and cost of disconnection is profound and palpable. I believe that the disconnection at work cuts deeper and causes even greater pain, as it impacts your team, yourself, and the world around you.

Quantum mechanics describes a universe that is made up of space, containing fields of energetic vibration that are all interconnected. The internet was born from the merging of computer networks and now links up the whole world. Connections are everywhere we look—subatomic particles, the gut microbiome, and social network theory. We find that, when we map, understand, and strengthen the connections that exist within and around us, we can sustain and regenerate our resources with greater efficiency, discover fresh insight, and devise new solutions. This allows us— and our teams—to be fully present and *all in.*

Many leaders experience the impact of this connection and interconnection every time they answer complex questions and find themselves replying with the age-old adage, "It depends…" Let's look at an example. Sam works in supply chain at a food ingredient company that requires many different active components to create the proper mixture for customers. The company is already behind on customer delivery schedules, so the pressure is mounting. As if that isn't enough, the boat containing the key ingredients is blocked by a cargo vessel that is stuck sideways in the Suez Canal.

The customer service department asks the supply group, "So, when will we get our ingredients?"

Sam's response? "It depends...on when the obstructed vessel is removed and then on how many vessels they will let through once the canal is reopened, and also on whether we can get a shipping port, since they're going to be in great demand once everything opens up..."

Everything depends on everything else. Because everything is connected. The challenge is that leaders often struggle to navigate this interconnection in a way that secures the impact they're looking for. They find themselves stuck, faced with seemingly impossible choices and struggling to prioritize: "I can't do X without impacting Y." Instead of leveraging the connections that exist within and around them, leaders are often trapped in the paradigm of *either/or*.

We Can Rise above Polarity

The language we use in the world of work reflects this either/or paradigm and the many polarities that we see and experience within it:

- work/life
- remote/in-person
- risk/reward
- ideation/execution
- tasks/relationships
- strengths/weaknesses

When making decisions, we bounce between extremes: *Do we follow our head or heart? Focus on quantitative or qualitative data? Plow through the To Do list, or take the time to listen and build relationships? Slow down and reflect, or jump in and act?* The struggle to choose between seemingly opposing forces creates an experience of separation and anxiety. It shifts our focus to division and separation, forcing us to play a zero-sum game. That age-old experience of being caught between a rock and a hard place—such as the earlier example involving Sam—illustrates the fact that, when we're torn between two extremes, either choice tends to leave us feeling unfulfilled. For instance, many leaders who we work with at Human Edge believe that prioritization is impossible because it requires an impossible choice: *How can we say "No" to the projects or initiatives that will bring the business forward?* This is a challenging situation because they are looking through the lens of polarization.

Operating in this context often leads us to defend the choices we make; in an either/or world, we are either right or wrong. We rise and fall by our judgment, so we may resort to justifying and maintaining the side we're on, dismissing and criticizing others who have different points of view. We become entrenched and isolated, causing us to get stuck in our behavior patterns and limiting our ability to collaborate effectively, grow, and change.

Alternatively, we start to doubt ourselves and fear we've made the wrong choice, are on the wrong side, are failing, and don't have what it takes. We may hide away, make ourselves smaller, stay silent, and hope nobody will notice, or else we charge in and overpower others to prove we add some value to the world. Our anxiety and frustration cause myopia, as we lose our awareness of the space between these extremes and fail to step into a place of connection where *all is possible*. We've grown accustomed to living in a fragmented, binary, polarized, and disconnected world that is draining our energy and diluting our collective power.

It has been said by great sages including Eckhart Tolle that how we see the world is not how it really is but as a reflection of ourselves and our level of consciousness. So, what if we saw and accessed greater connection—to ourselves, each other, and our daily experience? Imagine what would happen to our teams, our organizations, our culture, and our world, if leaders were able to:

1. Step beyond the paradigm of either/or and access something new, better, and more profound.
2. Strengthen and leverage connections that exist around us to fill our emotional tanks and restore balance.

Can you imagine the unlimited potential?

As Aristotle observed—and Google later researched in their eponymous study into high-performing teams—*the whole is greater than the sum of its parts*. Google proved through analytics that employees achieve much more working together than alone. *The Human Edge Advantage* explores this concept on an even deeper level, elucidating how *interconnectedness* can help guide you and your organization into a new realm of exciting possibilities.

We All Need Connection

From the early days of human experience, connections have given us more than independence ever could. During prehistoric days, living as part of a community gave early humans safety, shared resources, support, and inter-action—and today is no different. Even as the world is changing, we still have a deep-seated need for connection.

Behind closed doors, our clients openly share what they are feeling when it comes to connection. The following is a common sentiment among leaders:

> *While things are slowly supposed to be getting back to normal after the COVID-19 pandemic, I'm still in the position of never having met one-third of my team. We're a distributed workforce, and we'll never again be in a position where everybody is working from the office. Hybrid and remote are now the prevailing working patterns for most of my people. I'll be honest, I hate it. I long for the days where you could connect informally—when my interactions were not just about the subject matter for the meeting of the moment, where you could bounce ideas with somebody on the way to the coffee machine. People get more done when they work in the same place. I really feel that, but I can't say it. I know it won't achieve anything to force people back to the way things were. Many of my team appreciate the time they gain by not needing to commute—time they can spend with their families. I want to feel like we're supporting people to work in the way that fits their needs...but, on a personal level, I can't help feeling I've lost something.*

In an eighty-year-long study on happiness, the Harvard Study of Adult Development partnered with Harvard Medical School and Massachusetts General Hospital to answer a simple question: *What makes life fulfilling and meaningful?* The answer: *relationships.* The stronger our relationships, the more likely we are to live happier, healthier, and more satisfying lives. In fact, the study reveals that the strength of our connections with others can predict our physical and brain health as we move through stages of life. Conversely, when we experience disconnection, we feel alone, experience increased levels of anxiety, and miss out on all the richness that our world has to offer.

Navigating the Paradigm Shift

Navigating the shift from either/or to a place of co-creation and possibility demands a new kind of leadership, one that can fully leverage the power and possibility of connection. Drawing on Human Edge's research and my experiences working with a multitude of leaders, we'll explore in these pages the behaviors that facilitate connection and the assumptions that hold us back. Our aim is to awaken you to the connections that are available to you in each moment, providing you the awareness and behavioral insights you need to master the art of being *all in*, all the time.

One of the hard truths of leadership is that it doesn't matter what is on your website, in your employee handbook, or in the company's vision statement. It's how others experience you that determines your effectiveness as a leader. This is shaped by what you think, feel, and do. Everything surrounding your thoughts, feelings, statements, and actions is contagious and spreads throughout the organization—whether by intent or not. Remember what we've already established: *Everything is interconnected.*

I learned this hard lesson years ago as a first-time leader at Chase Manhattan Bank. A woman on my team named Sibel oversaw training the staff to encode checks so they could be processed. I assessed that when Sibel entered the turnstiles each day, she left her passion at the gate.

At the time, I didn't have the experience to know what to do. Like most new managers, I spent my time thinking about Sibel's underperformance and what she could do to improve it, rather than what I might do to tackle Sibel's apparent disconnection and lack of engagement. We missed the fact that the two were connected. When it came time for Sibel's performance appraisal, I needed to provide feedback that her performance wasn't up to par. After I presented the negative message, Sibel looked me directly in the eye and said, "You wanted to get rid of me from the moment we met."

The truth of her words was like a punch in my stomach: I couldn't refute Sibel's words. I came to the realization that how we feel about a person gets transmitted and received, whether we verbalize it or not.

As you read this book, we hope that you will also have such an epiphany as you shift away from either/or choices. Instead, you will learn how to balance thinking, feeling, and being to access that place of all in.

We Have a Dream: Organizations That Are *All In*

As professed in the subtitle, our main goal in writing this book is to provide a holistic framework based on data and research that will enable leaders like you to address the paradigm shift and get everyone in your organization *all in*. In practical terms, what do those two words really mean?

Let's begin this exploration by first clarifying what we *do not* mean by the expression *all in*. We aren't referring to bringing people to a place of overwhelm and exhaustion, demanding so much of people (including ourselves) that they are forced to give without any boundaries or limits. If anything, *all in* refers to the state of being connected at an emotional, cognitive, and intuitive level. This connection can happen at three levels:

ALL IN = **CONNECTING TO SELF** Explore and integrate every aspect of oneself to achieve self-mastery, drive personal agency, and unlock potential. **+** **CONNECTING TO OTHERS** Establish meaningful connections with others and engage them to create a sense of belonging. **+** **CO-CREATE POSSIBILITIES** Hold space for others to contribute, generate and capture insight, and activate everyone's genius.

This achieves a desirable result—strength, fortitude, energy, etc.—with an endgame of achieving a whole that is much greater than the sum of its parts. This opens the door to the infinite possibilities we'll explore throughout this book. Our unique approach leverages the full potential of humans and serves as a journey to where *all in* is no longer about giving everything we have but discovering limitless possibility wherever we look.

How This Book Is Organized

We've organized this book into four parts that work together to create an overall map and guidebook for accessing and leveraging greater connections.

In Part I, we start with the innermost circle, "Integrating Head, Heart, and Gut." Here we will provide you with tools and techniques that support you as you leverage these gateways for connection that we all have within us. You will understand how to open your mind (your power to think), your heart (your power to feel), and your gut (your power of intuition), so that you can integrate and balance these vital aspects and bring strength, insight, and inspiration to yourself and others. We'll strengthen your capacity to simultaneously think, feel, and intuitively understand, so that you can use your experiences as a source of energy rather than as a drain on your reserves.

In Part II, "Cultivating Personal Power," we'll hone your awareness of all that you are, so that you can leverage your full self from moment to moment: in your experiences, interactions, decision-making, and understanding. We'll support you as you deepen your sense of purpose, values, strengths, and energy and channel these with the right balance of confidence and humility, so that others may access and benefit from these unique aspects of your leadership. We'll also explore our innermost fears and identify the masks we wear or our unresolved coping mechanisms stemming from childhood. Our goal is not to guide you back toward the past but instead to help you face your fears in the present moment.

Once you have developed a greater sense of the power within your leadership, you're ready for Part III, "Connecting to Others," where we support you to deepen and expand your relationships, so that your leadership becomes a powerful interaction with the team and a force that enables others to feel empowered. We'll support you to unlock the power of true collaboration and the diversity of perspective, experience, and insight that exists all around you. We'll distinguish among three commonly confused modes of relating to others: empathy, sympathy, and compassion. Additionally, we'll help you unlock the power of selfless collaboration and the diversity of perspective, experience, and insight that exists around you.

When you go *all in* and lead with your heart, others are invited and inspired to do the same, and true co-creation becomes possible. In Part IV, "Co-Creating Possibilities," we'll look at the different facets of co-creation and how to use your connections to the moment to spark insight, innovation, transformation, and new possibilities.

A Few Perks Along the Way

Sprinkled throughout this book, you'll find case studies and vignettes that introduce challenges, after which we'll propose solutions. Some of these examples are fictionalized or in the public domain; others are inspired by our work with clients from around the world. Out of respect for the privacy and integrity of these organizations and their staff, we have changed some names and basic details.

We also want this book to be a practical guidebook for you to use and apply to your own leadership experiences and challenges. With this in mind, we are providing the following digestible insights and tools to support you:

- *Leader Says/Colleague Hears* and *Colleague Says/Leader Hears:* These passages introduce each section of the book. We believe that most leaders have good intentions, wanting their workers to be *all in* without compelling them to work to the point of exhaustion. Similarly, we assert that most colleagues have similarly positive intentions, wanting to make a greater contribution to their organizations. However, sometimes our intent and impact as leaders are misaligned. Miscommunication and misunderstandings often occur because one party says something and the other hears something different. Our intention with these sections is to help explore some of the common blocks or barriers to the state of being *all in* that can operate below our level of awareness. By giving voice to these contrasting perceptions and perspectives, it becomes possible for each side to relate to the other and open the organization to a greater amount of heart energy.

- *Reflection* (callout boxes): Questions to ask yourself to help you dive even deeper.

- *Action Frameworks* (callout boxes): Specific follow-up tasks for you to perform.

- *Takeaways* (chapter endings): Summary statements on how to open your head, heart, and gut to unlock greater connection using the content in each chapter.

A Note about Human Edge

Human Edge has helped dozens of global organizations by taking executive teams on high-performance journeys. We develop leaders at all levels by leveraging experiential learning and assessing them through our integrated tools. Our work unlocks human potential so people and organizations can adapt and thrive; this is core to everything we believe and do. One by one, we seek to create a movement that will fuel transformational change with deeper insights and superior solutions to elevate individuals, teams, and leaders at every level. Our human-centric view puts you at the center of your leadership journey, cultivating greater self-awareness as a starting point for improved organizational performance and transformation.

You have the power to access and leverage connection in every aspect of your experience as a leader and ultimately transform your company into an agile, resilient, unstoppable organization where people are inspired to deliver their best work and co-create to take the business to new heights. If this sounds appealing, it's time for you to fully commit your time—along with your head, heart, and gut—and begin your journey.

Part I

INTEGRATING HEAD, HEART, AND GUT

Leader (Tamara) SAYS: Beth, I think it's time to give you a new challenge. You've been doing great work, and now it would be good for you to step up. I really want you to be the project lead for the new digital initiative. Not only will it add value to the company, it will elevate your profile.

Colleague (Beth) THINKS: I'm not sure I'm ready for this. I need time to gain more confidence in my current work. I feel like she's pushing me too much outside my comfort zone. She doesn't understand I don't want to get it wrong and look like a fool. I wish she'd just stop pushing. She talks about how it will elevate my career, but, in all honestly, I'm not as ambitious as she is.

■ ■ ■

Colleague (Beth) SAYS *(fiddling with her hands):* Hmm, Tamara, it seems like a great opportunity, but I have so much work already, and I'm just starting to get traction on the digital dashboard I created a few months ago. What about Sara? She seemed to be interested in taking on this assignment.

Leader (Tamara) THINKS: I see so much potential in Beth. Why is she so resistant to a greater level of responsibility? Every time I want to give her opportunities to help her develop, she resists at first—and I don't understand why.

Chapter One

IT TAKES COURAGE TO FULLY BE OURSELVES

What do we mean by *courage*? Is it one's ability to face fear or step into the unknown? Or to act even when you know it will cause discomfort to yourself and/or others? Perhaps more importantly, where does courage come from and what does it bring to leadership?

Over the years, while working with hundreds of leaders in developing their authentic self, I would conduct an experiment in which I would ask people to *point to themselves*. When I looked around the room, all the leaders pointed to their hearts without any direction or influence. When asked why, they would say something like, "The heart is the center of who we are."

It's no wonder, therefore, that the root word of courage is *cor*, the Latin word for *heart*. Brené Brown, author of the bestsellers *The Gifts of Imperfection* and *Dare to Lead*, discovered that one of the earliest forms or meanings of courage is "to speak one's mind by telling all one's heart." If you want to have courage, it requires you to walk through life with an open heart, so you can be accessible to yourselves, your family, your co-workers, and the people you lead.

Courage has been evoked as an essential component of character among effective business leaders. Out of the University of Istanbul, Asım Şen, Kamil Erkan Kabak, and Gözde Yangınlar found that courageous leaders are brave, and they have heart, spirit, and exceptional intellectual and emotional capacity to make drastic changes. Courageous leaders take risks to face and deal with difficult problems to move the organizations and nations forward instead of minimizing or ignoring them. They are creative so that they can make an objective analysis and select the most effective strategies. Today, leaders are expected to demonstrate this trait amidst challenging circumstances. This trait serves as the foundation for other favorable attributes to build upon in leaders. Most of our clients have added this principle to their leadership framework. However, many leaders bypass courage and take the path of least resistance, not wishing to risk their illustrious careers by stepping out, making bold moves, and potentially losing everything. It's safer and easier to toe the line and follow the rules and expectations. Of course, there are exceptions to this, such as Alan Mulally, who was brought in to Ford to turn things around. In 2006, Ford Motor company anticipated a loss of $17 billion with their declining product quality and lackluster design. Mulally needed to reshape the culture, reengage the employees, and lead the company to profitable growth. One of most important keys to his success was transforming the culture from leaders ignoring the blaring truth and downplaying situations to becoming truthsayers and honestly reporting on the state of the business and then actively addressing the issues. Five years after joining Ford, Mulally returned the company to profitable growth with $20 billion in profit, Ford's second-best year ever.

We must ask ourselves: *What stops us from being courageous?* Some sort of stop gap in the brain triggers warning signs and pushes us toward what is known and safe. We rarely talk about it openly, but *fear* is often the number one undercurrent driving us at work. In our pressurized climate, we are almost always afraid of *something*—real, imagined, or with exaggerated personal impact or consequences. Workers at every level are secretly uncomfortable nearing the edge, pushing themselves to unleash their potential. These are just a few of the things people worry might go awry at one time or another on an individual or more expansive level within the organization…

Blame for an error, whether it's their fault or not

Missing a deadline

Not meeting revenue goals

Competition winning out

Disagreement with a manager over a simple misunderstanding

A statement made at a meeting (or an email sent) that they later regret

Whispers of a possible department restructuring

Rumors that the company is up for sale

Not being good enough

A fear of being kicked out of the tribe (social isolation)

Loss of status

Financial dependence to support your family

Gossip about looming company layoffs

This emotional undercurrent of fear is driven by our primal fear of not being accepted, not feeling worthy, and not feeling safe. When we allow anxiety to rule, it becomes about limitation and restriction. We tend to focus our attention on what we *can't* do or what barriers are in our way, rather than directing our energy and focus on the things we wish to create. In essence, fear shuts us down and makes us feel small, whereas hope expands us into new possibilities. We spend too much time consciously or unconsciously worried about what we will lose as opposed to what we might gain. A good present-day example of this is how workers are fretting more and more over work-life balance. *Fast Company* reports that 49 percent of full-time employees and 42 percent of part-timers feel at least "somewhat anxious" about being forced to choose the demands of their careers above those of their personal lives. We find ourselves in a world of duality in which we must make uncompromising choices that lead to high levels of anxiety, separation, and disconnection.

With the stakes in our modern workplace so high, it's no wonder that fear-induced stress is one aspect of our emotional makeup that is suppressing desirable positive feelings, such as courageousness, confidence, curiosity, interest, hope, and awe. Shouldn't work be a place of meaning, fulfillment, accomplishment, and connectivity, rather than a source of never-ending stress?

Do We Need to Be So Stressed Out?

Fear plays a vital role as a protective mechanism for all life forms. Even though the frontal lobe of our brains has evolved for complex thinking and problem-solving, we still find ourselves reacting and scanning our environments and looking for potential danger. It has been ingrained in human DNA dating back to when we were cave people and needed the *fight or flight* response—the instinct to decide whether we should head into battle to attack the threat or run for cover—to protect us from harm, notably being devoured by predators. This mechanism also came in handy to warn a society of impending danger arising from a rival community of humans.

There are two additional, less discussed fear responses: *freeze* and *fawn*. *Freeze*—also referred to as *duck and hide*—is what causes a person to feel stuck in place; it occurs when your body doesn't think it can respond with fight or flight. *Fawn* is when your body responds to stress by trying to please someone to avoid conflict.

 REFLECTION

From the list below, check off what causes you to feel the most fear in the workplace.

- Giving bad news to your leader
- Conducting a performance review with a direct report who is failing to meet company expectations
- Making a high-stakes corporate decision
- Facing certain changes in the company
- Taking a company in a new direction

Next, take ten minutes to reflect by asking yourself: What are you most afraid of? And what could you be protecting?

Close your eyes and picture your worst fear coming true, allowing yourself to feel the sensations in your body. Then picture the opposite: What would success in this area look like? Notice how the feelings change in your body. Keep going back and forth to the extremes until the fear no longer grips you.

Leaders: Do we need primal responses to fear in our present-day *business* environments?

In most instances, the answer is *No*. The four primal mechanisms exercised at work not only cause rash decision-making, they also create profound stress and anxiety that often go unresolved and may cause ailments ranging from chronic issues (such as migraines and neck and back pain) to digestive problems (such as gastritis) to heart conditions (such as high blood pressure and risk of heart attack) to depression.

Fear grips the workplace in yet another detrimental way. People who are fearful stay in their comfort zones, protect what they have, and avoid change and risk at all costs. That means that when fear pervades a company's culture, innovation suffers.

Fear Leads to Disconnection

Fear is such a powerful force that its undercurrent can be felt in the deep recesses of our minds. It shows up when we least expect it through our avoidance or reactive nature in everyday life and work experiences. It leads to disconnection on three levels:

Level 1: Disconnection from our feelings and intuition
Level 2: Disconnection from our dreams and imagination
Level 3: Disconnection from others and society at large

Along the way, we've somehow lost the connection to ourselves. There seems to be a chronic issue pervading society in which we go through the motions or *functioning* rather than having the courage to live our best lives. We cut ourselves off from our emotions and intuition because we don't want to face our truth. If we listen to our inner guidance, it will require us to make significant changes and disrupt our lives. We buy into what society expects, and we bury our inner callings and dreams. Many of us are dying while we are awake with our dreams unfulfilled. It reminds me of having ripe fruit hanging from a tree that will never be picked and enjoyed.

There is another downside to so much fear-induced stress flooding the workplace, one that isn't nearly as measurable in terms of productivity or financial cost. In the Introduction, I mentioned that feeling overwhelmed by data and technology leads to disconnection. The stress inflicted on workers by the daily grind also causes them to feel as if they are inhaling their own fumes from working so hard at breakneck speed 24/7—given the full-time access to email and company systems—without any let-up, end in sight, or even an acknowledgment that their breaking point is not far away.

The rift has widened since the start of COVID-19 lockdowns and continues through today. With so many people working remotely, it's not unusual for managers and direct reports to have never met face to face. The same may be said for teammates, interdepartmental colleagues, clients, vendors, buyers, and customers (purchasers and end users/consumers). It's not so easy to accurately "read the room" during a Zoom meeting and especially challenging for individuals to interpret body language and facial expressions. Without proximity to one another, we've become suspicious, mistrustful, and fearful because we don't know each other as well as if we were sitting across from each other at a conference room table. When issues and/or conflicts arise, how do we identify ways to work better together when we hardly know each other? It's difficult to open up to others and be vulnerable when we haven't broken bread together and eased into our relationships.

The disconnects among various individuals are clear-cut, but underneath resides the impact they have on the individual psyche. Working apart from one another through various technology, we feel personally disconnected from people and greater society. Does a worker feel that they truly have a *sense of belonging* to an organization, a department, and a team? Does a leader even feel she *has* a team when everyone is so spread out?

Distance is only part of the challenge and, of course, there are distributed teams where connection thrives. The overarching issue is how we get to a place in which we are willing to open our hearts to each other and truly care about our colleagues and the business—regardless of how geographically close or distant we are.

With such a prevalent sense of disconnect and fear running through organizations, it often feels like a fool's errand to even attempt to bring everyone *all in* on the company's vision, purpose, and mission. This is precisely where leadership courage plays such a crucial role in connecting the dots and unifying a business.

REFLECTION

Ask yourself these three questions:

1. Which levels of disconnection are you experiencing?
2. How are you listening to your emotions and inner guidance?
3. What dreams have you put on hold that you would like to bring to fruition?

Courage Requires a Leap of Faith

Courage is an essential ingredient for being an exceptional leader and moral courage plays a key role in long-term decision-making anchored to personal values. This attribute has been directly linked to being an *authentic leader*: one with the ability to display hopefulness, optimism, and resiliency while demonstrating high moral character. But being courageous doesn't come easy. We often close ourselves off from the world to keep ourselves safe. We self-censor for numerous reasons, but a major one is that we long to be part of the tribe and don't want to risk being kicked out. We tend to withdraw from relationships because we don't want to be the only one to take the leap and be completely open and vulnerable. In our boldest moments in life, we allow our dreams to symbolize all the things we could do and could become. When our dreams begin to fade into the background, our inner fear emerges, and we become distracted by our everyday work and personal responsibilities. A leader's ability to reveal their true nature ends up hidden in the shadows. It's only those who take that bold step during pivotal moments who experience deep personal and professional transformation.

Certain films have a way of leaving a lasting impression on our psyches. One that comes to mind is *Indiana Jones and the Last Crusade*. In his quest, Indiana Jones sees the prize—the Holy Grail—in sight. He walks out of the cave to find himself staring into the abyss of a giant chasm. If he moves forward, it will mean instant death. He opens his father's notebook, where he finds a clue: "Only in a leap from the lion's head, shall he prove his worth." Realizing he must make a leap of faith to achieve his quest, he puts his hand over his heart and apprehensively steps forward—even though it might mean falling to his death. His courage is rewarded when he finds himself standing on an invisible bridge. The same circumstance is true in business; sometimes we must make that courageous decision without a guarantee of success.

French psychoanalyst and philosopher Anne Dufourmantelle argues that risk is an inherent part of living fully in the world. Avoiding risk, she argues, is not living at all. Courage is as much about living, despite knowing that you might look like a fool or fail at any moment. Dufourmantelle wrote: "To me, risking your life is not dying yet, it's integrating that you could be dying in your own life. Being completely alive is a task, it's not at all a given thing. It's not just about being present to the world, it's being present to yourself, reaching an intensity that is in itself a way of being reborn." If we want to live fully, we must summon the courage to explore ourselves.

Leaps of Courage

There is a saying by Socrates that encapsulates the idea that it requires courage to be ourselves: "The unexamined life is not worth living." To enter this self-exploration, we must take a few leaps of faith…

Leap 1: Let go of judgment and accept.
Leap 2: Confront your shadow side.
Leap 3: Take off your masks.
Leap 4: Pursue what really matters.
Leap 5: Dare to be uncomfortable.
Leap 6: Dare to care.

Leap 1: Let Go of Judgment and Accept

One of the most difficult things in life is to fully accept ourselves—our strengths as well as our flaws. We are taught to put our best foot forward and show the world "how good we are." Behind the veneer lurks a self-deprecating shadow that fills you with negative self-talk. A disparity forms between our internal and external world, leaving us in a place of imbalance. Our psyches decide that the only way to even the scales is by judging others. When we are unable to see or admit certain things to ourselves, we end up criticizing other people for these shortcomings, which leaves us with deeper feelings of unworthiness and disconnection.

At one time or another, we've all felt that we were judged unfairly; when this occurs, the pain cuts deep. Judgment will not dissipate until we face our shadow self. To make this shift, we must come to the realization that we can only judge another person when we're in our own head. Try being in a place of compassion while attempting to judge someone else; it just doesn't work. Having an open heart is the key to letting go of judgment and accepting.

You might be asking yourself: *How do I avoid using judgment?* Most company performance management systems today are built on the notion of judging and comparing. These systems make employees feel devalued, requiring leaders to reengage direct reports after each performance cycle, which can often be uncomfortable for both the manager and direct report.

I propose that we weigh options and solutions instead of drilling people on their shortcomings. This means remembering that what somebody does and what they achieve don't completely define a person. Similarly, what they're capable of doing and delivering today isn't all they will ever be able to accomplish. I've heard far too many times employees saying something along the lines of "I feel like I've been put in a box and there is no way out." When we let go of judgment, we give ourselves and others the possibility to become something more. Below are a few tips to managing judgment in your mind:

- Notice when you judge others. Turn it around and ask yourself, *How does this relate to where I dislike or reject myself?*

- If you do find yourself in a state of judgment, take a few deep breaths and move your energy from your head to your heart.

- When you catch yourself judging someone, see if you can find a positive attribute that you like and appreciate about them.

Leap 2: Confront Your Shadow Side

I've observed from my many years of working with leaders that they are under the delusion that others can't see their shadow side. The reality is they're swimming in a fish tank; we can see their every move, their strengths and where they need to grow. Oddly, many leaders believe that if they focus on the bright side of their personality the rest will be hidden from view. To dare to be our authentic self, we must embrace *all* of who we are. This is not easy, however, as we aren't trained to work with our shadow side or masks. It requires going deep into our fears and childhood patterns, which can be painful or daunting. No one wants to admit to behavior that may negatively impact others or limits reaching their deepest desires. Eva Chen, CEO of Trend Micro, stated in *Fast Company*, "I realized that I'd need to face my fear head-on, literally and symbolically, if I wanted to become the best version of myself."

We wear our masks to protect ourselves, but, at the same time, we are unintentionally hiding our essence and disguising ourselves. We occasionally get too attached to the fake image we are portraying. We use our masks as a badge of honor: "I never let anything bother me" or "being focused only on work has kept me at the top of my game." When we put on emotional masks, we prevent ourselves from having true connections. It's as if we're placing an impenetrable wall around our heart that keeps us from accessing our innermost thoughts and feelings while limiting our work and life experiences. Most importantly, it keeps us separate from our true self and acts as a shield protecting us from opening to the world. Our mask can lead to:

- Rejection of self
- Impaired relationships with others
- Fear of the future

Our masks don't always have to be permanent fixtures that block our most authentic self. They tend to show up more when we are under stress and revert to our childhood coping mechanisms, which we will explore more in Chapter Seven.

Leap 3: Take Off Your Masks

We tend to protect the small child inside ourselves—and our unmet needs—far too long. If we want to unlock the full potential of our teams and ourselves, we need to serve as role models, demonstrating vulnerability and revealing the imperfect humans that we are. When our childhood needs of safety, love, and feeling wanted are not fully met, we create coping mechanisms to deal with our fear and anxiety. This leads to a system of beliefs and programming that enables us to face up to our daily challenges. In some cases, our experiences help shape and guide us on the right path and build strong emotional intelligence. In other instances, however, we bury our true emotions—such as lingering pain from past events—and find ourselves exhibiting reactive behavior that impacts our performance and limits our potential. We wear masks to hide our underlying raw emotions and feelings of inadequacy and cover up areas we think will make us seem anything less than perfect.

Removing our masks can be scary. I remember one of the many times I arrived at the painful realization that I was wearing a mask—that of "pride" or being the "know-it-all." I relished the thought of being well-read and the smartest person in the room. This was not the truth, however. I was concealing a harsh memory from childhood when people told me—in words and otherwise—that I was stupid. My first-grade teacher once told my mother I would "never amount to anything." When I couldn't find my assignments, she would dump out my desk in the middle of the classroom with twenty-nine pairs of eyes staring at me. I can still recall the heaviness of my head and the shame I felt scrambling to find my paper. It wasn't until fifth grade that another teacher, Mr. Schellhorn, saw something intelligent in me that I didn't recognize in myself. Years later, I found I'm able to heal and improve myself by revisiting these experiences. It's painful, but it allows me to be fully present in the moment with others.

The secular leap of faith you, as a leader, must make is to summon the courage to remove your mask and trust your inner self, to face the reality of your most unfulfilled primal needs not being met and explore them with a sense of compassion to further grow your self-awareness. The greatest challenge is internal; you must bravely lower your guard and allow yourself to be seen as vulnerable. By doing so, you open the world to a full set of your capabilities—heart, mind, and gut (intuition)—that will help you reach a higher level of resonance or coherence that is the clarity of thought, speech, and emotional composure. It's only when we cultivate our self-awareness that we can become ready to take off our masks.

Leap 4: Pursue What Really Matters

We must dare to pursue the things that matter to us, even if they don't feel rational and the world seems to be holding us back. It requires strength and courage to step into our personal power and move beyond societal and family programming. When we do so, we can author our own lives to create and shape our life experience.

An example that comes to mind is the story of actor Ke Huy Quan. As a child, he starred in such films as *Indiana Jones and the Temple of Doom* (1984) and *The Goonies* (1985). By early 2000, acting roles were few and far between, and he shifted to working behind the scenes. When he reached the age of fifty, he had a nagging feeling to give acting another try. He made some inquiries, but industry people discouraged him, saying it's almost impossible to break in at his age. His wife encouraged him to go for it anyway, and he sought out an agent. His efforts paid off when he was cast in the film *Everything Everywhere All at Once*. Not only did Quan make a triumphant comeback, he won the Academy Award for Best Supporting Actor in 2023.

Acting truly matters to Ke Huy Quan—so much, in fact, that he never gave up, despite the currents pushing against him. What things matter to you? What obstacles are holding you back from achieving your dream?

Leap 5: Dare to Be Uncomfortable

Ginni Rometty worked her way up the corporate ladder and became the first female chief executive officer of IBM in 2012. "Growth and comfort do not coexist," she says.

What does it mean to really be uncomfortable? It involves stepping up and taking on the greatest level of challenge possible. It could also refer to failing, although I prefer the word *experimenting*. The skill required here is how we can use these experiences to help with our transformations when we do miss the mark.

When we grow and extend ourselves into the unknown, we move out of our depth and out of our comfort zone. An ideal professional goal would be to continue to grow, learn, and expand our comfort zone to build greater capability and ensure that we remain employable.

In my experience, a good rule of thumb is to stay 80 percent in your comfort zone and 20 percent in your stretch zone. If you want to grow and develop, you must be willing to feel uncomfortable while you move from "unconsciously incompetent" to "unconsciously competent." If we want to accelerate our learning, we need to cultivate a growth mindset.

Several decades ago, Dr. Carol Dweck, a renowned Stanford psychologist and author of *Mindset: The New Psychology of Success*, developed a theory that fundamentally changed our understanding of human mindset. Having observed that some young students naturally rebounded from setbacks whereas others gave up right away, she drew the conclusion that there are three types of mindsets: *fixed* (negative and unchangeable); *growth* (positive and resilient); and *mixed* (a combination of the first two). Our brains have innate tendencies to reside in one of these areas to some extent, but family dynamics and how we are treated when we are young also play a central role in our mindset. If, for example, our parents are highly critical of us and attack our every mistake when we are young, it's likely—though not definitive or permanent—we'll get stuck in a fixed mindset. On the opposite end of the spectrum, an encouraging household that lavishes praise and support on us would more commonly result in a growth mindset. In both cases, the unknown factor of brain chemistry can tilt the circumstances the other way—if it's strong enough.

Fixed, mixed, and growth mindsets are present and visible in the workplace every day at every level. By the same token, we've all also witnessed people who have remarkable growth mindsets and believe they can accomplish virtually anything—even after having experienced repeated failures.

Which mindset would you rather have? Which mindset would you prefer among your team members? Obviously, the ideal is for everyone to tilt toward *growth mindset* while also being grounded and realistic when it comes to decision-making and expectations. The wonderful news is that Dr. Dweck's research bears out the fact that the human brain is remarkably malleable and adaptive, enabled with enormous potential to improve mindset. Her techniques for fostering outstanding achievement have been effective for managers, as well as parents, teachers, and athletes. As Dr. Dweck writes in *Mindset*: "In a growth mindset, people believe that their most basic abilities can be developed through dedication and hard work—brains and talent are just the starting point. This view creates a love of learning and a resilience that is essential for great accomplishment."

Leap 6: Dare to Care

In most companies, while collaboration is a sought-after principle, leaders struggle to describe what they mean by it and how to create the conditions that make it possible. It's rare for companies to adequately explain what they mean by collaboration, which leaves people confused and frustrated. Some employees and leaders may have a blind spot in this area, not realizing they are approaching their relationships in a different way (such as only one person's needs being met) or from a transactional perspective (meaning, they are focused on getting the task done or their own needs met). These relationships are hollow and foster little personal connection or trust. The opposite of these blind spots—*mutuality* and opening yourself up to your co-workers—are required for true collaboration and caring. You must make your emotional self and resources available to those with whom you interact. To make this shift away from transactional behaviors, consider these shifts:

- Professionally distant to true caring
- Self-interest to mutual interest
- What you get to what you give
- Stay in touch to keep informed
- Understand the process to the person in the process
- Judge the results to evaluate the relationship
- Win conflict to resolving it
- Agreement to acceptance
- Evaluate the results to how the other person feels about the results

To truly have courage, we must *dare to be ourselves*. When we take a leap of courage, we step beyond the limitations that fear presents. Courage isn't the absence of fear; it is choosing to leap *despite* the fear. As the Wizard of Oz explains to the Lion at the end of his journey to the Emerald City: "There is no living thing that is not afraid when it faces danger. The true courage is in facing danger when you are afraid, and that kind of courage you have in plenty."

Courage is a strength that exists within us all, there to be found and recognized. In fact, we can use doubt, fear, uncertainty, and challenge as opportunities to access the courage deep inside of us, accessing the inspirational energy that can drive us to leap forward and gives others permission to do the same.

TAKEAWAYS

- Fear is often the undercurrent that limits our potential.
- Recognizing and facing our fears is the key to being authentic.
- Disconnection is a major factor hindering an organization's ability to bring everyone all in on the company vision, purpose, and mission.
- To become a great leader who is connected to yourself and your team, recognize that you will need to take several leaps of faith.

Chapter Two

HEAD

The human intellect seems to have no boundaries when it comes to ingenuity and achievement. We can split an atom, travel to outer space, construct skyscrapers towering high in the sky, build microchips the size of a quarter containing ten trillion bits of data, develop vaccines that save innumerable lives, and globally produce 760 million tons of grain each year to feed massive populations.

The human brain is a sophisticated and remarkable machine, capable of originating and managing complex thoughts and directing actions that turn ideas into reality. Unlike a machine, however, the brain is an organ and part of a living, breathing human entity; it processes intangible emotions as much as it does tangible data and it perceives, learns, grows, channels, and adapts. No matter how much technology evolves to the point of mimicking human thoughts, responses, sounds, and even appearances, a machine will be a product of human invention—such as a supercomputer—that can never truly replace the sophistication and integration of what our own supercomputer can do. At the same time, we are on the brink with the rise of artificial intelligence (AI) that is evolving at a rapid rate to mimic many of these simple brain processes. In many cases, AI can "think" faster and more accurately than a human brain, but, currently, there is a gap in the nuances, discernment, and depth of thought that may be achieved by technology.

How the Head Works for Us

The mind is our reality builder, serving as the playground of thoughts that shape how we live and operate. It offers us a multitude of choices that determine our life experiences and help us know and understand ourselves better while deepening our sense of self. The mind is also always in the process of opening or closing experiences: *Will I go live in a foreign country or stay put in my home country? Will I play basketball or choose swimming instead? Will I take the next big role or stay where I am with what I currently enjoy doing?*

The head has the capability of sifting through, storing, and applying data on a grand scale. The collected unconscious and conscious mind processes eleven million bits of information every second. Our ability to think helps us determine reality and drives complex problem-solving and decision-making unlike any other organism on Earth because we constantly seek data and facts and have intense curiosity about the world around us and the unknown.

The brain enables us to give structure to our dreams and allows us to activate our unique purpose in the world. A good example of this is an invention known as the Lomi Composter, developed and sold by Pela Earth. While on vacation in Hawaii, company founder Jeremy Lang witnessed the damage that plastic refuse was doing to our oceans. His firsthand experience led him to dedicate his life to creating alternative environmentally safe materials for use in everyday products. The result of his company's efforts was the Lomi Composter, a machine that sits on your countertop and turns food waste into plant food in less than four hours, reducing greenhouse gas emissions. It became the number one crowdsourced environmental product of 2021.

Once the mind helps successfully model, produce, and test a product, we then develop operational excellence to support and improve it. We establish processes and systems to help the business operate and scale with continuously better accuracy, speed, and resulting functionality.

We Are Not Our Thoughts

Our minds are constantly chattering to us, from the moment we wake up to the instant we fall asleep. All this noise gives us the illusion that "we are our minds." This is far from the truth. Instead, the mind is an empty container in which we produce our thoughts and identify the thoughts that will receive our attention and focus.

When unmanaged, our minds tend to become fixated on what flickers through the screen of life. For most of us, the mind is using us, rather than the other way around. Imagine, for example, a blind man being assisted on the street by a seeing-eye dog. Since the dog is the one helping the blind man avert a potentially dangerous misstep, one might think the animal oversees the relationship. This is obviously not true; the blind man always remains in charge and dictates where he'd like them to go.

However, when properly directed, the mind can serve as one of our greatest tools to help us bring into reality the deeper expression of who we are. With a focused mind, we can create clear goals, habits, and actions that bring our full potential to life. Instead of our thoughts arising from our fears or misguided or outdated belief systems, we can channel them and create our own realities, putting us back into the driver seat of life.

Deconstruction of the Head's Five Functions

To understand how the mind works and how to leverage its full power, we must first break down its five functions, two of which are *subconscious* (existing in the mind but residing in such a hidden place that we are unaware of it) and three of which are *conscious* (being aware and having the ability to perceive things that are internal and/or external). The opposite of *conscious* is *unconscious*—which refers to a state in which the mind is unable to be aware. In this situation—such as with a person who has passed out—the conscious mind might not be functioning, but the subconscious mind could be quite active.

1. *Simulation (subconscious)*: This is where the mental constructs or paradigms of our life are created. The mind has the power to create mental images, and this shapes our reality in real time. If I were to ask you to picture a blue house, your mind immediately

FIVE FUNCTIONS OF THE HEAD

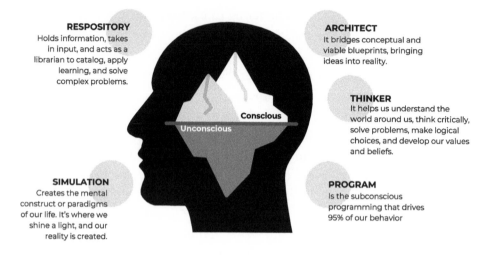

RESPOSITORY
Holds information, takes in input, and acts as a librarian to catalog, apply learning, and solve complex problems.

ARCHITECT
It bridges conceptual and viable blueprints, bringing ideas into reality.

THINKER
It helps us understand the world around us, think critically, solve problems, make logical choices, and develop our values and beliefs.

SIMULATION
Creates the mental construct or paradigms of our life. It's where we shine a light, and our reality is created.

PROGRAM
Is the subconscious programming that drives 95% of our behavior

Conscious

Unconscious

begins to construct a visual image. The more detail ascribed to it, the more real it becomes. This is significant because the brain doesn't know what is true or false; it receives the input it is provided and then creates. Roman Emperor Marcus Aurelius wrote: "A man's life is what his thoughts make of it." This greatly changes our perspective, as our world is not happening to us; we are simultaneously creating it together. If we want to have more creative agency, we must pay attention to what we think about and where we focus our attention. Two individuals might experience the same event yet interpret it in completely different ways based on their own mental constructs. For example, one person receiving constructive feedback from her manager might view it as positive guidance on how to grow and develop; another person might interpret the same comments as criticism and take it personally, shutting down and continuing to make the same misstep.

2. *Program (subconscious)*: We hold certain beliefs, or programs, and most of them form from when we are in the womb to about seven years of age. All these—such as what we think of ourselves

and consider to be acceptable versus unacceptable social behavior—are absorbed beneath the surface. Such programming may be good or bad, depending on the inputs and how our brains are wired. When we hear things often enough, we believe them to be true and find it challenging to move beyond them and step into a new space. Beliefs, combined with life experiences, generate the stories of our lives that we often repeat to such an extent that we become stuck. Limited beliefs, such as "I am stupid" or "I will never amount to anything," make us feel powerless. We accept that we will never be able to learn certain things (i.e., a new language) or fulfill our dreams, which then become self-fulfilling prophecies. By contrast, empowering beliefs—such as "I can find solutions to even the most difficult challenges"—foster confidence in our abilities and open new possibilities.

3. *Active Thinker (conscious)*: This represents the active notion of thinking, which consists of four types of skills: convergent or analytical thinking; divergent thinking; critical thinking; and creative thinking. We need all four of these skills to understand the world around us, determine what we will accept as fact, problem-solve, and develop new ideas.

4. *Architect (conscious)*: Most companies have a robust process for strategy development, but 50–90 percent of those strategies fail due to weak strategy implementation. In many cases, there is a gap between vision, strategy, and implementation. The secret to addressing this problem is leveraging the architect's function, which is a set process that serves as a bridge converting general concepts into viable blueprints. The architect turns ideas into reality and abstract thinking into tangible contextual points.

5. *Repository (conscious)*: Warren Buffett is not only a billionaire investor but also a top influencer in the financial community. He attributes his success to spending five to six hours a day reading—including at least a half dozen different newspapers—which

informs his decision-making. The repository function of the brain makes a significant difference in the level of success you can achieve. Like a librarian, it houses information and then catalogs it, so it may be found and applied when needed. Our ability to solve complex problems is reliant upon new information processed by our minds. Our midbrain contains a location known as the substantia nigra/ventral segmental area (SN/VTA), which serves as something of a "novelty center" of the brain. When it is stimulated by fresh data, experiences, and emotions, dopamine—the neurotransmitter that sends signals to and from our nervous system and is responsible for registering pleasure in the brain—triggers improved learning, long-term memory, innovative thinking, and renewed creativity.

We will return to these five functions later in this chapter, where we will use them to counter the detrimental aspects of the negativity that lurks in the deeper recesses of our mind and learn to get our mind to work for us.

The Dark Side of the Mind

Depending on the source, scientists believe that human beings have between 50,000 and 80,000 thoughts per day. To say we have lot of negativities rolling around in our heads would be a gross understatement: 80 percent of our thoughts are negative, and 95 percent are repetitive.

By contrast, professional athletes—especially the crème de la crème—have only 30,000 thoughts per day. In their case, thinking less achieves a lot more. Athletes require intense concentration and focus, so more thoughts would hinder their performance. In the split-second it takes a hitter in baseball to decide whether to swing or not, the slightest distraction in a wandering mind can cause a miss. The same is true for a soccer player deciding whether to pass the ball or kick it toward the net. For this reason, such legendary athletes as Michael Jordan, Katie Ledecky, Wayne Gretzky, Gabby Douglas, Novak Djokovic, and Tiger Woods have all used hypnotherapy and visualization techniques to develop mental prowess and gain an edge over their opponents.

With little brain training, we are naturally wired to think negatively and worry about what can go wrong rather than what can go right. In the lower center of our brains is an almond-shaped area known as the amygdala, which regulates emotions and interprets memories. It's in this region that the "fight or flight" survival mechanism originates. The amygdala's signals are primordial and powerful; they had to be, given their importance when early humans were in survival mode every moment of the day. Moreover, the human brain has an affinity for the familiar and is generally resistant to change. New ideas that are contrary to our previous understanding can seem threatening to us, triggering an amygdala hijack that usually results in the knee-jerk reaction of shooting them down.

Our amygdala is programmed to keep us safe, which means it seeks out what is familiar and known and raises alarm bells when this status quo is threatened. At these points, it may resort to dragging up past encounters—incidents in which we were humiliated, let down, or failed in some way—as a protection mechanism. The amygdala encodes the painful emotions associated with those events, gearing up to produce a distress flare of emotion whenever our current circumstances evoke a memory of one of the experiences. When this occurs, the cave brain—as Daniel Goleman, author of *Emotional Intelligence*, refers to it—takes over and causes us to react too emotionally and block knowledge we need in the moment.

Hijacking the amygdala with negativity can work both ways in professional environments: direct report to leader and leader to direct report.

For a direct-report-to-leader example, let's suppose Darren is a junior-level engineer who has an idea that he believes can streamline the company's production process, saving time and money. He presents the concept to his manager, Angelica, who has twenty years of experience with the company. After Darren explaining his concept, he asks, "Well, what do you think?" Angelica sits back in her chair and replies, "Great idea, Darren, but we tried it eight years ago and it failed. Besides, any change needs to go through the executive team and then undergo a rigid kaizen process. It would be a waste of your time to even try." Angelica rejects Darren's suggestion because something similar failed in the past. She doesn't consider the possibility that circumstances might have changed since then or that Darren might have devised a more effective way of enacting the changes.

As you'll discover later in this chapter, there is some good news: Negative wiring is reversible. The ability to control your thoughts can be learned. To quote Norman Vincent Peale, author of the classic *The Power of Positive Thinking*: "Change your thoughts and you can change the world."

The Head Can Only Take So Much Before Going Haywire

The same organ that instills us with so many wondrous powers has also been known to steer us off course, especially when it becomes overtaxed, fixed in our way of thinking, misused, or misinformed. Despite all its remarkable abilities to create, the human brain is equally as adept at destruction, having been responsible for air pollution, the deaths of somewhere between 150 million to one billion people in warfare, and continuing societal injustices against one another for their race, religion, political affiliation, and other categories that make each group special and unique.

We also tend to *overuse* our minds by stressing out and causing exhaustion, which can lead to poor decision-making and wreak havoc on the body. Overthinking impacts our ability to get a good night's sleep. Our cardiovascular, nervous, and muscular systems pay a steep price, with migraines, back and neck pain, and stomach ailments.

Overthinking also gets in our way by precipitating second-guessing and throwing us into self-doubt; we search for the logical "right answer" rather than generating the spark of insight that will move us forward. Nobody can deny the power of logic and reasoning. But, when unchecked, our logical brain can also fall prey to assumptions, default reasoning, and some of the nuances, possibilities, and connections that exist beyond reality. Thinking too much—especially unconsciously—yanks us out of the current moment, distracting us from subtle messages, cues, and warnings that could be beneficial if they were given enough head space to flourish. In business situations, for example, we can miss the connection of more holistic thinking that leads to improved problem-solving and communication.

Our educational systems and decision-making in business is tilted toward being left-brained and sequential, both of which have their place—but also major limits. Left-brain dominance can be equally as dangerous for leaders when working with people who think and react to situations more logically than emotionally and can miss opportunities to deal with sensitive human issues. If you're among those leaders who prefer logic, you've probably been surprised or caught off guard by others' emotional reactions in the workplace. When trying to influence others, you can probably recall yourself saying, "It's a no brainer, just look at the data" or "Come on, just get on board"—only to find your great recommendations falling by the wayside because your team's needs weren't met or even considered.

While most people commonly believe that decision-making is logical, research findings prove otherwise. Portuguese American neuroscientist Antonio Damasio discovered that patients who had suffered damage to the emotional side of their brains couldn't make even the simplest of decisions, such as what to eat. This explains why logical arguments in business negotiations tend not to work; the individuals on the other side of the table are far more likely to be convinced by something that appeals to their emotional needs and wants.

When you make your next decision, consider the following:

1. Ask: *How can I appeal both to my audience's logical and emotional needs? What question do they want answered?*

2. Ask more open-ended questions that activate the right-side of the brain (e.g., *What's another way of solving this problem?*).

3. When feeling stressed or overtaxed, determine if it's essential to make the decision that moment or if there is a benefit to taking a step back, allowing different aspects of your brain to support you.

The Myth of Multitasking

If you believe multitasking is your best friend, think again. You may seem to be accomplishing more in total, but you are coming up short in terms of performing each task to its fullest potential.

Dr. Sandra Bond Chapman, author of *Make Your Brain Smarter*, asserts that multitasking is "the bane of our society," as it taxes the brain, strains our relationships, increases stress, and causes illness. If that isn't enough, it isn't even an effective way to get things done.

When you juggle too many things, your brain isn't communicating at full capacity because so many ideas are flying around in your frontal lobe that they are conflating and confusing details. We also miss or misunderstand much of what is reported to us from other people because our attention is being diverted to performing other tasks, while our minds are probably ruminating on the next half dozen things we must accomplish.

ACTION FRAMEWORK

Leaders, pay attention: When you are meeting with someone—anyone, that is, including a direct report and especially a client—turn off your phone, text, email, and social media notifications. Resist all temptation to check your screen and don't attempt to do "other work" when your primary work should be listening and conversing. Don't just pretend to be engaged.

Imagine, for a moment, a direct report (Sally) is meeting individually with her manager (Amara). During the session, Sally expresses her frustration with a client who is being difficult and treating her disrespectfully. While Sally speaks, her manager's eyes are everywhere except on Sally. Amara's phone buzzes from a phone notification. She flips over the device, reads the message, and sighs with exasperation as she flips it back over. Her phone rings a moment later; she picks it up as she instantly recognizes the caller. "I'm sorry," she tells Sally, "This is super-important." She spins her chair around and initiates a private phone conversation for five minutes while Sally wipes her moistened eyes and blows her nose into a tissue. When Amara returns, she apologizes for having to take the call and says, "Now where were we?" Feeling hurt, Sally quickly says, "Forget it, I'll make it happen—is there anything else we need to cover?" before rising and leaving. Amara is obviously a busy leader who prides herself on her ability to multitask—but at what price? As she splits the screen in her mind by answering a phone call, she misses Sally's insight on the customer and potential blocks to sales, as well as an opportunity to coach her on how to better handle a difficult situation. What are the chances that Sally will bring this subject up again with Amara? Can you identify a time when you weren't fully present when one of your direct reports needed you?

The Cluttered Brain

If you suffer from lack of focus and mental fatigue, it doesn't necessarily mean you have attention deficit disorder (ADD) or a similar challenge. In fact, 50 percent of the population admits to struggling with focus issues. This shouldn't be surprising, given the deluge of information coming at us each day via texts, emails, the internet, and social media. We are bombarded by distractions and notifications. If we want to have control of our thinking, we need to take control of our environment, rather than letting it control us. On average, professionals check their email fifteen times per day or every thirty-seven minutes. Most leaders I work with complain that they are stuck in meetings from 8:00 a.m. to 6:00 p.m. with little time for biological or mental breaks. When we arrive at our next meeting together, we are still processing the last one. Sometimes we find ourselves in the midst of scheduling conflicts when we are double—and perhaps triple—booked. If we want to be successful leaders and have a somewhat balanced life, we need to start asking ourselves: *How do I manage the conditions for my success? How can I take back control over my time?* When coaching leaders, I ask them how much time they need to clear their emails and respond to everything on their desks. The answer is usually two hours. When we present this "gift" of an extra two hours to ourselves, we find that we can fully be present with others. Otherwise, while we are sitting in meetings or one-on-one with our direct reports, our minds are wandering to all the critical things we need to address.

David Allen, an organizational guru and author of *Getting Things Done*, asserts that each one of us can only handle a certain amount of chaos or floating things in our minds at one time, which he refers to as "open loops." If we want to master our minds, we must understand our limit for managing chaos and close more loops. Chapter Six, which is dedicated to mental mastery, will demonstrate how to take control and become masters of our mental domains.

Amidst all the thoughts stirring in our minds, we are processing and responding to external stimuli. The questions we must ask ourselves: *Are we even aware of what we think about? Do we know how much time we are wasting on unproductive, distracting thoughts? How much more could we accomplish without them?*

Eckhardt Tolle wrote: "Knowing yourself is to be rooted in Being, instead of rooted in your mind." While I don't seek to diminish the importance of the mind for all the reasons detailed in this chapter, I find great wisdom in Tolle's words, as far too many of us are "stuck in our own heads." We don't invite enough room for the heart, which, as we'll discover in Chapter Three, is the true gateway, or channel, to defining who we really are.

TAKEAWAYS

- Contrary to commonly held beliefs, we are not our minds, and we are not our thoughts.
- The five functions of the mind are: *simulation, program, active thinker, architect, and repository.*
- Despite all our intelligence, skills, and talents, humans are wired to think negatively.
- In our current era, our minds tend to be overused and distracted, which causes us to miss intuitive opportunities and invaluable connections.

Chapter Three

HEART

The heart is our entryway into existence, and our souls, the doorway to our humanity. It's the first organ to emerge when we are fetuses, materealizing even before the brain. For these reasons, there is no greater joy or excitement for a parent than seeing the miniscule pulsating miracle of life flapping on the ultrasound monitor screen for the first time.

The heart represents the bridge between the physical and the metaphysical. It gives us the capacity to feel and take in all facets of life experience in its wholeness. Think of a beautiful sunset; it has a physical quality but, when we take it in with our heart, it's magical and leaves us with a feeling of awe and completeness. The heart symbolizes the truest expression of who we are.

How many times have you heard the expression *What is in your heart?* We know full well that this isn't suggestive of romance but rather a feeling of connection to something greater than ourselves. Leaders often rely too heavily on their heads when running their organizations, at the expense of their and others' hearts. This extra current of power is what they've been lacking to take their organizations to the next level.

The Heart of the Matter

The heart has the potential to fill our lives with meaning and purpose. As the center of emotion in our bodies, it serves as a symbol for how we absorb and share the energy of our experiences. The heart connects us to our needs, desires, and values—as well as those of other people—producing a wide range of potential feelings. The more emotions our hearts experience, the greater the opportunity for our capacity to grow as human beings. If you seek to honor your heart and the hearts of others, you'll need to learn a new language of needs and feelings. According to Dr. Marshall Rosenberg, author of *Nonviolent Communication*, our needs typically fall into seven major categories:

- Connection
- Physical well-being
- Honesty
- Play
- Peace
- Autonomy
- Meaning

Our feelings manifest as an expression of met or unmet needs. In the Appendix, you will find a list of needs and feelings, courtesy of the Center for Nonviolent Communications.

While the energy produced by emotions can't be seen or held in your hand, it has properties that may be measured. As far back as a century and a half ago and using magnetic induction coils, scientists proved the existence of fields generated by the human heart. Since then, studies have concluded that the heart is the most robust source of electromagnetic energy of all organs in the human body, creating an energy field *sixty times* greater than that of the brain. This is how you can feel when someone entering a room is happy, frustrated, or angry.

Our emotions are generative, meaning that they create energy and have a kinetic force that may be either positive or negative. Dr. Paul Ekman and Dr. Eve Ekman have partnered with the Dalai Lama on their "Atlas of Emotions" project, based on a survey of 248 leading researchers and their consensus regarding five universal emotions: enjoyment, sadness, disgust, anger, and fear. If you visit their website, Atlasofemotion. org, you'll find that each of the five universal emotions have a least intense to most intense expression. For example, sadness starts at disappointment and goes to the most intense, which is anguish. Fear moves from trepidation to terror with anxiety somewhere in the middle. These facts alone are more than enough reason for you to pay close attention to the emotional energy your heart expends—and in what capacity. By the same token, you also have the power to nurture and inspire other people with your emotions.

Our feelings are part of how we "code" our experience; they influence the way we store and access memories in our brains. As you've no doubt gathered, our emotions are fluid and can change in a heartbeat, but traces of feelings can linger and surface at any time. The stronger the emotion in either extreme—positive or negative—the greater the impression on your memory. When you hear a song that you loved during your teen years, for example, you may be flooded with warm emotions that bring you back to that time in your life, if not a specific occurrence. We explored in the chapter on courage that the amygdala can hijack us with memories of painful experiences to place us somewhere else that is familiar and safe. Fully connecting to our hearts can help us process the pain of these past experiences so they're less likely to resurface. It can also enable us to access positive memories, along with their associated emotions as a source of energy, inspiration, and motivation.

Positive Emotions Require Intelligence

To truly connect, we must learn the language of the heart—something most of us aren't taught. This is problematic, because *emotional agility* is as essential to our education and development as learning how to walk, talk, problem-solve, and many other basic human skills necessary to succeed in society.

Dr. Susan David at Harvard University refers to agility as the ability to "be with your emotions with curiosity, compassion, and take the time to align and communicate with your values." When you face your real feelings and don't ignore the uncomfortable ones, you can detach from emotions to see your true options and use your core values to set goals that reflect the real you. This fills you with the power to be yourself and move into wholeness. It is only when you master this for yourself that you become able to open up to being your most authentic self and can then view others in their own truth. It is entirely possible to improve our emotional agility by intentionally building the vocabulary pertaining to the heart.

When we become more emotionally agile and available at work, we find ourselves more at ease and in greater alignment with who we are at the core level. We develop core values that guide us through life and become our North Star (which we will cover in greater detail in Chapter Four). When we stand by our core values and make wise life decisions, we become open to greater collaboration and communication with our colleagues. Recognizing and understanding our emotions and values gives us the capacity to express our emotional truth, which increases engagement, creativity, and innovation.

Jo, a coach and senior consultant at Human Edge, describes an example pertaining to her own working life. She began her career as an actor and, like many in this profession, had to find supplemental work between roles. Initially, she approached other forms of employment with a degree of frustration and disappointment resulting from not being in a rehearsal room with her fellow actors. Allowing herself to feel those emotions led her to see the deep value she has for creativity and connection, which she then applied to her non-acting jobs. In one temporary assignment, she made it a mission to understand the stories of the customers and sales reps she engaged with, as well as explore ways to make her day more creative. She introduced new rituals to bring colleagues and customers together. She realized that she loved attending trade shows and sharing information about the products in new and creative ways. Her new approach to this temporary role helped her find value in the position and, in turn, made her more valuable to the company. Her employer hired her on a more permanent basis, still allowing time for her to step out and accept acting roles when they came along. These experiences may have taken place more than two decades ago, but the core values of creativity and connection remained to help Jo navigate her working life. They give her work meaning.

When we recognize that we have the capacity to move through our feelings, we become connected to the underlying needs and values that drive them. It is only then that we can start to use our emotions with greater intention. Using our core values as a guidepost, we can proactively generate the feeling that aligns with them through our actions and behavior. For example, if one of our core values is creativity, we can define micro-actions that instill this experience in our daily lives. We might sketch our meeting notes instead of writing them; deconstruct and rebuild a process in a new way; or simply listen to music that gets our creative juices flowing.

ACTION FRAMEWORK

Take a moment to regard your emotional agility as a reflective process, meaning being an active observer of your feelings like watching them on a movie screen without emotional attachment. While you note them in your mind, write down your answers to the following: *How are these feelings connected to the seven core needs (connection, physical well-being, honesty, play, peace, autonomy, meaning)? How do they define your most cherished values? How do you express them at work? How do you communicate them to others to create connection?*

A Heart to Heart with Workplace Emotions

Here is the paradox summed up in one pointed question: *If the heart is who we are, then why are we conditioned to leave it behind at work?*

Over the years, we are hammered by our parents, teachers, coaches, managers, and colleagues to "control our emotions" at work. We are led to believe there are certain emotions that are acceptable in business and others that are taboo. Work is a "serious" place where emotions need to be checked or you'll be considered "unprofessional."

Does this mean we must cease being human the moment we log in at work? Isn't that a rather tall order, given our programming and how much emotional energy we produce? The emotions are always within us—what do you imagine happens when we bottle them all up? According to Totaljobs research, we express six emotions at work—joy, surprise, anger, sadness, disgust, and fear—and yet, Brené Brown, author of *Dare to Lead* and *Atlas of the Heart,* asserts that most people only identify three: happy, sad, and pissed off. The result of this repression is that we only notice something is wrong when lines are crossed and feelings are hurt. We end up putting out fires instead of building bridges.

It feels as if we are expected to "check our emotions at the door," but this simply isn't possible. We are complex human beings with deep feelings that can't be stored away like a file in the cloud. At the same time, we would never want to collectively create a culture in which the norm is to have outbursts of emotion at the smallest occurrence.

What, then, do I mean when we encourage inviting emotions into the workplace? I am referring to expressing our authentic, vulnerable selves in a way that allows us to connect with one another on a deeper level. Brown put it this way: "In order for connection to happen, we have to be seen, *really seen.*" Sometimes we bend too much with our need to be accepted, and it has the opposite effect.

Outside our conditioning and perceptions of what is considered "proper, acceptable" workplace behaviors, there are three additional reasons why people don't express emotions in professional settings:

1. *They are afraid they we will be exposed as failures and embarrassed.* Some leaders continue to believe the fallacy that they must "get it right" all the time and set an example for the organization. They believe any admittance of imperfection or *not knowing* will reflect badly on them and perhaps the organization; they are convinced the teams won't follow someone who is flawed. This is an absurd notion since *all* human beings have some kind of imperfection. When leaders hide their shortcomings, they are wearing masks that lead to mistrust. By letting their guards down and being vulnerable in front of others, leaders are sending a *positive* message to everyone that it's *safe* to admit a mistake and leave room to develop.

2. *Leaders fret they will be perceived as "weak."* If you are a soldier heading into battle or a professional boxer entering the ring, yes, vulnerability can be interpreted as a weakness. However, by

displaying this aspect of their personalities in a work environment, business leaders are demonstrating that it's "okay to be human." The upside is that they become more relatable and earn greater trust among the ranks. If a business leader admits, "I have some concerns we'll make our fourth quarter earnings," the team doesn't feel she has her head in the sand, pretending everything is rosy when it isn't. This goes a long way toward workers taking her seriously enough to work alongside her and solve the problem.

3. *They don't want to be the only ones to expose their emotions, which feels uncomfortable.* The only way to break the ice on this front is for leaders to be courageous and put themselves out there. It doesn't have to be an all-out dramatic scene; as a starting point, a simple moment of heartfelt public acknowledgment to a worker who overcame an obstacle would suffice. When the leader demonstrates that it's okay to express emotion, others will be more inclined and feel safe to follow the example.

Leaders: Have a Heart

Leaders must acknowledge and accept that emotions exist and play an important role in every workplace culture. Not only do they need to be comfortable with showing their vulnerability when appropriate and respond appropriately according to the situation, they must learn how to cope with feelings expressed by a diverse group of people. This is not an easy matter for any leader, as most people don't have training in psychology. Interacting with a person's complex emotions can be tricky business with risk of misinterpretation.

There are four good rules of thumb for adapting to employees' emotions:

1. *Enable people to process making a mistake.* Leaders are still empowered to identify when errors occur and politely hold parties accountable. The idea is not to reprimand them but to allow employees to process their emotions in relationship to making a mistake. Most employees experience shame and embarrassment,

so it's important to give them the space and support to fully process their emotions. It's easy to downplay upset emotions, but, when fully processed, employees will learn, improve, and internalize important lessons while keeping their self-esteem intact.

2. *Set the example.* If you are sympathetic, understanding, and compassionate in your business relationships, you earn trust and leave little room for people to be suspicious of your motivations when something controversial occurs.

3. *Show caring.* Leaders who take the time to interact with their team members and get to know them have a good chance of building strong relationships. An effective method is for you to stop by an employee's workstation or check in virtually on a regular basis and ask questions that probe how she is feeling both personally and professionally, such as: "How are you managing the workload?" or "What do you think of the new sales tool?" or "How are you settling in with the new move?" The fact that you took the time to stop by for a check-in goes a long way toward gaining loyalty. As U.S. President Theodore Roosevelt once said, "Nobody cares how much you know until they know how much you care."

4. *Pay attention.* Many leaders are excellent speakers. They often have just the right inspiring words at the right time, whether they are speaking one-on-one to a direct report or presenting in front of a large audience. *Listening*, however, is an entirely different matter; many leaders are much more comfortable giving advice than listening to others. If someone is expressing an emotion to you, the best response is to pay close attention and listen deeply to what is being said—as well as what is *not* being said. Watch for word choice, tone of voice, and body movements showing discomfort. When you are certain she is done, acknowledge her experience and validate her emotions with statements such as: "Currently, you're covering for Allison, who is out on

maternity leave for six months. By handling this new project, you have more work than expected. It's not a surprise that you're feeling overwhelmed and are worried about your own work-life balance. Anyone in a similar situation would feel the same way."

Propelling Results with Positive Emotions

As we've explored throughout this chapter, emotions help us navigate our environments and connect with others. However, we shouldn't regard emotions as just nice touchy-feely things to welcome into our office culture only when it's convenient to do so. When properly channelled, emotions have the power to improve an organization's ability to collaborate, innovate, and problem-solve.

Wharton Professor Michael Parke discovered that emotional sharing often leads to productive conversations and "more creative outcomes." The best results occur when teams put their feelings on the table and then work them out as part of a natural process without casting judgment. When the leader of a brainstorming meeting in this type of open organization asks the group, "How does everyone feel about that?" she expects honest answers that can be aired out and discussed by the group on the spot. Genuine issues end up being brought into the light and then resolved before they fester into something less manageable later.

If the culture sets the right tone and embraces emotions, even the most introverted or reserved team members become more inclined to speak up and raise concerns or, better yet, offer ideas that otherwise would not have been heard. When you hear a reserved individual say things like "I don't know, guys, I have a weird feeling about this," or "Hey, I have a crazy idea," that's the time for the group to stop and listen because there is high probability of a breakthrough. This is an opportune moment for the leader to ask the individual, "Please, tell us more."

Closer to the Heart: Words of Connection

Words have enormous power: They can connect and inspire, or they can hurt and destroy. We've seen how ugly politics can be when words are used as weapons to insult other people and incite others to perform acts of violence. In the reverse, speeches from great orators such as Martin Luther

King Jr. and Nelson Mandela unified people and created massive social change. On a smaller scale, we've all witnessed how praising an employee's abilities with the right words can boost his confidence to excel at performing certain tasks.

Be mindful when it comes to choosing your words. What you say may not matter to you, but your words may stick with someone else for a lifetime. Words don't disintegrate in the air after being voiced, especially since we now have cameras on our phones and social media apps that can broadcast them to the world and save them for all posterity. A tongue doesn't have any bones, but it has the capability to instantly break someone's heart.

As leaders, we secretly desire to be inspirational. As we are all aware, this doesn't always come easily. Our word choice can make the difference between shifting people from understanding to excitement to commitment. If we want to have a greater impact, we need to be cognizant to use words that create an emotional state.

The following are some examples of word choices that create an emotional state:

- A call for change—urgency:
Our competitors have increased their market share to 30 percent. If we don't do something quickly, we'll continue to lose market share.

- Greater emotional resonance:
Our competitors are edging us out and eating up our market share— they've already captured 30 percent. It may be uncomfortable, and you may feel alarmed, but we'll need to transform our business now or we'll be left behind.

- An opportunity:
We have an opportunity to launch a new product that can drive $10 million in revenue.

- Greater emotional resonance:
We are ecstatic to announce that we are first to market with a product

that will skyrocket sales and create an additional $10 million in revenue.

Words can be so potent their impact goes far beyond anything humans are capable of hearing, reading, or otherwise detecting. Depending on their context and how they are expressed, negative words contain emotional vibrations that enter our hearts and assault our bodies and souls.

Scientists have proven this theory by demonstrating how toxic language can harm humans. Researchers acquired data from 5,616 college students on the subject of verbal abuse from differential sources, such as parents, peers, and supervisors. They found that verbal abuse is a form of emotional abuse intended to inflict intense humiliation, denigration, or extreme fear, as perceived by the victimized person. Perceived parental verbal abuse in childhood and peer-related verbal abuse in adolescence have been associated with a risk of depressive mood, anxiety, anger/hostility, suicidal tendencies, or drug use in young adulthood. Moreover, experience of perceived verbal abuse has been associated with changed patterns of brain maturation, compromised brain resting state functional connectivity, and decreased brain gray matter volumes in regions responsible for sensory processing, emotional regulation, and social interaction-related cognitive functioning, such as language and memory. Adults who perceive verbal abuse with their intimate partners or in the workplace often experience serious issues with their mental health and ability to function.

The impact of harmful language is tangible and denigrating, whether for a child or an adult. In the workplace, we must, therefore, choose our words wisely and recognize that they have the capacity to linger and fester.

I couldn't illustrate this better than by sharing a nineteenth-century folktale involving a young fellow who slandered the town's wise man. One day, the young man felt so guilty about having spread lies that he decided to go to the wise man's home and beg his forgiveness.

The wise man, who didn't believe the young man had fully internalized the gravity of his transgressions, said he would forgive him on one condition: He must take a feather pillow outside his house, cut it up, and scatter the feathers in the wind.

The young man was puzzled by the request but happy to be let off with such an easy penance. When he returned home, he cut up a pillow outdoors and watched the wind blow the feathers in all directions.

Feeling a sense of accomplishment, the young man made a return visit to the wise man's home. "Am I now forgiven?" he asked.

"Just one more thing," replied the wise man. "Go now and gather up all the feathers."

"But that's impossible. The wind has already scattered them."

The same exact thing happens when words are released.

ACTION FRAMEWORK

Think of a relationship you were in that made you feel happy and connected. What words would you use to describe that relationship?

Now think of a relationship that involved friction. Compare how you spoke to this person one-on-one versus how you talked about her when she wasn't around?

In the latter scenario, think about how changing your words around might convert the conflicted relationship to one of connection.

Lassoing the Power of Emotions

The workplace has been so dominated by the head that the heart is only just beginning to be recognized and applied as a valuable business asset. The heart provides the courage we need to put ourselves out in the world, successfully connect with each other, build trust, inspire others into positive action, and create a caring culture.

As leaders, one of our roles is to shape culture. If we don't do this consciously, the culture evolves on its own. We must change our focus and reflect on how we want people to feel and experience their work. It is only then that we become capable of creating work environments that are motivating and engaging. For this shift to occur, we must focus on the needs and feelings of others and not just on what we value or want. You have an opportunity to implement this in every conversation. There is one big caveat, however: You need to know your direct reports on a deeper level. You must learn what they care about and recognize their cherished core values.

Leaders have the potential to help others identify their emotions and needs, especially when they find they are stuck. By acknowledging their experiences and validating their emotions, you can shift them into problem-solving or innovation mode and access their head and gut—which we will explore in the next chapter—more readily.

TAKEAWAYS

- The heart is the entryway into our being and allows us to fully experience life.
- The heart gives life meaning and serves as the vehicle to explore our needs, feelings, and most treasured values.
- Vulnerability is a strength in the workplace, not a weakness.
- Emotions determine how we code our life experience; we tend to remember negative experiences more than positive.
- In the past, we were taught to leave our emotions at the door when coming to work; now we must realize that emotions drive connection, collaboration, and productivity.
- Words are enormously powerful; they can connect and unify or be divisive and destroy.
- You can unlock your team's potential and shape the company's culture by decoding emotion and intentionally thinking about how people want to experience their work lives.

Chapter Four

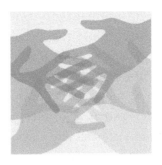

GUT

Unlike the mind and heart, the *gut* isn't suggestive of a connection to a visually flattering part of human anatomy. If you've ever gone with your gut feeling or felt butterflies in your belly, you've already experienced your second brain. The "gut brain" (or second brain)—which scientists at Johns Hopkins Medicine refer to as the enteric nervous system (ENS)—is hidden in the walls of your digestive system. It consists of two thin layers of more than 100 million nerve cells lining your gastrointestinal tract and alerts the brain when something is amiss. The digestive system doesn't conjure impactful symbolic images to help us orient ourselves to the meaning and significance of our gut. It is, therefore, the most difficult of the three for people to grasp and embrace as something tangible.

In simple terms, the gut is our highest form of intelligence and symbolizes the root of deep and powerful insight. Adaptable to whatever interpretation fits your belief system and world view, the gut serves as a guidance system for the soul. If it makes you feel more comfortable, you can replace *gut* with the word *intuition*, as they are interchangeable for our purposes.

The word intuition derives from the Latin verb *intueri*, which means "to look inside" or "to contemplate." Today, it refers to our greatest tool that connects us to our hearts and helps us hear our inner wisdom. It provides us with the ability to integrate our five senses, step beyond them, and move through time. Touch, hearing, sight, smell, and taste enable us to experience, identify, and recall things that occurred in the past or present based on evidence that happens to be available at the time. By contrast, intuition opens doors for us to glimpse *future* unknown pathways.

Our intuition is how our subconscious communicates with our conscious mind. Seymour Epstein, a former professor of psychology at University of Massachusetts–Amherst and author of *Cognitive-Experiential Theory,* put it this way: "Intuition involves a sense of knowing without knowing how one knows." Often the information passes through us like "a strange feeling" or "sensation" that can become difficult to describe or prove. Some people are tuned in and claim to have intuitive experiences on a regular basis, whereas others might have them but lack the awareness to access them and miss the broadcasted message.

I have yet to meet a strong leader who doesn't attribute at least some of their success to a powerful "gut instinct." If you currently have difficulty accessing or listening to your intuition, the first step is to accept that we all have some degree of intuitive ability, especially since many notable thinkers—including Malcolm Gladwell (author of *Blink*), Daniel Kahneman (author of *Thinking, Fast and Slow*), Isaac Asimov (biochemistry professor and science fiction author), and Steve Jobs (co-founder of Apple)—have welcomed the concept. Even Albert Einstein—largely regarded as the greatest physicist in world history—espoused the virtues of human intuition. As he eloquently wrote: "I believe in intuition and inspiration. Imagination is more important than knowledge. For knowledge is limited, whereas imagination embraces the entire world, stimulating progress, giving birth to evolution. It is, strictly speaking, a real factor in scientific research."

As you'll discover in this chapter, the power of human intuition exists not just in some of us but in *all* of us, and it can have a significantly beneficial influence on many aspects of business. The question is how much we choose to pay attention to our gut and follow its guidance when it calls to us.

Our North Star and Protector

Whether we are aware of it or not, our intuition connects us to our life's purpose and keeps us on track, like our North Star. Some people—such as a writer who tells stories from the first moment she holds a pencil or pen in her hand or sits with a keyboard—know exactly where they're headed in life right from the beginning. Others embark on lifelong journeys to determine where their North Star is trying to lead them. Once we have found our purpose and direction, our intuition may communicate to us when we veer off-track. This might appear in one of many forms: as a soft inner voice (which we discuss later in the chapter), as an unusual feeling, or as an external sign to help us reset and get back on course.

Our intuition has also been known to sound alarm bells to warn us when we might be in imminent danger or prepare our psyches for incoming tragic news. There have been accounts of people who have had such ominous feelings about flying on a certain aircraft that they changed their plans, later finding out that the plane they didn't board had crashed. There have been documented cases of such intuitive warnings saving people's lives, such as individuals who didn't board planes associated with the fatal 9/11 flights. On a smaller scale, most of us admit to having known they were about to hear about something upsetting just from the sound of a phone alert or ringtone.

There remains a great deal for us to learn about intuition and how it enables us to accomplish such remarkable things without fully understanding how we did them. However, many researchers have accepted its existence and are continuing to map out and build upon what is provable by scientific fact.

Spider Senses Are Tingling

Whether we've realized it or not, the comic book, film, and TV character Spider-Man's "Spidey sense" is a genuine form of heightened intuition inspired by innate talents displayed by arachnids. Creatures such as spiders may not have ears, but they sense things—especially a coming threat—through vibrations with 100 percent accuracy. Human beings have this same ability but to a much lesser extent, partly because we have other senses—such as hearing—to rely upon.

The HeartMath Institute, a nonprofit that "empowers individuals, families, groups and organizations to enhance their life experiences using tools that enable them to better recognize and access their intuitive insight and heart," identifies three types of human intuition:

1. *Implicit knowledge or learning:* Connects information that you've already been exposed to and makes new connections quickly to drive problem-solving and rapid decision-making.

2. *Vibrational:* Picks things up before they occur from an unseen external electromatic field. Like "Spidey sense," this is when a person predicts an event before it happens, such as an approaching tsunami.

3. *Interconnectedness:* This is how we connect to the infinite intelligence and receive or download information from it, providing us with deep insight and unlimited energy. In an NPR podcast, Lulu Miller and Alix Spiegel brought up the interesting idea that entanglement happens everywhere in nature. Despite the idea that we are all independent entities, we can become entangled with anyone we encounter. This relationship embeds itself in shared emotions, actions, and fears, suggesting that all human bodies are interconnected to some extent.

Have you ever personally experienced one or more of these three types of intuition? Were you aware of your intuition at the time—or did you realize it later? Can you recall what circumstances triggered the event?

Intuitive Alignment

Dr. Gerard Hodgkinson, a professor at the University of Manchester, concluded that our intuition derives from a perfect analysis of both our internal and external cues. When we experience our intuition, it's because both our internal and external worlds are working perfectly in sync. Our brain is not only protecting us from danger but also calculating the best decision to make in what may be a fraction of a second.

There have been documented cases of such intuitive alignment. In the 1940s, Argentinian Formula One driver Juan Manuel Fangio dominated the sport. During the 1950 Monaco Grand Prix, as he exited a tunnel on the second lap, Fangio inexplicably braked when he normally would have continued at his accelerated pace. In that split-second—without the benefit of any conscious evidence—he was able to make a decision that helped him avoid becoming involved in a horrendous accident that had just occurred around the bend, beyond his vision. If that's not enough, he won the race.

Miniscule fragments of information coalesced in Fangio's subconscious that protected him from danger. For starters, the racer had keen peripheral vision that picked up details most people would miss while driving at such a high speed. He noticed that spectators in the stands were looking in a different direction from usual. They should have been watching his car and others exiting the tunnel, which meant Fangio would have seen their faces. Instead, he saw the back of their heads—a subtle change in color that instantaneously signaled to him something was wrong up ahead and that he should stop.

The following quote from Malcolm Gladwell in *Blink* says it all: "There can be as much value in the blink of an eye as in months of rational analysis."

Unleashing the Power

Whether you've been aware of it or not, you've had intuitive superpowers all along. The next few sections direct you to four ways you can tap into intuitive energy: Relationship Connector, Problem Solver, Imaginator, and Navigator.

Relationship Connector

This ability enables us to communicate with others without the use of modern technology and is an acknowledgment of Miller and Spiegel's entanglement theory by having shared emotions, actions, and fears even across distance. A common example of this is when we sense the passing of a loved one, although there isn't any tangible evidence suggesting this occurred. The Relationship Connector doesn't have to be an extreme circumstance, however. You may be thinking about a friend you haven't heard from in some time when you suddenly receive a phone call from her. Or, while you are involved in the sales process, you think of a potential client who happens to contact you at that moment.

When you activate the Relationship Connector, you can tune into a person or group at all levels and pick up what is and isn't being said. This enables you to better navigate and build trust with others in the workplace. You can invite people to explore their fears and concerns, whereas in the past they would have kept their cards hidden.

In your personal life, the more discerning you are about the people you welcome into your inner circle—especially in terms of trust level—the more harmonious your relationships will become.

Problem Solver

Sometimes our intuition leads us to find the best solution to a problem based on past experiences or seemingly out of nowhere from the infinite intelligence. Once we broadcast our problem, need, or desire to the world— via what I refer to as the Magnetizer—we begin to attract information or people who seem to show up at just the right time with the answers we were seeking, or at least pieces of the puzzle.

Sometimes the Magnetizer leads you to an unexpected but welcome circumstance. On one occasion, while I was driving home from our family vacation home in Pennsylvania to New York City (where I lived at the time), I slammed into hours of bumper-to-bumper traffic. There weren't any alternate routes to take. Suddenly, my inner voice spoke to me, ordering me to get off the highway. The message was so direct and forceful that I didn't hesitate to turn at the next exit ramp. The voice guided me into the parking lot of a do-it-yourself hardware store. Something compelled me to enter, although I had no reason to be there. I walked down the aisles searching for something, but I couldn't identify what it was. My inner voice became more fervent as it sent me toward a middle-aged black man at the back of the store. We didn't know each other, but we started up a conversation right away. He shared with me that he was struggling with his career and was lost about what he should do. Enquiries and words of advice flowed out of me. The interaction didn't last more than fifteen minutes, but he listened intently, responded to my questions, gained new insight into his dilemma, and seemed receptive to my suggestions. He thanked me profusely. I left the store without having bought anything and returned to my car. When I turned onto the ramp for the highway, I couldn't believe what I'd found: The traffic had cleared up.

The point of the story isn't that I found a productive way to pass the time during a traffic jam. It's that I believe the man in the store had broadcast a signal for help via the Magnetizer, which my intuitive receptors had picked up.

The intuitive area of our brain often knows the correct answer to a problem long before the analytical part. Data can be extremely useful for decision-making, but many leaders use it as a crutch or excuse to procrastinate, overthink, or just say *No* and avoid taking a risk. If, however, they listen to their gut—even if it may contradict the data—they will make faster, more effective decisions, usually with greater upsides. In one study involving three dozen top CEOs, 85 percent confirmed that intuition—in the form of rules of thumb—was central to their decision-making process.

ACTION FRAMEWORK

Here is an effective way to tackle a new problem: Actively ask yourself questions about challenges or opportunities you are experiencing, such as: *Why aren't our clients engaging with our product as we expected?* Instead of attempting to solve the dilemma right away, consciously take a step back and remain in discovery mode. Write down as many questions and reflections related to the topic as you can. Once you identify a perspective that you haven't experienced before, try implementing it as a potential solution.

Imaginator

Intuition, the basis for our imagination, has two pathways that can lead to:

- Discovery, breakthroughs, and new concepts.
- Creativity and the ability to produce something tangible (e.g., a book, a painting, a new process, or an innovative framework).

In his masterwork, *Critique of Pure Reason*, eighteenth-century German philosopher Immanuel Kant put forth the notion that some knowledge exists inherently in the mind—independent of experience—and that intuition exists as an ability separate from objective reality. He identified a progression of three stages or representational types: intuition (*Anschauung*), to image (*Einbildung*), to concept (*Begriff*). Essentially, this means that, once a creative thought enters the mind, it becomes converted into a visual representation and then shaped into a tangible idea ready to be further explored.

For the Imaginator, this builds a concrete framework for the creative process that may be applied to all endeavors, including product development and innovation at work.

Navigator

The Navigator gives us instinct that helps us deal with our ever-changing environment, where the answers or right path forward are far from obvious. The Navigator gives us the fortitude to progress through ambiguity. We live in an increasingly uncertain world, where change happens at an accelerated pace and the context isn't as clear, linear, or logical as it had been in the past. In 1987, leadership theorists Warren Bennis and Burt Nanus coined the acronym VUCA—which stands for *volatility, uncertainty, complexity, and ambiguity*—as a way to describe and manage continuous change. Then in March 2020, futurist Jamais Cascio coined the acronym, BANI, which stands for: *brittle, anxiety, non-linear, and incomprehensible*. Intuition is one of his suggested ways to navigate our BANI world, as follows:

- *Brittleness* requires *capacity* and *resilience*.

- *Anxiety* may be handled with *empathy* and *mindfulness*.

- *Non-linearity* benefits from *context, flexibility,* and *adaptivity*.

- *Incomprehensibility* needs *transparency* and *intuition*.

It stands to reason that a person who is visually or hearing challenged relies more heavily on other senses to function at an optimal level. However, there is scientific evidence to support the notion that intuition also plays a significant role in adapting to such circumstances. There have been studies in which blind people placed in blackened rooms were able to navigate around furniture and other objects without colliding into a single thing. This remarkable skill, dubbed *blindsight*, has been known to occur among individuals who have functioning eyes but a damaged visual cortex, which is essential for seeing and interpreting images. In the future, scientists believe *intuition training* will be invaluable for navigating a wide range of challenges—and as a resource for improving business skills.

Why We Ignore Our Intuition

Intuitive skills are innate but often dormant, ready to be awakened and summoned. Every so often they call out to help us connect, problem-solve, imagine, or navigate. The problem is that gut feelings are often ignored or submerged, due to learned prejudices against accepting them.

Our intuition absorbs available information and infers an outcome based on our experiences and/or imagination. If there isn't a specific event in our minds to latch onto, we defer to examples of whatever empirical data happens to be available—even if it's tangential. When this "evidence" fails, it becomes locked in our minds as a learned prejudice, often negative.

This is why business leaders often dismiss new ideas; they are convinced these have failed in the past and therefore will never work in the future. Logic is considered more acceptable because it's tangible, which is why we are trained to solely rely upon provable data at work. It's rare for people to openly speak about intuition in the workplace.

Constant fearful thoughts can induce powerful emotions, often hijacking our intuition. When we're afraid, we tune out gut feelings because they can make us physically uncomfortable. Why stick your neck out on a longshot concept when the only available facts (or lack of them) indicate it won't succeed?

Of course, intuition can be misinterpreted and lead us astray, especially when we are filled with fear and anxiety, causing our intuitive capacity to weaken. The mission is to recognize when we are facing fear, explore where it is coming from, acknowledge it, and move through the feeling until it leaves us. To accomplish this, we must calm our limbic system—the part of the brain involved in behavioral and emotional responses—through whatever practice works best for us, such as meditation, yoga, exercise, or soothing music. Once your mind is relaxed, your intuition becomes freed and can communicate with you.

What Happens When We Ignore Our Intuition

In ancient Greek mythology, Cassandra was a beautiful Trojan priestess who was given the gift of foresight by the god Apollo in exchange for certain (presumably prurient) favors. After being blessed with the ability to foresee the future, she reneged on her deal. Apollo cursed her by making it so that she could continue to make accurate predictions—but no one would ever believe her. This had dramatic repercussions, as no one heeded her warnings about the fated destruction of Troy.

Imagine what happens to us when we ignore our inner voice and listen to what others think is best for us. If Jack Ma had listened to his critics, he would still be teaching instead of being the founder and CEO of Alibaba, a Chinese multinational technology company specializing in e-commerce. Ma first experienced the internet in Seattle in 1995, when he typed "beer" and found every type of the beverage except for Chinese beer. He became convinced that the internet would change China, and this intuition became the foundation for his business ideas. As of 2023, the company's network is valued at $318 billion.

There are equal downsides of ignoring our intuition when it cautions us about impending danger. Sometimes we are in such a precarious situation at work that we feel like we are Cassandra warning everyone about the fall of Troy—but no one will listen. This happened in the case of Gustavo Cisneros, CEO of the media conglomerate Cisneros Group. His board, family, and management team were all in favor of partnering with AOL to form AOL Latin America. Gustavo had a gut feeling that Latin American consumers wouldn't respond the same way as Americans, but he dismissed his intuition and caved to the pressure. Flash forward five years: Cisneros lost nearly $1 billion and faced bankruptcy.

Have you ever been in a situation where you've regretted not having paid attention to your gut? What would you do differently next time?

A Guide to Accessing Your Gut

Unlike what we might see in popular culture such as films, television, and books, intuition isn't a magical tool awarded to some people but not others. It's a gift we're all born with and must learn to hone.

Our intuition comes alive when we engage all our senses to absorb and understand our experience. The goal isn't to try to "fix" the messages we receive but to become curious about them and listen to what they are trying to tell us.

The concept of a "flash of insight" conveys the fallacy that intuition always strikes us in an unexpected way, rather than as something we can detect, mine, and develop. There are, of course, some occasions when ideas strike us with such a rapid fury that we don't take the time to write them down and then *poof!*—they're gone forever. There are also times when ideas seem nowhere to be found, but, when we step back and make space for something to strike us, we can generate that insight for ourselves.

When we don't focus on our current challenges and instead shift our focus, our subconscious mind is let loose, allowing the quieter part of the mind to integrate newly acquired data. If we want to listen more to our gut, we need to silence our minds and tune into what is floating around in there as if we're listening to a radio broadcast. If your thoughts are overcrowded and buzzing, the sound will resemble static between stations, and you won't receive the ideal transmission.

Our consciousness doesn't stop when we're asleep; it makes connections in a different manner. Invaluable intuitive thoughts can come to us while we are sleeping or dreaming, jolting us awake with an epiphany in the middle of the night or when we arise in the morning.

Many of us have been known to say, "I get my best ideas in the shower." The soothing hot water, steam, and auto-pilot cleansing ritual puts us in a relaxing state that enables the active mind to quiet down enough for intuitive, flowing thoughts to roam free.

REFLECTION: PAYING ATTENTION TO YOUR INTUITION

Write in your journal about your senses, experiences, and energy in different situations. Keep the notebook by your bed, so you may capture intuitive thoughts that come to you in dreams, in the middle of the night, or first thing in the morning. Throughout the day, too, take special note of when your gut decisions proved to be more accurate than your logical ones.

- Where did you feel the intuitive sense in your body?
- How did your intuition communicate with you?
- What steps, if any, did you take (or not take) to receive an intuitive signal?
- How does location play a part in your experience?
- What activity were you involved in at the time?
- What state of mind were you in?

It may seem counterintuitive, but a similar experience occurs when we become hyper-focused during exercise, such as running, walking, or yoga. Athletes refer to this as *getting into the zone.* On both sides of the spectrum—at rest or during exercise—what's left is pure intuition that must be consciously recognized and nourished.

After a few weeks, review your writings and determine if there is a pattern to what triggers your intuition to communicate to you. Do more of whatever routines seem to improve your decision-making and powers of prognostication.

Where Our Bodies Receive and Feel Intuition

Throughout this chapter, I've pointed out how intuition can act sometimes as a guardian angel or other times providing deep insights. This phenomenon is known as *clairaudience*: the quiet voice that whispers ideas—or sometimes screams that we are in danger. Going back to the "Spidey sense," it might convey something along the lines of "Don't get on the train" without any comprehensible frame of reference or explanation. The way to tell the difference between this voice and the regular one in your head is that the communications are short, sweet, and matter of fact—not long rambling sentences—and they never come from a place of fear.

In 2016, lauded film director Steven Spielberg spoke about clairaudience during his Harvard commencement speech. He stated: "At first, the internal voice I needed to listen to was hardly audible, and it was hardly noticeable—kind of like me in high school. But then I started paying more attention, and my intuition kicked in." He continued, "And I want to be clear that your intuition is different from your conscience. They work in tandem, but here's the distinction: Your conscience shouts, 'Here's what you should do,' while your intuition whispers, 'Here's what you could do.' Listen to that voice that tells you what you could do. Nothing will define your character more than that. Because once I turned to my intuition and I tuned into it, certain projects began to pull me into them, and others, I turned away from."

The problem for us today is that our world is so cluttered with incessant noise that our internal voice becomes drowned out. Notifications, texts, emails, social media posts, alerts, direct messages, and the like bombard us every minute on our phones. As a result, we don't give ourselves enough time to enjoy peace and give our intuition a chance to express itself and be heard.

The importance of silence cannot be underestimated. It's during these quiet times that we develop the ability to receive deep insights into what we truly need and/or want in our lives that will light the passion in our hearts.

There are three more central ways we feel our intuition communicating with us:

- *The gut (the physical stomach):* This form of intuition is the most common. Even people who are skeptics of a sixth sense will admit they have experienced gut feelings over the years. These sensations may be either positive or negative. Regarding the former, it might be a sense of nervous excitement ("butterflies in the belly") that good news is on the way. When it comes to the former, the stomach might issue a queasy feeling telling you that you are on the wrong path and need to say *No* to whatever it might be.

- *Vision in the mind:* This form of intuition—sometimes referred to with the word *clairvoyance*—arrives as an image or scene in the mind, usually as a metaphor. It can arrive in waking hours or can be seen in dream state or shown to you right when you wake up in the morning. This can also show up in the form of visual signs or coincidences, as described in the next Action Framework.

- *Brain download:* Known as *claircognizance*, this is when our brains get an immediate rush of information out of the blue that drives idea generation, innovation, or helps solve a problem. Nikola Tesla, creator of such remarkable inventions as the alternating current (AC) electricity supply system, once said: "My brain is only a receiver, in the Universe there is a core from which we obtain knowledge, strength, and inspiration. I have not penetrated the secrets of this core, but I know that it exists."

Intuition can be one of your greatest strengths when harnessed and developed, but it requires you to stay connected to your inner self. Now that we have the framework in place for the head, heart, and gut, we are ready for Part III, where you will discover how to identify your power, cultivate it, and turn it into a superpower.

ACTION FRAMEWORK

Intuition can also appear in the form of mysterious "signs and wonders," if we pay enough attention to them. For example, if a couple is visited by a dove on their wedding day, that may be mere coincidence—or it could be interpreted as a symbolic sign of new beginnings, fidelity, love, luck, and prosperity.

Spot the coincidences in your life and see what happens as you regard them as deeper signs or opportunities for discovery. Are you able to determine how/where the occurrences are related/connected? Ask yourself: *How are these messages related? What are they trying to tell me?*

- Our gut (or intuition) is a tool and a flash of insight that enables us to tap into infinite intelligence.
- Leveraging our intuition can lead to improved relationships, sharper problem-solving, a broadened imagination, and the ability to navigate the unknown.
- Our intuition can help us avoid disaster or lead to high levels of performance.
- All humans are born with intuition, but we must learn to cultivate it and listen to it.
- There are four main ways that intuition can be received in the body: Relationship Connector, Problem Solver, Imaginator, and Navigator.
- Quiet time is essential to being able to receive frequent and clear intuitive signals in our mind and gut.

Part II

CULTIVATING PERSONAL POWER

John (external to peers, brimming with excitement): I'll take the lead on this strategy project—no problem, I did something like this in my last organization and feel I can add a lot of value.

(self-talk): Wow, I can't believe I'm leading this new strategy workstream. This is a big stretch for me. I hope I'll be able to do it. I feel like I am an imposter.

Samantha (external to peers): John, if you need any help on the project, I'm happy to support you.

(self-talk): I'm so mad at myself, why didn't I jump in and volunteer to lead this project? I know I can do it. I'm ready to show everyone what I am made of. Why do I always hesitate and let others steal my thunder?

Angel (external to peers): This will be a very complex project, as it requires input from so many key stakeholders. How are you going to accomplish this?

(self-talk): I'm so glad I won't be working on this project; they'll never be able to deliver on time. The deadlines are too tight, and they'll be at the mercy of everyone else for information and input. There's no way I'd want my name on this project.

John (external): I agree it won't be easy, but with the right focus and support from the team, we can manage to accomplish this. We just need to believe we can do it.

(self-talk): I hate it when Angel undermines me. He said that on purpose to create self-doubt and make me look stupid. Now I'm even more nervous about taking this project than I was before.

Chapter Five

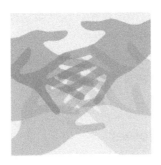

WHAT IS PERSONAL POWER AND WHY DO WE GIVE IT AWAY?

Power can make people feel uneasy—and with good reason. When we think of traditional hierarchical power, we imagine leaders at the top of organizations or governments who have authority and control over those who are underneath them. The reason we resist this dynamic is because the power is seen as finite, meaning we live in a world in which only a tiny minority control it. However, we can't be naïve and think that power dynamics don't exist in all our relationships, whether spoken or unspoken.

The concept of someone "having power over us" takes away our own agency—the ability to act without constraints and consequences—which causes us to hold back what is deep within our hearts out of fear that it might be stripped away, crushed, or stolen. The hierarchical structure—with power concentrated at the top—creates a culture that discourages employees from volunteering solutions, experimenting, and innovating—either because individuals feel they don't have permission or fear their suggestions may get shot down by those who are in charge. A scarcity mindset has its origins in the belief that power is something we are either given or that we take. We then need to hold on to it and protect it once it's in our grasp. To combat this scarcity, we seek external sources of power that can be taken or given.

We need to ask ourselves: *Is this type of external power still legitimate where fear is the underlying motivator? As we move to networked organizations where power is distributed, is* power over *the best approach for leaders? If human capital is our greatest resource, is this the right organizational model for today and in the future?*

New Concepts of Power

In her 1990 book *Truth or Dare: Encounters with Power, Authority, and Mystery,* Starhawk challenged the traditional notion of power as something that could be taken and used over people, writing: "Power is never static, for power is not a thing that we can hold or store, it is a movement, a relationship, a balance, fluid and changing. The power one person can wield over another is dependent on a myriad of *[sic]* external factors and subtle agreements."

The idea of *power* being a fluid concept has led researchers to expand its long-accepted application—*power over others*—to include three alternatives that are gaining greater acceptance in the business community:

1. *Power with:* This is all about collaboration and working with others. This requires a fundamental acceptance of equality (e.g., gender, race, religion) and the firm belief that everyone has the skill and talent to participate and contribute. Here power is shared and based on social power and influence. We are motivated by mutual support, empowerment, and solidarity, and we seek to collaborate to create connection and collective action. If we lack *power with,* we can't build bridges across organizations and shift to an enterprise mindset as the goal is to act together and as one mutually beneficial organization. As Aristotle professed: "The whole is greater than the sum of its parts."

2. *Power to:* Not every assignment requires a team or the opinion and influence of a committee to ensure strong execution. This power refers to the individual's ability to create independently

without the need for them to be dominated or to exert power over others. This is the power to make a difference, create something new, or achieve goals.

3. *Power within:* This is the ability to write your own life through productive or generative power that is derived from an internal sense of self-esteem, self-knowledge, internal connection, and sense of being present. When we are driven by our own sense of agency, we can recognize individual differences while respecting others. By tapping into *power within*, we have limitless possibilities; we uncover our unique potential to shape our personal lives and organizations, while inspiring and igniting a pathway for others to do the same. Moreover, when we access *power within*, we are driven to make a difference by creating meaning for ourselves and others.

We've established that *power over* is not a desirable model for any organization. Does this mean we must now choose from among these three emerging types of power? I suggest not. Rather, I recommend an entirely new paradigm shift that blends the best of all worlds.

You Have the Power

At the end of the classic film *The Wizard of Oz*, Glinda (the Good Witch) gives Dorothy an epiphany: She'd had the power to go home "all along." The same is true for everyone in the business world—from interns and entry-level workers to long-time leaders. We've had a special ability—*personal power* or *power within*—to command our own destinies the entire time. We've been sitting on a treasure chest and didn't even know it. This level of power has always been there, but we now need to shift our view from the external world to the internal. It can be concluded that our power within has been diluted for so long because of operating within organizations and cultures that value the paradigm of *power over*.

Personal power is a new way of being and thinking. We give up our craving for external power as we awaken our true selves and enable others to do the same. This requires us to take charge of our lives, which some of us might not feel ready or even capable of doing as we've grown accustomed to acting the role of victim or playing by someone else's rules. Personal power gives us the capacity to navigate any challenge and difficult situation. Along with this gift comes several important responsibilities:

- *Ownership:* If you say you are going to do something, you get it done—no excuses, no one else to blame, no characterizing yourself as the victim. You are responsible for your own actions and outcomes—positive or negative.

- *Collaboration:* Personal power doesn't mean working in a silo and excluding others. It shouldn't be used as a source of power over others. We must hold space for others' power and unique gifts and work together toward a common goal. An integral part of our self-knowledge is understanding our impact on others and the need to seek and accept feedback to deepen our knowledge in this area.

- *Transparency:* Key stakeholders have a right to know what you are working on, how things are going, and where you stand compared to benchmarks (e.g., deadlines, budget). The more you share with others, the more personal power you have, because you are signaling that you have nothing to hide.

- *Integrity:* When you are clear about who you are and what you stand for, you set the tone for a shared responsibility to create an environment in which psychological safety prevails. The ideal is to encourage people to speak their minds without ridicule or consequence, which enables teams to raise concerns, share errors, and create breakthrough ideas.

- *Trust:* Personal power isn't a one-way street. You need to respect the personal power of others and have faith that they will get their jobs done to the best of their ability and according to accepted standards (if not better). You are welcome to be curious-minded, asking questions and providing feedback—which also demonstrates engagement and support—if you don't dictate *how* something should be done or become judgmental.

When we learn to master personal power as individuals and then as leaders, we become adept at helping others discover their own power and accomplish things they never thought were possible. In this way, you build a team of individual leaders who are so confident and energized they become even more skilled at executing, problem-solving, decision-making, and innovating.

	Power Over	Power With	Personal Power
Definition	This type of power is built on force, coercion, domination, and control.	This type of power is shared, co-active, and linked to social power and influence.	The ability to author your own life through productive or generative power that is derived from an internal sense of worth, self-knowledge, inner connection, and being.
Underlying Motivation/ Function	• Fear	• Mutual Support • Empowerment • Solidarity	• Creation
Associated Beliefs	• Power is a finite resource or a scarcity mentality. • Power is held by individuals. • Some people have power, and some people do not.	• We are equals. • We can build bridges within teams and across organizations. • We can act together.	• Possibilities are limitless. • Each person has unique potential to shape their own life and world. • Respect/leverage individual differences.
Focus	External	External	Internal
Seek	• External approval and love	• Collaboration and connection • Collective action	• Make a difference. • Create meaning. • Awaken to your true self. • Enable others to awaken to their true self.

Adapted from "The New Concepts of Power? Power-over, Power-to, and Power-with," by Pamela Pansardi and Marianna Bindi, University of Pavia

The Elements of Personal Power

When we fully integrate the head, heart, and gut, we develop our internal guidance system that guides our life's decisions and brings to light our own truth and deep sense of who we are. When we focus on listening to this inner guidance system—rather than relying on the external world for advice—we have boundless energy and a deep sense of knowing, and we activate our personal power.

It can feel that some people have personal power and others don't, but when we understand the elements of personal power, we can all learn how to cultivate it in ourselves. We each have a unique purpose to fulfill in this life, our soul's blueprint. Some people know what it is from when they were young; others discover it as life experiences unfold. In either case, it's not something your mind can "figure out" or look for on store shelves. As I touched on in the previous chapter, your purpose comes from within—your intuition—and may be revealed through deep reflection and identifying what you care most about. Your purpose should provide sustainable meaning for yourself and others. Once you know your purpose, you feel as if it's what you were born to do and you develop a passion for fulfilling it.

Personal power is broken into three distinct segments:

1. *Personal power and agency:* Focuses on the perceived level of influence; an individual must shape a situation and her own life, including how she knows, and act in accordance with her purpose and values across situations (i.e., how true she is to herself).

2. *Personal power and mental mastery:* The ability to remain focused to deliver the best results; taking time to reflect and quiet the mind with an awareness of their own thoughts and how they think.

3. *Personal power and self-mastery:* Focuses on how well an individual knows, believes in, and accepts herself for who she is; includes how mentally and emotionally present she is, as well as her openness to embracing new experiences.

Personal Power and Agency

Authorship refers to how we shape, believe, and create our lives and handle life's challenges. It represents the idea that we firmly believe we are the authors of our own lives. We are writing our story every day, determining what focus and actions we will take and who gets to play with us on stage. While we may be proud of our successes and feel we created them with our hard work and fortitude, we often do the opposite when it comes to failure, pointing a finger externally at someone else to blame. This keeps us in victim mode and limits our power.

It's important to acknowledge that our story will never be 100 percent linear; there are always bumps in the road, detours, and recalibrations. When setbacks occur, we need to be resilient, learning to bounce back and recover.

One of our greatest sources of agency is the power to make decisions. When we are intentional about our decisions and integrate guidance from our heart, mind, and gut, we increase our personal power. However, there are times when we are indecisive and avoid making decisions; in reality, *no decision is a decision*. Sometimes, when we are afraid of facing our truth, making a choice can be painfully difficult.

As leaders, we need to be attuned to how we let others decide for themselves. It's so easy to take over and make decisions on their behalf, but that removes their power to choose and be responsible. Sometimes our actions lead people to be too dependent upon us, and they fail to stand on their own two feet and be accountable in their own lives.

Connect to Your Purpose and Core Values

We each have a unique purpose to fulfill in this life, our soul's blueprint. Some people know what it is from when they were young; others discover it as life experiences unfold. In either case, it's not something your mind can "figure out" or something you can shop around for. Your purpose comes from within—your intuition—and may be revealed through deep reflection and identifying what you care most about. Your purpose should provide sustainable meaning for yourself and others. Once you know your purpose, you feel as if it's what you were born to do and you develop a passion for fulfilling it.

Our sense of personal purpose is individual and can operate on many levels: family, community, industry, country, and the global world stage. All can be equally valuable, enabling personal transformation and contributions to society that create a better world for subsequent generations.

Once we figure out our personal purpose or calling, it becomes time to accept it, develop a plan, and put it to work. *Harvard Business Review* refers to this as a "purpose-to-impact" plan: how you are going to execute it and make a difference in the world. The purpose-to-impact plan is a personal expression of who you are, written in your voice and style to ensure it will remain meaningful to you. You want the document to include a concise purpose statement, an explanation of it, annual goals with specific

ACTION FRAMEWORK

The stories of our life and our experience can reveal our purpose and passion in life. Below are four prompts (storylines) to help you gain greater insight into your purpose. After you've fleshed out your own story for each prompt, reflect on what you've written and see if you can identify patterns that lead you to create your personal purpose statement.

1. *When I was young:* Think back to your childhood before you knew what was the "right" or "expected" thing to do. What did you love to do? What did you enjoy spending your time doing, and where were you at your happiest?

2. *Crucible: The challenge that shaped me:* Think about your life in general or your career so far. When have you faced a real issue? Why was it so hard? Did it challenge your skills, values, or identity? Were you with people or in a place that made it difficult for you? What did you do, and how did that challenge shape you? How did it change how you see yourself?

3. *Sparking my interest:* Outside work, what do you most enjoy doing? What got you interested in it? What is it about this activity that energizes you? Has there been a special moment for you involving this activity?

4. *My success story:* Think about your career and your life outside work. When have you been at your best? What do you think made you successful? What motivated you to achieve these things? Why did it make you feel proud?

steps you'll take to implement them, and an examination of how your key relationships fit into the big picture. To begin the process, use the Action Framework on the previous page to begin to craft your personal purpose.

Core Values

If we want to direct our lives and navigate the world, we need a map and compass to guide our journey. Our personal core values keep us on course and direct our lives. They express what we value most and enable us to make decisions that are aligned with our personal belief systems. When we make decisions in line with our personal values, we'll feel like our truest selves. When push comes to shove and we feel like we are in a position that requires making difficult or tough decisions, core values define who we are. Ask yourself: *What are my five most cherished values, and how do they guide my life?* As a leader, ask yourself: *What are each of my team members' cherished values?*

Personal Power and Mental Mastery

Getting our minds to work for us is not an easy feat, as it takes a high level of awareness to train and direct ourselves. *Mental mastery* is a framework for improving the mental aspects of performance. It helps manage anxiety and keep us in the present moment while identifying what we can control—our personal emotions and reactions—and what we are able to influence. Our attitudes and beliefs may be consciously shaped, which can lead to how we view ourselves and the world at large. Mental mastery drives our focus and concentration and helps ensure that we have mental toughness to weather the storms that come and go.

It might surprise you to know how many leaders we work with struggle with self-talk and imposter syndrome and have little awareness of word choices they make that reveal their innermost thoughts. Many years ago, I was having a thoughtful conversation among a group of friends (whose names I'm changing for privacy reasons) when Monique expressed her self-talk outwardly: "I'm not smart enough to go for this promotion."

Yvette snapped: "*Whoa*—What did you just say? Would you talk to your best friend like that?"

"No," Monique sheepishly replied.

"Then why do you talk to yourself like that?" Yvette demanded.

The rhetorical question was an obvious truth that has guided my personal development to this day. I have come to realize that self-talk is one of the most important aspects that drives our self-confidence and self-esteem, which are key elements of personal power. Mental mastery gives us an awareness and capacity to manage and regulate these negative thinking patterns that can keep us stuck. When we achieve mental mastery, it can be a game changer in our personal and professional lives. (We will cover mental mastery in greater depth in the next chapter.) This is known as *grit*—a trait successful people and leaders have in abundance.

Personal Power and Self-Mastery

We have full mastery when we own and leverage our greatest capabilities, are willing to reinvent ourselves when needed, and know our deepest worth. Leaders with this personal power are seen as calm, in control (but not of others), patient, understanding, and steady, even when faced with stressful or unexpected situations. They also wield a growth mindset, seeking to stretch and grow their breadth of knowledge.

The following are five self-attributes needed for self-mastery of personal power:

1. *Self-trust:* Self-trust involves more than just confidence. Successful leaders are optimistic about their ability to deal with demands, tasks, or situations in a capable and responsible manner.

2. *Self-awareness:* Self-awareness deepens our understanding of our intent (purpose and values) and how it evolves as we grow and change. Successful leaders see themselves accurately and accept feedback and insight from others, so they can address their blind spots. They also must recognize when they are overwhelmed and engage the support of others to move forward with their energy. When leaders demonstrate an awareness of how they are perceived by others and impact those around them, they build widespread trust and support.

3. *Self-compassion:* Successful leaders demonstrate warmth and understanding toward themselves, moving past self-criticism and processing negative emotions in a balanced, non-judgmental manner.

4. *Emotional agility:* Successful leaders demonstrate willingness to be in the moment with their emotions and reactions, taking time to explore and move through to move forward, expanding their thinking and emotional position.

5. *Receptivity:* Successful leaders demonstrate being open to experiences, moving past personal fears and saying "yes" to what life presents.

Personal Power and Receptivity

Receptivity, or presence, is how we use our bodies to express how we show up to the world and exert our power. "To be or not to be, that is the question," Hamlet's famous line in Shakespeare's play, is the character's deliberation about life, death, and suicide. It also begs the philosophical question: *Are we receptive, or present, to what life has to offer?*

British theatrical vocal coach Patsy Rodenberg best describes presence in terms of three different circles of energy:

1. *First circle:* This circle is when the performer's focus is on herself. Rodenberg believes such introspection can be valuable if it isn't held for more than a few moments. After that, others might suspect that you are concealing your true presence. When we are in our first circle of power, we tend to be focused on the past, which limits our access to others in the present moment.

2. *Second circle:* In this instance, the performer is fully present. The second circle is critical for anyone in business who must engage with other people. It involves an equal exchange of energy among all parties, granting the space to forge deeper connection and intimacy. When we are in the second circle, we establish an

environment for attentive listening and new ideas to emerge. We become so confident and secure in ourselves that we allow others' personal power to shine.

3. *Third circle:* When a performer recites a monologue on stage, she is sending a message outward to the unknown universe, unaware that others continue to pick up these signals. We've all experienced leaders who are stuck in the third circle, who are unaware they are talking at people rather than with them. When a leader is in the third circle, she comes across as having all the answers, being too directive, and showing concern about the future, which is masked as fear. This kills all measure of psychological safety; people become too afraid to speak up and experiment with new ideas. This is the least effective way for leaders to present themselves, as it relates back to the hierarchical business model and demonstrates limited use of empathy.

 REFLECTION: TAPPING INTO YOUR PERSONAL POWER

Ask yourself these questions:

- How much personal power am I willing to accept?
- Where do I resist my own power?
- Which aspect of personal power do I need to strengthen?
- Which aspect of personal power may I be overusing?

What Happens When We Give Away Our Power?

Throughout our lives, we inadvertently outsource our power, which causes us to feel weak or less than other people. When we do this, we allow outsiders to define our self-worth and control our time and energy. This may manifest in terms of changing our mind to align with the views that others have of us or by comparing ourselves to others. Would a rose ever compare itself to a tulip? Of course not. They are both beautiful, but, as humans, we are in a constant state of comparison. This can lead to being trapped in a victim mindset and believing that we don't have control over outcomes or the ability to shape our lives.

Every relationship is a continual dance of power, and if we have weak boundaries, we lose the delicate balance that creates harmonious relationships. We inadvertently let others define our moods and end up in a state of continual emotional turmoil, which can bring out our worst traits and behaviors. Even when bad stuff happens—and sometimes it will, even in business—we have control over how we respond. Do we behave with grace and dignity, or do we get caught up in another's drama, leaving us off-balance and confused?

Sometimes we confuse power with control and give away our power due to:

- *Lack of confidence:* We don't believe we can stand on our own, forge our own pathway, and make our life decisions. We give up control to other people who we see as more competent.

- *The fear of making a mistake:* When we have a compulsion to ensure everything is right all the time, we give away our power. We let others tell us what to do, enabling us to feel safe and maintain our sense of perfection without having to put ourselves out there. When we do this, we don't learn and end up having a victim mentality.

- *A craving for certainty:* Many of us are uncomfortable navigating ambiguity, so we choose the most familiar path, the one of least resistance. This keeps us small and in the risk-free zone.

- *The desire for comfort and security:* We look to others to provide us with the comfort and security we crave, rather than trusting our own capacity to create it. This can lead to spending time in a job that isn't suited to us because it's the only place we feel provided for and safe. Although we want to do something else, deep down we convince ourselves the current pathway is *good enough*.

When we understand our patterns of behavior, we recognize where we need to reclaim our power and feel whole and valued once again. The first step is recognizing that power isn't an external factor but rather an internal source of strength and knowing. The key is to stop looking for validation from the external world, so we can access the magic of our inner compass. This gives us the strength to move mountains and achieve anything that our hearts desire.

ACTION FRAMEWORK

Identify specific instances when you have intentionally or unintentionally given up your power. The following are a few general scenarios to trigger your memory.

- Allowed others to make decisions for you.
- Didn't speak up and say what you truly felt.
- Believed you were less than someone else.
- Said one thing but did another.
- Were unhappy due to someone else's behavior.
- Kept yourself so busy with activities that you didn't feel life's past pains.
- Failed to align your habits with your goals and desires.
- Played the victim role, blaming someone else for your life circumstances.
- Compared yourself to others.
- Complained about your life.
- Lived by societal or parental expectations rather than what you want to do.

Balance of Power: A New Approach to Leadership

Rodenberg once said, "At the center of every Shakespeare play is a central message that we must not misuse our power." As leaders, it's our role to guard against the misuse of power and call it out when we see it.

Being a leader is no longer about having control over others. This form of leadership is no longer useful or valid in our fast-changing world. Our goal as leaders, therefore, is to move into a place of *power with* and encourage fostering personal power in others. This will create a culture of shared power in which all people feel secure and can show up as their most authentic selves, offering and receiving their greatest talents to and from others and their organizations.

When personal power becomes the mantra of everyone involved in a business culture, there is no longer any room for victim mode. You will no longer hear workers say things such as: "We have no way to influence this. It's up to top management to make this call." We look to instill hope and confidence in our team, so they may forge ahead and find new solutions to current problems and innovate.

As you continue to cultivate your personal power and that of others, ask yourself these questions at least once a week:

1. How much power am I willing to share?
2. How do I misuse my power and try to control others?
3. How can I encourage more second circle energy and more *power with* environments?
4. How do I encourage others to step into their personal power?

I promise you that asking the above four questions on a regular basis will prove invaluable to you and your teams, as it's all too easy to fall back on old habits where power is concerned. To have the greatest impact, we must embrace our truest power, which is an integration of *power with, power to,* and *power within*. It is only then that we stand in our own power and know ourselves that we become willing and able to share power with others.

TAKEAWAYS

- The traditional model of hierarchical power is unsuccessful in today's work environment.
- There are three newer types of power that have replaced *power over: power with, power to,* and *power within*.
- Personal power is a new way of being and thinking that requires us to take charge of our lives and no longer leaves room for victimhood.
- Personal power is broken into three areas: personal agency, mental mastery, and self-mastery.
- When we give away our power, we allow others to define our self-worth and control our time and energy.

Chapter Six

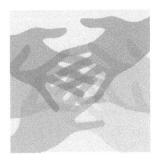

UNLOCKING PERSONAL POWER

Unleashing your personal power is a lifelong journey. Most of us have days when we're in our element and feel nearly invincible and other days when we fall back, stepping out of our personal power and letting external life circumstances direct us.

Owning your personal power is not for the faint of heart; it requires courage to explore yourself and be the best version of yourself. The overall purpose of this chapter is to offer some tools and support to further strengthen your personal power journey.

Mirror, Mirror on the Wall

If you want to fully step into your personal power, you must cultivate self-awareness. Research suggests that, when you see yourself more accurately, you become more self-confident and creative, make sounder decisions, build stronger relationships, and communicate with greater effectiveness.

Self-awareness is one of your greatest tools for growth and the realization of your goals. We all have blind spots, so when you look at your reflection in the mirror, self-awareness enables you to see yourself as you are and identify opportunities for continued growth and improvement.

There are two aspects to self-awareness. The first is understanding yourself, which entails identifying your values, passions, and aspirations. It also involves adapting to your environment and being able to master your thoughts, feelings, behaviors, strengths, and weaknesses.

The second aspect is recognizing the impact you have on others and how their impressions of you compare with those you have of yourself. Organizational psychologist Tasha Eurich, author of *Insight*, conducted studies in which she revealed that, while 95 percent of people think they're self-aware, only about 10-15 percent have this ability. The following are three strategies from Eurich to help cultivate your self-awareness:

1. Make the decision that you want to know the truth. This requires being braver and wiser.
2. Ask for more feedback. Other people can see us more honestly and objectively than we can see ourselves.
3. Ask others *what* you can do to improve. (Example: *What can I do to improve my work relationships?*) Action plan

Maximize Your Personal Power

Truly unlocking your personal power requires a shift in thinking and acting in three areas: from *taking to giving*, from *selecting to creating*, and from *acknowledgment to self-esteem*.

Taking to Giving

We have been conditioned to achieve and/or attain things to satisfy our egos. We feel exhilarated when we accumulate possessions, get promoted, receive praise, or win an award. The more status symbols we collect, the greater our sense of importance in our society. But materialistic things, titles, and accolades don't satisfy us for long because the ego always wants something more.

Early on in our careers, achieving certain goals may satisfy our needs

Solicit feedback ... draw diagram

while building our self-confidence. It doesn't take long, however, before the need to achieve begins to evolve. If we continue to pursue goals that serve ourselves, the gratification gets shorter until we begin to feel empty and lost. Then we feel satisfaction and contentment only when we transition from *taking* to *giving back*, devoting our unique talents to serving others. Deep down, our psyches crave one reward more than anything else: figuring out how to make the world a better place than how we found it.

Selecting to Creating

When we first start out on our own, the world can seem like a giant candy store, with several options from which to choose: the place we want to live, the career we want to pursue, and the people with whom we want to associate. Alternatively, we can get caught in a sense of panic about the limited options that seem to be available to us. When we shift from selecting to creating, we can move from simply operating within a set of given options to generating multiple paths forward for ourselves. Our true power lies in being able to become the author of our own lives, as we began to explore in the previous chapter.

If we only look to the outside world to fulfill our greatest desires, we can only choose from what already exists, which doesn't call for ingenuity or big dreams. We need to leverage our intuition and marry it with our unique gifts and talents. Our ability *to create* is our ultimate growth engine and welcomes us to play in a game that doesn't have any limits. Once we step through this door, we never see the world in the same way.

All the leaders I work with have powerful dreams, but few of them have dreams that are big enough and do justice to their abilities. They tend to extend their arms as far as they will go physically and then stop there. They don't reach for the stars.

I sometimes ask leaders: "What would really *blow your mind*?" I use those words intentionally, as our minds tend to keep us small and limited to the world of *selecting* or *trade-offs*. When we become creators, we open new doors and enter a world of possibilities. As Walt Disney stated, "If we dream it, we can create it."

Acknowledgment to Self-Esteem

We live in a world of *likes* in which our personal data is visible for the entire world to see. Yet *likes* on our posted content doesn't mean a thing if we lack self-esteem—the confidence instilled in our worth and abilities. When we have self-esteem, we are rewarded with a sense of feeling loved and worthy. Unfortunately, many of us are far too reliant upon other people's opinions of us. We spend too much time trying to get everyone to acknowledge, like, and praise us, so we feel validated. This can be *exhausting*. Worse yet, when we don't receive the expected attention, we become upset and believe no one sees our true worth. This triggers a downward emotional spiral that trudges up our childhood fears and causes our old coping mechanisms to kick in.

Building self-esteem and determining our self-worth are not only invaluable for helping us feel good, they also light the way to help us:

Give example.

- Recognize the difference between *confidence* and *arrogance*.
- Ask for constructive feedback.
- Avoid seeking approval or validation when it's not necessary.
- Know when it is necessary to seek approval.
- Lean into conflict instead of hiding from it.
- Set healthy boundaries.
- Voice our needs and opinions.
- Take care that things get done properly but not come across as pushy.
- Drive for excellence and stop before perfection.
- Deal well with setbacks.
- Avoid fear of failure.
- Feel neither inferior nor superior.
- Accept who we are.

One tool for improving self-esteem is to practice *self-compassion*. We sometimes beat ourselves up for not getting things right, but it takes time to master our work and relationships. We are never expected to get things perfect the first or even second time. Embracing self-compassion is asking ourselves: *Did I do the best that I knew how, given the situation?* If the answer is *Yes*, then take a step back and ask, *What can I learn from that situation?* This is the formula for achieving rapid growth, high self-esteem, and more personal power.

Stand in Your Integrity

Integrity doesn't just refer to having strong moral principles and making the right choices. It also means being *true to yourself* and making decisions that are in line with your intuitive path and informed by your intelligence. When you act with integrity and follow your inner compass, you strengthen your personal power.

It's easy to betray ourselves. At work, our manager might convince us to accept a "good development opportunity," although something deep inside tells us we shouldn't. We might remain in a company because it offers security—income and benefits—even though it's sucking the life out of our souls.

The cliché "the truth will set you free" couldn't be more accurate when it comes to standing in our integrity. It means *telling ourselves the truth*, no matter what. This opens doors for true and lasting change in our lives. This is never easy; it means facing the unknown every day. At the same time, if we listen to our guidance system and learn to trust it, we come to realize that we don't need to be fearful, as we've been guided by our hearts and intuition all along. Being guided by our hearts and intuition doesn't mean we have all the pieces of the puzzle, but it does provide us with enough strength to move forward into uncharted territory with confidence.

 REFLECTION: ACKNOWLEDGING THE TRUTH

Spend some time ruminating on these questions:

- When have you avoided or ignored the truth?
- How did it impact you in the end?
- What actions can you take to align with your truth?

Being vigilant to your life's vision obligates you to set healthy boundaries and say *No* to others' requests. Sometimes, to be true to yourself, you must disappoint others who have expectations of you. It might entail declining a promotion because it isn't aligned with your inner compass—even if it doesn't make logical sense. To carry out your vision, you must be fully committed with your head, heart, and gut. As eighteenth-century German playwright Johann Wolfgang von Goethe wrote, "At the moment of commitment the entire universe conspires to assist you."

As leaders, we also want to encourage our colleagues and direct reports to align with their respective purposes. McKinsey & Company, in their study entitled "The Search for Purpose at Work," discovered that nearly seven out of ten employees reflected on their purpose because of COVID-19. Those employees who indicated that they live their purpose at work are 6.5 times more likely to report a greater amount of resilience. They're also 4 times more likely to enjoy better health, 6 times more likely to want to stay at the company, and 1.5 times more likely to go above and beyond to help their company be successful.

Mental Mastery

To fulfill our highest potential and claim our inner power, we need to master our minds and get them working *for* instead of *against* us. Since the mind has the power to create our reality, it can also manifest anything we want to achieve in our personal and professional lives, if we devote enough time and attention to the things that matter most to us. To master the mind, we need to focus on the following five areas, which we will next explore in greater detail:

1. Visualize your future.
2. Monitor your thinking and beliefs.
3. Quiet your mind and leave time for recovery.
4. Collaborate with your mind.
5. Fill your repository.

Visualize Your Future

Visualization can be a wonderful tool to channel and fulfill our dreams. If we use our hearts to become clear on our purpose, then we can activate it with the mind. If finding your purpose becomes too daunting, start by identifying your strengths and using those skills to direct your professional life.

Visualization techniques, as introduced in Chapter Two with reference to professional athletes, can be an excellent way to create a desirable simulated environment. Visualization grants you the power from within to fulfill a major goal, obtain something meaningful to you, or influence events in your favor. By focusing all five senses—sight, smell, taste, feel, and hearing—on the intended objective, your subconscious becomes conditioned and prepared for a situation before it happens. The most important ingredient to ensure visualization takes hold is to focus on what it will feel like once the goal has been achieved. You must pay attention to and connect with that emotion every day to accelerate success. On an intuitive level, what you project in your mind filters outward and connects to the cosmic ether, sending signals into the world that turn your visualization into reality.

 REFLECTION: HOW TO VISUALIZE

Visualization can be powerful and effective, but it doesn't work with a mere snap of the fingers. It's not based on "wishful thinking." You must be in a relaxed state, practice regularly, imagine your goal in relation to all five senses, emotionally connect with it, and truly believe that it will happen. Hold the visualization for at least sixty-eight seconds. Visualization doesn't work if you're distracted or self-critical; be focused and positive.

To begin, find a comfortable place where you can close your eyes, relax, and avoid interruption. Sit in a chair with your spine tall. Take ten to twelve deep breaths and slow your breathing. In your mind's eye, picture your success. Fill in as many details as you can, including where you are and what you are wearing. Most importantly, focus on how it will feel to achieve this goal. Hold the picture and the feeling for a full sixty-eight seconds. Repeat these steps three to four times per day.

Monitor Your Thinking and Beliefs

It requires intention and self-awareness to make our subconscious *conscious* and become aware of what we are thinking. It's only when we do this that we can create our desired paradigms and shift our thinking. If we want to change our programming, we need to begin with our current identity, since we can't move beyond our view of ourselves. Creating a new perspective is like getting a software update. On the other hand, repetitive current stories and thoughts keep us activated in our old programming and identity.

The way to truly make fundamental changes in your life is to become more aware, present, and conscious. When you step away from running on automatic pilot, you become able to see how you interact with the world around you, including strangers, family, colleagues, and friends, as well as your self-talk. While awareness is the first step to change, this alone isn't enough to make significant shifts in your life. Intention, focus, and action are key.

Step 1: Create awareness—This includes behaviors, thoughts, beliefs, and values and how they may be impacting the outcomes you are getting in your life—both positively and negatively. Be the observer of your thoughts and stories without judgment.

I see myself in the moment reacting to criticism.

Step 2: Accept—You can't change unless you accept your current experience. By accepting how you operate, you can take accountability for the outward results and break through your resistance to change.

I accept that I might not be doing something the best way.

Step 3: Make conscious choices—Repattern the brain by choosing a different pathway; this results in a new level of empowering thoughts and stories.

I view criticism in a new way and see it as an opportunity to grow.

Step 4: Create moments of awareness—Catch yourself in the moment that you are ruminating on old thought patterns and exhibiting detrimental past behaviors. In this moment of awareness, you can make a new choice instead of returning to former conditioning. This is where change really occurs.

I observe myself feeling criticized when my manager gives me feedback on my work. Instead of getting defensive, I am curious about her comments and will explore how they can help me improve my performance.

Step 5: Practice integration—Continue to practice making different choices. As a result, you'll see yourself transforming from within, and it will become second nature.

Sometimes I fall back into feeling criticized, but I don't let it get in the way. Now I use it to help improve my performance.

Having compassion for yourself is the most important aspect of the change process. You'll find there will be many times that you catch yourself *after* behaving in the way you want to change, instead of in the moment. It's easy to beat yourself up and get angry and frustrated; it's only with patience and time that you will find yourself in the moment of awareness. The more you follow these steps and practice, the easier change will come.

Quiet the Mind and Leave Time for Recovery

The active thinker often becomes so overtaxed that it can't focus enough to adequately deal with the important matters at hand. At times, we get so wrapped up in our work that we aren't even aware that we're overtaxed until we stop. A client of mine was working ferociously on a big mergers and acquisitions deal for a few months straight–working nights and weekends. When the deal was complete, he slept for three days straight. He didn't realize how much he had taxed his physical body, as his mind overrode the signals to slow down and pace himself. Sporadically peeling yourself away from work and granting your mind a bit of a rest recharges your batteries and enables you to return with a clear head. In my case, I recognize that I've been pushing myself too hard when the bottom of my feet hurt when I wake up. It's a sign for me to step away from work and get some rest. *How do you know when your mind goes into overdrive, and you are pushing yourself beyond your limits?* Optimally, you want to work for no more than ninety minutes at a time and take fifteen-minute breaks in between.

ACTION FRAMEWORK

The ancient Buddhist practice of *mindfulness* is an exceptional way to quiet the mind and increase the strength and stamina of your active thinker. Dr. Jon Kabat-Zinn, author of numerous bestsellers and the developer and founder of MBSR (mindfulness-based stress reduction), has brought mindfulness to Western medicine and philosophy. He describes mindfulness as both a way of being and a formal meditative discipline. It has broad applications that can be mined to improve one's overall mental state, spiritual outlook, and even physical health. For leaders, mindfulness means mastering thoughts in a way that balances the left and right brain while also boosting a person's ability to tune out distractions, focus on what matters, and listen to the inner voice that is jam-packed with brilliant creative insights waiting to be released into the world.

The following are a few commonsense tips:

- *Commit yourself to doing mind/body practice.* This might be yoga, walking in nature, or deep breathing.

- *Declutter your desk.* The less paper and junk on it, the more psychological space you have in your mind to think freely and/or concentrate.

- *Stay in the alpha wave of the brain.* Alpha is one of five such waves—the others being delta, theta, beta, and gamma—that represent the level of electricity occurring as a pattern in the brain. Alpha waves, which register 8-12 Hz (hertz), are the most relaxed state. We are naturally in this reflective Alpha wave state when we wake up in the morning. See how long you can remain in it.

- *Avoid technology when you wake up in the morning.* There are several benefits of this, but primarily you avoid seeing anything negative—such as something unpleasant in the news—that can distort how you feel and then carry throughout the day.

- *Give yourself some needed breaks to relax your mind.* Take breaks, and solutions to unsolved problems begin to emerge. To recharge, do nothing and just unwind, or do something that brings you intense joy. Here are a few tips for recovery:
    - *Shorten your work meetings: Shave a mere fifteen minutes off four meetings and you give yourself an extra hour.*
    - *Leave two hours of unwinding time before you go to bed. This may be as simple as reading a book, connecting with a partner or loved one, listening to music, or playing a game with your kids.*

Collaborate with Your Mind

Hypnotherapist Marisa Peer, in one of her TEDx Talks, explores four key concepts that are at play when you collaborate with your mind:

1. The mind "always does what it thinks we want it to do" and "the words you use matter." If you were to say, "I hate doing my department budget," you are going to procrastinate. Instead, if you say, "I just need to focus and get the budget done," you will find ways to devote the requisite effort necessary to complete the assignment.

2. The mind is "hardwired toward pleasure and away from pain." Identifying what you love to do—as well as the things you perceive as hurtful—can be beneficial. You must train your brain to limit the time spent on pleasurable things that are distractions—such as scrolling social media feeds—and focus on what is most pressing and will advance you the most—even if it means dealing with things you regard as difficult.

3. The images you form in your head and the words you tell your-self determine how you will feel. If you picture favorable out-comes in your head and describe them with optimistic words, you'll feel happier and the odds of a positive result tilt in your favor.

4. Your mind is "programmed to focus on the familiar." If you want to succeed at something, you must make it as identifiable as pos-sible. The more familiarity you have, the greater your comfort level and the more your brain wants to return to it. This also works with enabling your team to deal with change at a higher level of effectiveness. The more you discuss it, the more familiar it becomes, and the better chance team members will embrace it.

Ask yourself the following questions: *How well are you collaborating with your mind? What words do you most often tell yourself?* If you find that you often "trash talk" yourself in your mind with statements such as "I'm no good at it," "I can't," and "It won't work," flip the script: "I will be good at it *after I've practiced it a few times.*"

Fill Your Repository

As a reminder, the repository is the place where new information is stored and cataloged in your mind. To become mental masters of our personal libraries, we must stimulate the brain with exciting inputs that awaken the mind and challenge our current way of thinking. To quote Albert Einstein: "We cannot solve our problems with the same thinking we used when we created them." If we want to solve our complex problems, we need to chal-lenge our assumptions, approach problems with a beginner's mindset, gain others' perspectives, and foster intellectual curiosity.

Reframing Situations

Sometimes just looking at a situation from another angle—or reframing it—can resolve a difficult decision when you aren't getting the results you want. Ask yourself questions such as: *How can I view the situation differ-ently? What assumptions do I have about the problem or situation? Are there any upsides or potential opportunities from the situation that I haven't considered?*

Let's look at an example of reframed conflict resolution. Suppose a colleague publicly disagrees with you about the release date of a product; she wants it to come out as soon as possible in the spring to capture some immediate revenue, whereas you want to release it in the market in the fall during the prime season. Your feathers are riled up. You just want to nail down a plan. Instead of saying, "No, you're wrong" or dismissing the suggestion entirely, you can view the situation differently by initiating the six-pack rule—looking at a situation from six different viewpoints. Below are three to get you started:

1. What if she has a point? We did ask the team for creative ways to build quick revenue to make the goal for spring...

2. What assumptions do I have about the problem or situation? I'm assuming that releasing in the fall will give the greatest revenue—but what if I need to rethink this?

3. What potential upsides or opportunities are there if I consider her perspective? I suppose we could develop a complementary follow-up product in the fall that piggybacks on this one in the spring. Maybe we could even bundle them together later. Aha—revenue opportunities from just a simple shift in release date!

What other three would you add? As you can see from the above scenario, reframing your thoughts has the potential to shift your perception, allowing something new to emerge and creating win-win situations all around.

Foster Intellectual Curiosity

Above all, we must foster our intellectual curiosity to ignite our personal and professional dreams. Whenever we venture out into the world, we want to think of ourselves as wide-eyed children who are experiencing things for the first time. The objective is to take on the role of a seeker who is still absorbing and growing, rather than one who is always trying to force our ideas and perspectives onto the world. By doing so, we add value to what we already know, which helps us dive deeper for answers to complex questions and innovate beyond our wildest imaginations. The following are four added benefits of heightening our intellectual curiosity:

1. *Curiosity makes our minds active instead of passive.* Curious people ask questions and search for answers. Their brains are always active. Since the mind is like a muscle that becomes stronger through continual exercise, the mental exercise initiated by curiosity makes it sharper.

2. *Curiosity makes our minds observant of new ideas.* When we are curious about something, our minds expect and anticipate new ideas related to the subject. If the ideas happen to come from reading a book or another source, we'll recognize them. Without curiosity, ideas fly right by us because our minds aren't prepared to spot them.

3. *Curiosity opens new worlds and possibilities.* By being curious, we become able to see things that are normally invisible. They are hidden behind the surface of normal life, so it takes a curious mind to search underneath and find them.

4. *Curiosity adds excitement to our lives.* Curious people never lead boring or routine lives; they always have new and adventurous things to try. People gravitate toward the curious-minded for one simple reason: They are fun to be with!

Below are four tips to help you create a repository as grand as the Library of Congress (Washington, D.C., United States), Bodleian Library (London, England), or the National Library of St. Mark's (Venice, Italy):

- Travel to new and exotic places.
- Develop new and varied interests and hobbies.

- Review interesting blogs, newspapers, or magazines or listen to podcasts.
- Be open to new ways of thinking and don't discount things if they don't fit into what you already know.

TAKEAWAYS

- There are two aspects of self-awareness: understanding yourself and recognizing the impact you have on others.
- Unlocking your personal power requires a shift in three areas: from *taking to giving*; from *selecting to creating*; and from *acknowledgment to self-esteem*.
- In addition to having strong moral values, integrity means being true to yourself and making decisions that are in line with your intuitive path.
- To master your mind, you must: visualize your future; monitor your thinking and beliefs; quiet the mind; collaborate with your mind; and fill your repository.
- When you aren't getting the results you want, try reframing the situation.

Chapter Seven

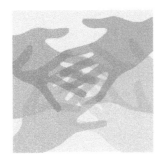

THE GATEWAYS TO A DEEPER PART OF YOURSELF

The journey of stepping into our personal power requires us to look inward to reclaim our true selves and let go of the masks we sometimes wear and that can hold back our authenticity. Few of us are ever encouraged to enter this personal journey or even taught where to begin. Instead, we find ourselves directed by everyday experiences that impact us one after another. Many of us believe these life experiences shape and define who we are, but this isn't entirely true; rather, they indicate how our perspective of the external world is informed. This includes the stage of human development we are in, which provides clues to help us find ourselves as we head on our respective journeys.

The Five Stages of Human Development

Dr. Robert Kegan—a psychologist who built on the work of predecessors such as Jean Piaget, Lawrence Kohlberg, and William Perry—referred to five stages of mental complexity or what he described as "orders of mind." According to Kegan, becoming an adult isn't about learning new things or adding things to the "container" of the mind. Rather, it's about *transformation:* changing the way we know and understand the world or the actual *form* of our container. Western psychology asserts that these stages of development are cumulative and follow in sequential order; we can't bypass a stage without fully realizing all the qualities and mindsets that each one provides. As the statistics in the list below reveal, most people fail to move past stage three, which severely limits their potential. If we wish to widen our possibilities, we must strive to advance to stages four and five, where we co-create and maintain the highest level of awareness possible.

Kegan's five stages (levels) of adult development—also known as *Constructive Development Theory*—are as follows:

- *Stage 1: Impulsive mind:* This takes place during early childhood. When you are a baby and then a toddler, your mind doesn't yet have a rulebook. The whole world is your "playground" in which your imagination can roam free and help you learn through the senses.

- *Stage 2: Imperial mind:* The second level primarily includes older children and adolescents, but 6 percent of the adult population—those who haven't progressed to full emotional maturity—fit into this population as well. While in this stage, we lack perspective and tend to be rebellious and unknowingly selfish. Essentially, we are unable to understand and process the needs and wants of others at the same time as our own and are unaware of the resulting consequences.

- *Stage 3: Socialized mind:* This adult group has the largest population at approximately 58 percent. Here we develop internal values based on external influences that guide us on how we view the world and make decisions. When faced with conflict, we must rely on information and support from outside sources, or we become confused or even lost. Since this level compels us to look externally and eschew ownership and responsibility, our "selfish" reliance upon others becomes so habitual that many of us end up stuck in the Socialized Mind and don't proceed to Stage 4.

- *Stage 4: Self-authoring mind:* An adult of any age has the capacity to reach Stage 4, but only 35 percent of the population make it to this level. In this stage, we access information and views from all sources—external and internal—and form our own individual belief systems based on the *self*, enabling us to make informed, independent decisions.

- *Stage 5: Self-transforming mind:* This stands as the smallest group at only 1 percent of the adult population, occurring during or after midlife. In this stage, you display the power to let go of your current ways of thinking and upgrade them. You become a master at decision-making and dealing with conflict and controversy.

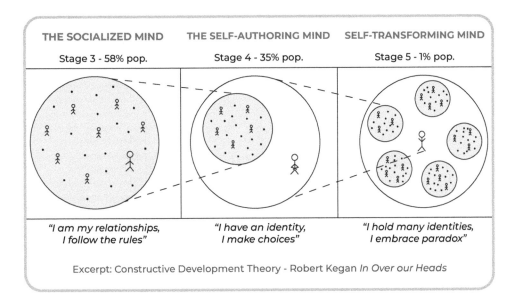

THE SOCIALIZED MIND	THE SELF-AUTHORING MIND	SELF-TRANSFORMING MIND
Stage 3 - 58% pop.	Stage 4 - 35% pop.	Stage 5 - 1% pop.
"I am my relationships, I follow the rules"	*"I have an identity, I make choices"*	*"I hold many identities, I embrace paradox"*

Excerpt: Constructive Development Theory - Robert Kegan *In Over our Heads*

Which State of Development Are You In?

Stages	I am/I have	Guiding Questions	Additional Characteristics
Stage 1: Impulsive mind	I AM pure impulse.		
Stage 2: Imperial mind	I AM needs, interests, and desires. I HAVE impulses and perceptions.	• Will I get punished if I do something or other? • What is in it for me?	• We can recognize that others have perspectives • We can control impulses • We have stable needs and habits • Self-interested • We act based on consequences
Stage 3: Socialized mind	I AM interpersonal relationships and mutuality I HAVE needs, interests, and desires	• Will you still like/value me? • Will you approve of me? • Will you still think I am (good, excellent, smart, etc.) at X characteristic?	• We can internalize feelings and emotions of others as guidelines for how to think and act • What we know and believe we get from others vs. from our own independent thinking • We take personal responsibility for how other people experience us and think about us • We validate our sense of self externally (the approval of others, acceptance into a group) • We can focus on following rules, traditions, and norms • We have difficulty letting go of harmful relationships

Stages	I am/I have	Guiding Questions	Additional Characteristics
Stage 4: Self-Authoring mind	I AM self-authorship, ideology, and identity I HAVE interpersonal relationships and mutuality	• Am I maintaining my own personal integrity, standards, and values? • Am I living, working, and loving to the best of my ability? • Am I achieving my goals and being guided by my ideals?	• We can listen to other's opinions, ideas, and beliefs and decide for ourselves what we think • We can take stands and set limits based on the things we believe and feel are important
Stage 5: Self-Transforming mind	I AM all and nothing I HAVE self-authorship, ideology, and identity	• How do I know what I am saying or thinking is true? • Are there multiple truths to be seen and understood? • What lens am I looking at this through? Is there a perspective I'm missing or don't understand? • Am I unattached to ideas, beliefs, and identities? Am I seeking truth, or am I seeking truth through my own filter?	• We are self-reflective and constantly looking to refine our sense of self as well as align it with how we act • We can reflect on our own actions and modify behavior to achieve different results • We make decisions to be consistent with ideology or identity • We see beyond ourselves, others, and systems we are a part of to form an understanding of how all people and systems interconnect • The mind is no longer subject to its filter (i.e., identity, ideologies) but can step back and examine, update, or hold multiple filters • We put entire way of thinking and identity at risk with each interaction, understanding that both are fluid and ever-changing • We hold opposite viewpoints and different identities, embraces paradox in the search for a deeper truth

> **REFLECTION:** WHAT STAGE ARE YOU IN?
>
> Using the table above, reflect on which stage you might be in using the questions below as guideposts. Note: It's possible to move from one stage to another—backward or forward—at various junctures of your life.
>
> ■ What holds you back from going to the next stage?
> ■ How do I need to think or act differently to move to a higher stage?

There is another approach to achieving a higher state of human development, one that may be found in many Eastern philosophies: *a state of awareness* or *being in unity*. People have been known to achieve such higher consciousness with various types of activities, including:

- Devotional practice
- Meditation
- Sex
- Yoga
- Chanting
- Fasting
- Exhaustion
- Illness
- Self-enquiry

While it is possible to access higher consciousness intentionally or unintentionally through these experiences, one particularly useful philosophy to leaders is self-enquiry (or *self-inquiry*), which was described by Indian guru Bhagavan Sri Ramana Maharshi as the only tool you need to fully realize your human potential and bypass duality. The purpose of self-enquiry is the constant attention to the inner awareness of *I* or *I am*. This provides you with the ability to question everything you believe to be true and frees your mind to expand and break free. I invite you to practice using this powerful tool—it can *blow your mind!*

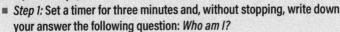
In the following sections, you'll discover several additional ways to
reach Stages 4 and 5: *being present, processing your experiences,* and *allowing
yourself to transform.*

Being Receptive or Present

Digging deeper into who we are requires us to be fully present with ourselves and others. For most of us, this doesn't come naturally; it takes effort
to stay focused in the moment. When we're fully present, we gain full
access to our feelings, senses, and intuition. In doing so, we open ourselves
to creating a wide universe of possibilities that can bring about unexpected
outcomes.

To begin, you must say *Yes* to everything in the moment—not necessarily to an idea, personal request, or recommendation but rather to the
experience being presented. Carl Jung coined the phrase "what you resist
persists." It's better to deal with things when they are presented, rather than
having to constantly revisit the same issue or challenge. The first level of

this concept requires you to stay present and head further into the experience, even if it feels uncomfortable or painful. The second is to explore your feelings that arise while being present. To go further, it might be necessary to ask yourself: *How does this present situation trigger reactive behavior in me related to past experiences?* This allows you to fully process your emotions and draw out a learning. Lastly, it means moving beyond the little voice in your head that says, *Don't do it, you'll look like a fool.* Instead, step up and move things forward!

Saying *Yes* in this way is not an easy thing for many leaders to do, as it requires you to fully trust yourself in the moment. It could mean having the courage to speak up when you would normally stay quiet, postponing a request from a senior leader, or volunteering to work with a challenging colleague. When we stay present, a deeper part of ourselves emerges and we allow the same to happen for others.

Processing Your Experiences

In our personal and professional lives, we flit from one activity to the next so often we become unable to process what happened in the last meeting or conversation before we must dive into the next one. No wonder we find ourselves so exhausted by the end of the week that we search for ways to unwind. Sometimes in life, we can have greater impact by slowing things down, so we may properly take them in and process them. This provides the opportunity to deal with the complexity of life and to process our emotions and allow our mind and intuition to work for us. As I reached higher levels of leadership roles, I realized that, when people asked for my thoughts on an issue, the question "May I reflect on this and get back to you?" bought me time to think deeper, integrate my thoughts, and provide a more thoughtful response.

Tackling challenging experiences and taking the time to process them opens the door for deeper reflection and self-discovery. For example, if you notice a co-worker is not herself and in reactive mode, a few paused moments followed by an inquiry into what is bothering her has a good chance of being received as compassion. Similarly, if your business is in a rough patch, self-reflection can help you realize that conferring with a coach or mentor would be beneficial. While I'm certainly not wishing "bad things to happen," there are discoveries and revelations that can be made during these raw, vulnerable moments.

Taking time for extra reflection also offers us the opportunity to avoid unnecessarily being in reactive mode, as it gives space to ask the question: "Is this my emotional baggage or someone else's?" When we reach this level of awareness, we reduce the amount of self-imposed angst brought about from past experiences that may not even relate to the issue at hand.

Allowing Yourself to Transform

Sometimes we become stuck because we are wedded to our positive or negative life experiences and permit them to define us. When this occurs, we must release the self-impressions that are holding us back. Several years ago, for instance, I was coaching a highly respected female leader. Throughout her career, she believed she had to work harder and faster than everyone else to prove her worth. Once she landed a senior role in a Fortune 100 company, she still couldn't let go of her preconceived notions and absurdly high standards. Not only did this make her feel exhausted, it also limited her team's potential because she felt she always had to prove she was the smartest person in the room and come up with all the solutions herself.

When we let go of self-expectations, we give ourselves the freedom to fully transform and grow. We should strive to be in a state of exploration and reinvention and place ourselves and others in a position where we can accomplish even greater things.

ACTION FRAMEWORK

To move beyond yourself and your limitations, try the following experiment. Spend fifteen minutes a day repeating three words: *I am that.* As you view things in your external world, recite these three magical words while paying attention to identifying things that you dislike about yourself. Notice how it feels when you connect to the parts of what you judge or reject. Do you now feel greater motivation to try something new that will help you discard the unlikable attributes you pinpointed?

What Guides You and Gives You Meaning?

There are many external actions that can bring you satisfaction and sustain you: perhaps a dip in the ocean, a chat with your best friend, or a hug from a loved one. What you need to identify, however, is what sustains you from the *inside*—and how do you find meaning and purpose? This is one of the deeper questions that Dr. Viktor Frankl explores in his book *Man's Search for Meaning*. Having personally endured and observed the worst human conditions in a Nazi concentration camp during World War II, Frankl wondered why certain fellow prisoners lost hope and withered away during the experience, whereas others found joy in even the smallest things and thrived after being released. What determined one individual's mindset and resiliency versus another? Frankl proposed that those who could draw meaning from the inside could cope in the face of such atrocities.

Meaning isn't only important to us when we are forced to deal with extreme circumstances. In a study at Johns Hopkins University, social scientists discovered that only 16 percent of students who were surveyed identified "making a lot of money" as the most important thing to them. However, an astounding 78 percent singled out "finding a purpose and meaning to my life" as their primary motivation.

German neurologist Kurt Goldstein coined a term referring to the process of becoming a holistic "self" to instill meaning and purpose for the individual: *self-actualization*. Humanistic psychologist Abraham Maslow expanded on this premise and defined self-actualization as "everything you are capable of becoming," by which he meant the highest level of consciousness a person can achieve according to her or his framework. In his research, Maslow discovered a common thread among those who were most self-actualized: They had found their *own religion*, meaning that they had devised and lived by a personal practice and ideology—not necessarily affiliated with any specific organized group—that connected them to something bigger than themselves.

The goal is to define your own meaningful practice and create rituals that work toward you achieving your unique purpose. The moments you devote to this practice must be deemed so important and sacred to you that you will be compelled to *take a break in time and space* from your routine to honor it. For some of us, this means carving out time for reflection, such as by writing in a journal; for others, it might entail taking a long walk along the beach. Others might fill this space by connecting to loved ones. The main thing is that the ritual is personal and provides meaning to you that you knowingly or unknowingly access whenever it is needed or desired.

Address What Zaps Your Energy

Earlier in this chapter, I suggested that you say *Yes* to everything in the moment without judgment. There is one important exception to this philosophy: Do *not* say *Yes* to something that will *drain your energy*. For example, if you know that joining a certain committee at your child's school will also mean getting dragged into political entanglements—which you truly despise—you should politely decline.

Every time you say *Yes* but mean *No,* your energy is reduced, and your power blocked. You must agree to the right things or else risk experiencing a *disconnection tax* that slows down your growth. The following are a few examples of actions that come with a steep emotional, mental, or spiritual price:

- Repressing or avoiding your emotions
- Limiting your emotional expression
- Saying one thing and doing another
- Communicating violently
- Ignoring your intuition
- Turning down something risky that fits your purpose and has a major upside
- Failing to pursue your dreams
- Staying in an unfulfilling job
- Failure to communicate disappointment in a relationship
- Disrespecting others
- Avoiding relationships
- Being self-serving
- Cutting yourself off from society

Sometimes we sabotage ourselves and keep ourselves small without being aware of it. Usually, this occurs when we cling to something that is outdated, like obsolete software running slowly on an electronic device. This includes things such as holding onto old perspectives, continuing the same bad habits, and repeating the same poor decisions. In the end, such baggage weighs us down and enslaves us, zapping our energy and preventing us from moving forward.

 REFLECTION: THE THINGS THAT ARE HOLDING YOU BACK

Ask yourself these questions:
- Where are you paying a disconnection tax?
- Where do you sabotage yourself or stay stuck?

Riding the Waves of Emotion

While there are myriad emotions, they boil down to a half dozen that are considered primary: happiness, anger, sadness, surprise, disgust, and fear. Among these six, there is potential for expressing a wide spectrum of extreme emotions: hate/love; anticipation/shock; boldness/terror; and so forth. To fully experience and embrace life, we must learn how to feel comfortable experiencing *all* these emotions. When we don't fully experience and process them, they find a way of leaking out and negatively impacting our mindset, decision-making, behaviors, and relationships.

To have true emotional agility, it's especially important to be able to recognize, understand, and respond appropriately to strong reactive emotions of other people. If someone becomes overly assertive and lashes out at you—especially in a work-related environment—the worst thing to do is counter with an equal amount of force. Instead, take a breath, pause, and then ask the other person, "Is everything okay?" This calm and caring disruption gives the individual permission to reflect on their own emotions in a safe way while preventing escalation.

We all become frustrated when unresolved conflict or lack of progress arises at work. When this occurs, we often judge others' reactive behaviors and feelings that likely stem from their past experiences. Since we don't know what's under their icebergs—needs, values, beliefs, and fears—misunderstandings become inevitable. What we must realize is that someone may be stuck in an emotional tunnel of their own creation. Authors Emily Nagoski and Amelia Nagoski in their book, *Burnout: The Secret to Unlocking the Stress Cycle,* cite the two reasons why we get trapped in a tunnel and can't fully process our emotions. We might regularly find ourselves in situations—at work, in our personal lives, or both—in which the people around us expect us to sit politely, smile, and do our best, even as our bodies stew in stress juice.

"No, no, it's fine. I'm fine. This is fine," you say, from the darkness of the middle of the tunnel.

Sometimes we get stuck because we can't find our way through the raw emotions by ourselves. The most difficult feelings—such as rage, grief, despair, and helplessness—may be too treacherous and painful to move through alone. We find ourselves lost and in need of someone else—a loving, supportive presence—to help us find our way.

It's fascinating to explore where we get stuck in our own emotional tunnel and stall out. We all have certain emotional areas that are more comfortable to deal with than others. For example, I once worked with a colleague who lost her mother at an early age. Her grief became so overwhelming that she never fully processed the emotion and became lost in the tunnel. As a result, she expressed anger more than other emotions and lashed out at people when something troubled her. Beneath the surface, she longed for connections, but she didn't know how to attain them due to her broken upbringing. If she had learned how to work through her sadness when her mother had passed away, she would have been better equipped to make deeper connections and know how to properly channel and express her emotions.

External events can impact our worldview and internal belief system. One negative incident at work can trail us and taint how we react to similar future occurrences—just like childhood trauma. For example, if your manager embarrasses you in front of the entire organization, you are likely to feel stupid and small. From that point onward, you will be cautious about expressing yourself in front of your manager, as you fear being on the receiving end of even more humiliation. In fact, after the first incident, the manager doesn't have to say much to trigger you and bring you right back to that dreadful moment. When we fully allow ourselves to process the emotion of the manager embarrassing us, we might take the time to talk to them about it, share it with a friend, or go for a walk to use our body's energy to move through the emotion. We're then less likely to be overtaken by embarrassment when we least expect it or if the threat has been imagined.

Masks

We all wear different masks to protect the fragile aspects of our innermost psyches. They are often a self-defense mechanism that helps shield us from hurt due to rejection or unfulfilled needs in our childhood and adolescence. We don them to protect ourselves from being outed for a self-perceived weakness, sensitivity, insecurity, powerlessness, or fear. At the same time, our masks hide our true nature and feelings and make us inauthentic and, therefore, unable to fully connect with others. When we wear a mask, we create a split screen and show one side externally while hiding another part from view.

Masks are not necessarily all bad; in fact, each one we wear was beneficial at one time in our lives, helping us become the people we are today. The masks become problematic when they become habitual, involuntary parts of our identities. While they sometimes serve as a protective barrier to get us through uncomfortable situations, they can also lead to stress, anxiety, and depression. When we wear a mask too long, it becomes so heavy that it exhausts us and negatively impacts our integrity. It's only when we recognize our masks and understand how they originated that we begin to have compassion for ourselves and others.

There is a small child inside all of us that is still experiencing fear that can easily get triggered. Sometimes we aren't even aware of the role these masks are playing in our lives, as we've grown so accustomed to hiding behind them. We need to ask ourselves: *When do these masks move from being useful to getting in the way of our moving to the next stage in human development?* The answer: *When we allow fear to grip our lives.*

While we can't fully dispose of our masks because it's not possible to turn back time and delete our childhood experiences, we can bring them from the unconscious to the conscious realm. Our goal is to shift our projected external view into greater alignment with our internal view, which exposes our underlying fears and the things that trigger us. When we accomplish this, we move beyond our reactive natures and experience personal growth.

German psychologist Karen Horney proposed an interpersonal theory of adjustment that revolutionized the science behind thoughts and behaviors underneath our shadow side or masks. She identified various neurotic needs that may be categorized into three types of personal behavior:

- *Self-reliant:* This is when people *move away* emotionally from situations or others during times of stress. Their emotional needs were probably not met during childhood, so they decided early on to be self-reliant and process things through the mind. They can be seen as extreme in business and are often described as unpredictable, suspicious, cautious, or aloof. Their inner work is to reclaim their emotions, open their hearts, and trust others to meet their emotional needs.

- *Dominant:* This is expressed when people under stress *move against others.* Leaders who exhibit these behaviors demonstrate a need to control other people, situations, and drive for results. They are often described as "go-getters" and "challenging."

When they were children, they most likely experienced a feeling of powerlessness or being ignored. Externally, they are self-confident, while internally they struggle with knowing their true self-worth. Their inner work is to stop proving themselves, accept their inner worth, and shift from a mode of fear driving their achievements to purpose and meaning. The key question to ask is: *Who are you when you are not achieving?*

- *Compliant and perfectionistic:* This is expressed when people under stress *move toward* other people. On these occasions, individuals go out of their way to seek acceptance and positive affirmation. During childhood, they most likely didn't feel fully loved for who they were or lacked a sense of belonging or healthy attachment. The inner work is self-acceptance and believing that we all hold equal power.

You've probably known more than your share of people who fell into one of the above groupings and struggled with how to best navigate those relationships. At Human Edge, we've identified ten masks based on psychoanalyst Karen Horney's work that can hinder success. We will never be able to entirely rid ourselves of them, but we can work toward being less reactive to reduce their impact.

Have you ever considered which factors might have led to your own coping behaviors? The more disconcerting question to ask yourself requires a deep (and rare) sense of self-awareness and intense self-reflection: *Where does my negative coping behavior impact other people and myself? How can I become more aware of my triggers?* It's only when we cultivate our self-awareness that we can become ready to take off our masks.

Removing Our Masks

We can't remove our masks until we've identified them and determined the roles they've served going back to our childhoods. If we examine the early stages of human development, we find that it's all about getting our basic needs met. We have limited experiences as children, so our perspectives are flawed, and we can't fully comprehend the nuances of life. At some point, we all experience similar situations of not having a childhood need met, which leads to confusion and anxiety. For example, when a newborn baby enters our home, we must deal with the emotional challenge of our parents' taking time away from us to care for the sibling. In my case, my middle sister needed more medical attention from my parents, which left me feeling less than adored. I responded by continually interjecting myself in the center of the family dynamics—even when it may not have been necessary or appropriate to do so. In my professional work, leveraging my masks led to attaining bigger jobs and a thirst for creating greater impact. It was only when I reached my early forties that I shifted to achieving with purpose and embraced the legacy I wanted to leave behind rather than what I hoped to accomplish for myself. I changed course and embarked on a career in which I could serve others, enabling them to unlock their human potential.

Let's examine the ten masks in greater detail, so you can identify any that may exist in yourself and others.

The Mask of...	Self-impact	Relationship Impact	Biggest Shift
Moving Away — Self-reliant			
Unease	Anxious and hyper-focused on what could go wrong in any given situation. Experiences more intense emotional extremes. Becomes fully immersed in projects	Sympathetic to others' anxieties or worries. Seen as unpredictable and volatile. Easily frustrated and disappointed when things don't go as planned.	Let go of their tight need for control. Manage expectations of situations and others. Learn to share their disappointments in a more genuine manner.
Underlying Fears	Fears losing control and/or being disappointed by others.		
Skepticism	Takes criticism personally and is unlikely to forgive or forget. Sees potential problems or negatives in most situations. Willingly passes up opportunities, or takes a critical view of these.	Perceptive and politically astute. Seen as argumentative, defeatist, overly cynical, and/or easily offended. Keeps a small group of trusted advisors.	Learn to trust again (self and others). Work through past grievances. Actively take time to counter inner critic and cynic.
Underlying Fears	Fear of being betrayed and/or being taken advantage of.		

The Mask of...	Self-impact	Relationship Impact	Biggest Shift
Moving Away – Self-reliant			
Emotional Control	Self-sufficient and task-oriented, trusting of their capabilities. May feel that they are unable to show their true selves to others. Keeps others at arm's length.	Able to make objective and independent decisions. Seen as tough-minded, aloof, and guarded. Avoids conflicts.	Embrace emotions, recognizing the value these bring to a situation. Shift view of vulnerability–seeing this as a strength and way to connect.
Underlying Fears	Fear of losing emotional control and/or fear of intimacy and vulnerability.		
Stability	Feels unsure when making decisions, preferring to stay in their comfort zone. May rely heavily on data and facts to mitigate potential mistakes. Overanalyzes or worries about even small actions, feeling stuck without outside guidance.	Requires reassurance, relying on the opinion of others. Worries that others will judge them or remember any mistake they make. Comes across as indecisive or hesitant.	Learn to trust themselves and their intuition. Shift view on mistakes–so that these are seen as a chance to grow and learn. Learn to be courageous in their actions.
Underlying Fears	Fear of making a mistake, and/or of being criticized.		
Moving Against– Dominant			
Originality	Always looking for their next area of interest, moving from one thing to the next. May become easily bored, finding it difficult to focus on one thing. May be overly confident in their ideas, becoming resistant to constructive feedback.	Sees things differently and is innovative. Changes focus quickly and in a manner that can be hard for others to follow. Disorganized and unpredictable.	Establish structure in their creativity. Embrace being ordinary. Learning to appreciate the benefit of tried and tested methods.
Underlying Fears	Fear of making a mistake, and/or of being criticized.		

The Mask of...	Self-impact	Relationship Impact	Biggest Shift
Moving Against – Dominant			
Eagerness	Focused on getting their own points or perspectives across. Impatient to share their thinking with others. Enjoys being center of attention.	Socially skilled and quick-witted. Dominates social situations and may not listen well to others. May speak over or disregard comments or perspectives of others. May come across as self-important.	Learning to love and respect themselves as they are. Recognize that they do not need to be at the center of the stage to be heard or make a significant contribution.
Underlying Fears	Fear of being ignored and/or not being fully seen or heard.		
Rebellion	Willing to take risks. Seeks out variety and excitement - may feel constrained or stuck if they are not doing this. Can be impatient and get bored easily.	Seen as adventurous–testing limits and transforming the external environment. Ignores others' resistance to change–overruling or dominating others. May ignore or brush past their mistakes	Learn to be in the present moment. Take not of other people's positions, fears, hopes and needs
Underlying Fears	Fear of missing out and/or of being boxed in with little room to expand.		
Pride	Strong sense of own ability–rating this above the abilities of anyone else. Strong belief that they can succeed–with any failure linked to external factors. Believes they should be given special treatment.	Socially and self-confident–taking the initiative in situations. Demands respect. Can be unwilling to give up or compromise. Unwilling to accept constructive criticism or feedback.	Build their internal self-esteem. Learn humility. Recognize the unique value of others.
Underlying Fears	Fear of losing and failure and/or fear of not knowing.		

The Mask of...	Self-impact	Relationship Impact	Biggest Shift
Moving Toward–Compliant and Prefectionistic			
Harmony	Highly flexible. Actively seeks a sense of belonging. Feel a need to be liked or viewed positively—experiencing anxiety when they believe this might not be the case.	Very amicable and get along with most people. Seen as "yes" people and tend to agree with everything that is said by those in power. Seen as highly accommodating.	Learn to step into their power and place themselves on same level of importance as others. Learn to consider and share their own opinions. Be authentic to themselves.
Underlying Fears	Fear of being kicked out of the tribe.		
Perfectionism	Strong attention to detail. Strives for excellence, with a high achievement drive. Believe that things can always be done better—with very high standards that can rarely be satisfied.	Diligent and conscientious. Can be judgmental of self and others when things don't meet their high standards. Tendency to rework their own as well as others' work. Can micromanage others.	Learn self-acceptance. Recognize that the process is just as important as the outcome. Understand that everything is evolving, learning, and changing–and perfection is not always the end goal.
Underlying Fears	Fear they are never good enough.		

👥 REFLECTION: IDENTIFYING YOUR MASKS

Read through the table and identify which masks you wear and how they impact your personal and professional life. Ask yourself these questions:

- How have these masks served me?
- Who would I be without these masks?
- What fears do I need to address to progress?

Transcending Our Masks and Facing Our Fears

To have greater impact in our personal and professional lives, we must face our fears and self-parent to meet our needs wherever possible. In some instances, we need to shift from a distorted child view to a more nuanced adult perspective. The only way to accomplish this is by transcending our masks and releasing childhood baggage. If we choose to resist, we will continue to blame our childhood—and perhaps even others—for our lack of progress.

It's easy to hold on to our past hurt like a warm blanket, but allowing it to fall away can be a gift. When we realize we no longer need our masks because they no longer define us, we become emotionally liberated. This process grants us space to spread our wings and soar.

There is no reason to concern yourself with how others will perceive or judge you. If you feel like you will be a fool if you release your mask, you will remain stuck in Stage 3 of Kegan's human development model. Transformation from one stage to the next requires you to look inward and resolve your own issues.

The following words are attributed to a variety of people, including Mark Twain, Satchel Paige, and William Purkey. Whoever said them first, they're worth repeating:

Sing like no one is listening. Love like you've never been hurt. Dance like nobody's watching, and live like it's heaven on earth.

Becoming the Best Version of Yourself

Imagination is perhaps the mind's strongest untapped tool, empowering us with the ability to paint our desired picture of the future. It enables us to decide what legacy we wish to leave behind; which people we wish to touch; and how we want to offer our gifts to our family, friends, and colleagues at work. Accomplishing this requires that we dig deep and align ourselves with the highest vision possible for ourselves and follow through on trying to achieve it each day. Before we know it, we will be creating the life that we've dreamed of and leaving the world a better place than when we found it.

TAKEAWAYS

- Robert Kegan presented Five Stages of Human Development: *Impulsive Mind, Imperial Mind, Socialized Mind, Self-Authoring Mind,* and *Self-Transforming Mind.*
- Your goal is to move into Stages Four and Five: *Self-Authoring Mind* and *Self-Transforming Mind.*
- Try these three methods to ensure you enter Stages Four and Five and don't lapse backward: *Being present, processing your experiences,* and *allowing yourself to transform.*
- It is critical for you to define your own meaningful practice and create rituals that work for you toward achieving your unique purpose.
- It's only when we recognize our masks, understand how they originated, and dispose of them that we begin to have compassion for ourselves and others.

Part III

CONNECTING TO OTHERS

Leader (Chris) SAYS: Hey, Tim, how was your weekend? Hope you got to enjoy some of the great weather.

Direct Report (Tim) SAYS: Yeah, we had Kim's parents over for a barbecue yesterday—it feels like summer is just around the corner, right? By the way, I just sent you the notes on the Sanderson case, so we're all set for 9:00 AM.

Direct Report (Tim) THINKS: I spent most of Friday evening and Saturday morning finishing up the due diligence on the Sanderson file. I missed my kid's football match and then Kim and I got into a fight because I forgot about the plants that she asked me to pick up. Just as I was about to unwind, I received an email from Chris outlining a few issues with the case, so I ended up having to finish up early Sunday morning, after everyone was in bed. I was wiped out, but we had Kim's parents over, so I spent the entire afternoon standing over the grill. I tried not to drink too much beer because I wanted to be bright for this morning's meeting... but, of course, that's not what Chris wants to hear. He expects me to keep my head down and my eye on the partnership track.

Leader (Chris) THINKS: Tim's a great guy, he's just what we need around here—so positive, focused, and relaxed. I wonder what he's thinking in terms of his future with the firm. Partnership is a lot of pressure, and I don't know if that suits his style. He's never asked for my thoughts or feedback on his future, so maybe he's looking at in-house counsel somewhere else...

Leader (Chris) SAYS: Good job, Tim, thanks.

Direct Report (Tim) SAYS: Yeah, no problem, Chris. See you tomorrow.

Chapter Eight

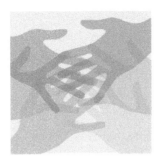

THE FOUNDATIONS FOR HUMAN CONNECTION

Most of us think we understand what the term *human connection* means—but do we really? If so, are we digging as deep as possible to enjoy its myriad rewards and benefits?

Everyone wants to feel significant, competent, and likeable. We achieve this through authentic connection–the relationship that is formed between people when they feel mutually seen and valued. This means knowing someone else cares about you, as well as your happiness and well-being. When you feel heard and understood and take the time to hear and understand others, the connection between you strengthens. It becomes a powerful source of energy and flow that generates a sense of engagement, trust, and belonging. During an *authentic* human connection, people exchange positive energy with one another and build trust. We might not be aware of it, but, every time we experience this positive energy flow, our metaphorical emotional tank gets filled. For this to occur, it is essential that we show up as our most authentic selves and move through life with vibrance and high energy. Continued positive human connection provides us with enough sustenance to help us deal with life's challenges.

A few years ago, I worked with a C-suite executive at a leading global insurance company. We discussed the 360-degree feedback that he had received from his team, notably his low rating regarding how he offered positive feedback and acknowledged his team members for their significant contributions.

When I pressed him on the matter, he became defensive. "These leaders get paid a lot of money to do their jobs," he explained. "Why do I have to tell them how good they are?"

I took a moment before replying, "They are human, too, and need recognition and acknowledgment."

"They got to this C-suite level, they know how good they are," he countered.

"Yes," I agreed in a calm voice. "They might see their rewards in their bonuses, but each of them wants to feel valued and know their contribution makes a difference. When you provide them with positive recognition, you fill their emotional tank. When their emotional tank is full, they will become better leaders themselves and achieve even higher levels of performance. In addition, when you offer positive feedback, you are setting the stage for anything that may occur down the road. For example, if you ever need to impart constructive criticism, they'll be able to listen and take it in stride."

He stepped back as his expression turned to one of recognition. "Okay…I get it now."

Hold Space for Others

When you experience true human connection, the heart expands—or, as people like to say, "your heart becomes full." This provides greater access to the higher functions of the mind, developing the ability to listen to and access your intuition.

True connection brings us into the present moment and takes away worry and concern. For instance, when my Dad passed away, my mom was stuck with grief. She came for a visit and cried non-stop. I acknowledged her sorrow and became fully present with her. I asked her a powerful question: "Do you have everything you need in this moment?"

She looked at me through teary eyes and said, "Yes, I am here in a beautiful garden with my lovely daughter."

It is only when we hold space for others to share their full selves with us—their perspective, emotions, aspirations, and values—that we can truly connect with them. Similarly, when we share what is in our hearts with others, the act of opening ourselves up to them creates a deep and lasting bond. Connection is a magical force, allowing you to find yourself able to shift and expand in the presence of others, while everyone gains access to a complete range of capability. This is particularly true in the workplace, where authentic human connections have largely been lacking due to outmoded expectations of professional behavior.

Colleagues and leaders are often not completely comfortable displaying emotion and asking for help. For instance, one of my peers once ran a performance management training session for a large investment firm that was specifically focused on how to deliver an engaging and motivating performance review. The firm had a clear directive: If somebody were to become upset—angry, sad, or disappointed—during a performance review, the leader must leave the room and grant the employee some time to compose herself before resuming the conversation. I would say the smarter policy would be for the leader to stay in the room and engage with the employee and the needs and values that are at stake. When the leader leaves the room, it's often about the leader's discomfort, not what the employee needs.

Why is it so difficult to make human connections when this is a state that should come naturally to us? Let's find out by searching underneath the foundations of what has turned into a worldwide concern.

All the Lonely People

It's not just in the workplace that emotional distance can tend to generate disconnection. Societal loneliness is at an all-time high. According to a 2021 global survey from Statista, approximately one-third of adults characterize themselves as feeling lonely. The nation with the highest percentage is Brazil, where *half* of the population feels lonely. The United States stands at about 31 percent, which is slightly below the global average but still shockingly high.

Loneliness was an issue before COVID-19 shutdowns, but the numbers skyrocketed during and after the pandemic outbreak. The prevalence of remote work has made workers feel even more detached and disengaged from their employers, which is especially problematic given that *their need for belonging* has risen 12 percent. People enjoy their flexibility and don't necessarily require physically working side by side, but they still have a burning desire to be part of something bigger at work, as well as connected to management and their peers.

It's only when you spend time with someone and ask questions that you open the opportunity for a connection to occur.

ACTION FRAMEWORK

It's impossible to know what people are thinking and feeling at work just based on what they say and how they visibly act. Someone who sits at his desk all day and doesn't interact with anyone may give the impression that they prefer to work alone, doesn't want or need work friends, or is standoffish. But maybe there is something else happening beneath the surface; the individual could be lonely but be too shy, uncomfortable, proud, or intimidated to reach out to anyone. To better connect with others, try the following:

- Ask about their day and what they're working on.
- Ask them for feedback, support, or to serve as a sounding board for one of your ideas.
- Remember details about their lives; if they tell you they're going away for the weekend or their child has a birthday party, ask about this upon their return.
- Take the time to see what energizes them and talk about that. You might say something along the lines of, "You really seemed to light up in there when you talked about the new software—tell me more about how you see the integration."

Human connection is a basic human requirement that is part of our DNA. When we feel unfulfilled at work on this front, productivity, engagement, collaboration, and cooperation plummet. The likely outcome is a ripple effect of high turnover coupled with reduced revenue and profit. There's no room for leadership to avoid this issue.

Sometimes we get so caught up on working on tasks and getting through the day we overlook connection or even reject it. When we want to connect with others, we must offer emotional bids, which is an invitation to connect. It could be as simple as saying hello to a colleague when you enter the office or inviting someone to lunch. When emotional bids are accepted, we feel a sense of belonging and that we are being seen.

But what happens when the emotional bids are ignored or even dismissed? At one time or another, we've all been immersed in a crucial piece of work when a colleague walks into our office or calls us. We might engage for a few minutes of light banter, but our minds are elsewhere, screaming at us that the work must get done. We turn our bodies away from them toward our devices and multitask. In essence, we are consciously or unconsciously giving the other person the cold shoulder, signaling that we aren't paying attention.

The simple solution is to explain, "Hey, I'd love to chat, but I have a tight deadline that needs to be met. How about I stop by later and we can finish the conversation then?" The colleague usually gets it and exits without any issue.

However, if we repeatedly give our colleagues, friends, and partners the cold shoulder and ignore their emotional bids, the rejected people will stop coming around. Then we become the ones who feel lonely and isolated. When we increase our awareness by accepting emotional bids wherever possible, we end up with more fulfilling connections.

 REFLECTION: HOW ARE YOU HANDLING EMOTIONAL BIDS?

Ask yourself the following questions:

- This past week, what emotional bids did I offer?
    - If they were accepted, how did they make me feel? If they were rejected, how did they make me feel?
    - When and with whom do I reject emotional bids? How has that impacted my relationships?

The Air That We Breathe

Dr. Vivek Murthy, the U.S. Surgeon General during two presidential administrations and author of *Together: The Healing Power of Human Connection in a Sometimes Lonely World*, concludes that loneliness has a devastating impact on physical and mental health, ultimately decreasing longevity. He reveals that we need three levels of connection to prevent loneliness

1. Intimate (such as partner or spouse)
2. Relational (circle of friends)
3. Collective (community)

The third level of connection is where work enters the picture. As we spend so much of our awake time at our jobs, our workplace often serves as that collective or community, where shared values and interests take on far greater importance than we might think.

At Human Edge, we liken human connection to "the air that we breathe" and believe we must foster it as much as possible. As with personal power, described in Chapter Five, we must first understand and adopt the principles of human connection for ourselves before attempting to apply it to interacting authentically with others. We accomplish this through the following four elements: *respect, empathy, integrity*, and *vulnerability*. (See the illustration on the following page.)

Respect

Respect is fundamental to connection—both for yourself and those around you. When you don't respect yourself, you are denying the personal power that is available to you and lock others out from receiving it. Respect means recognizing the relational connections between you and others. You don't believe you are superior or inferior in any way; in fact, you hold people in esteem, which means believing in their personal power as much as your own and being appreciative in advance of their potential contributions.

When we get this right, we honor every aspect of a person. We demonstrate respect for their values, opinions, and ways of thinking, which in turn forms the basis for trust and positive interaction. Respecting one another

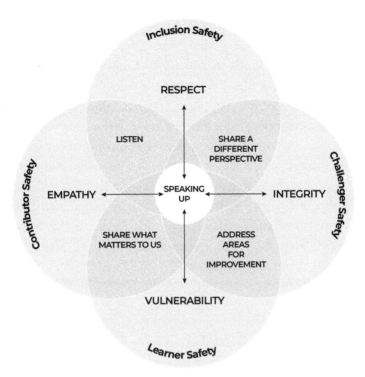

means that all parties are listening deeply to what is being said—or *not* being said—and they are sharing different perspectives without anyone feeling offended or diminished. Mutual respect among colleagues creates a safe space for everyone to feel comfortable and fully contribute.

Empathy

Many people often confuse the terms *empathy* and *sympathy*. The former is when you sense what other people might be thinking or feeling and are able to respond in a way that demonstrates relatability, humanness, and compassion. It requires you to hold space for what somebody is experiencing and, even if you've never been where they are, you acknowledge their experience and emotional response in a way that maintains connection with them. Empathy doesn't mean we join them in feeling exactly what they feel but rather that we hold space for what they are thinking and feeling without judgment or stating whether it's "right" or "wrong" to think or feel that way.

One component of empathy is *compassion*, the daily practice of recognizing and accepting our shared humanity, so that we treat ourselves and others with loving kindness and act with understanding in the face of suffering. The objective is to hold space for someone else's experience and then respond in a way that supports, respects, and values that person—even when the perspectives and feelings are different from one's own.

Sympathy is, by contrast, when you express support for someone else's dilemma—perhaps to the point of pity. It can mean we observe what somebody is going through from a place of superiority and think, "Thank heaven that's not happening to me!" Sympathy might also indicate that someone's emotional pain makes us so uncomfortable that we try to distance ourselves from it. As Brené Brown puts it: "Empathy fuels connection. Sympathy drives disconnection."

 REFLECTION: WERE YOU SYMPATHETIC OR EMPATHETIC?

Think about recent situations in which others shared a dilemma with you. How did you react?

- Did you rush to give advice? (sympathetic)
- Did you offer a "silver lining," such as "Oh, at least you didn't lose both of your arms." (sympathetic)
- Did you say something along the lines of "I'm so sorry that happened to you. It must have been really frustrating." (empathetic)

Empathy, therefore, is the true foundation for having emotional connections with others. It has the power to take us on a journey out of ourselves and enlighten us, unlocking our capacity to venture beyond our personal experiences and into the minds and hearts of others. Empathy can be a tremendous superpower to nurture, arming you with the ability to be on the same wavelength with someone who may have a completely different perspective from your own.

Research indicates that empathy is also the key to being able to exhibit positive behaviors, such as kindness and tolerance. Stanford University

Professor Jamil Zaki refers to it as the "psychological 'superglue' that connects people and undergirds co-operation and kindness." Karina Schumann, a professor of social psychology at the University of Pittsburgh, adds: "In general, empathy is a powerful predictor of things we consider to be positive behaviors that benefit society, individuals, and relationships." Ann Rumble, a psychology lecturer at Northern Arizona University, goes even further, asserting that empathy can override non-cooperation and prevent "harsh judgment"—both of which are critical for collaboration at work.

Psychologists Daniel Goleman and Paul Ekman cite the three following components of empathy:

1. *Cognitive:* This is the ability to understand another person's perspective. It enables you to sense how another person thinks about the world, which means you can communicate in terms they will understand.
2. *Emotional:* This is the ability to feel what someone else feels. Goleman and Ekman describe it as emotions that are "contagious."
3. *Empathic Concern:* This is the ability to sense what another person needs from you.

You can demonstrate how you care by perceiving something about another individual without being specifically told about it.

Brené Brown proposes an additional component of empathy: *non-judgment* of another person's situation. Judging is an attempt to protect yourself from the pain of the situation. Unfortunately, this also means discounting someone else's feelings, which will never help a person feel better.

The good news is that, even if empathy doesn't come naturally to you, it can be learned and honed. You must be willing and motivated to nurture this trait. Below are a few tips to increase your empathic ability:

- *Expose yourself to differences.* The more you widen your perspectives, the greater chance you will be able to recognize, understand, and appreciate situations you may not have experienced yourself.

- *Read fiction.* Studies have shown that literature improves empathy because written words and storytelling grant you access inside the minds of characters, which provides thoughts, emotions, and experiences from a new lens.

- *Identify common ground.* When you pinpoint areas of commonality, you automatically begin to relate to another person's situation from a place of familiarity.

- *Ask questions.* There may be things you simply don't know or understand about someone's situation. Asking questions shows that you are genuinely interested and care about the other person while also gleaning much-needed information.

- *Understand your empathy blocks.* You may have trouble empathizing with someone because of something you experienced in the past that caused you to form a preconceived opinion or bias. For example, if you were a child of an amicable divorce, you might not empathize with someone who experienced deep trauma from her parents' separation. While it's human nature to think of relatable things from your past, sometimes you must pull back to recognize that circumstances vary and not everyone experiences things the same way you did.

Integrity

Being able to stand in your truth is critical for human connection. We don't want to tell people only what they want to hear, but we also don't want to be brutal. When we speak our truth, we are choosing to share our full selves with others, not just what we believe they want to see and that we are comfortable showing. We don't make compromises or trade-offs for convenience or comfort that involve us hiding things from others or denying them access to our resources. We are consistent in what we make available to others, we honor our commitments, and our words and actions are aligned. This creates the space for building trust among colleagues and teams. When integrity is present, we become willing to share different perspectives and candidly address areas for improvement.

Vulnerability

Brown defines vulnerability as "the emotion we experience during times of uncertainty, risk, and emotional exposure." This involves letting our guard down enough to reveal our true underlying emotions, which often includes fear. In a work environment, a leader who exposes her vulnerability lets others know that she is willing to "put herself out there" by being honest and authentic, even if it means revealing a potential weakness. Not only do people relate to vulnerability, but it also gives them permission to do the same. If a leader says, "I must admit, I'm a bit nervous about my speech," a direct report will feel better about his own upcoming presentation because he knows he is not alone in his fear. Collaboration thrives when colleagues feel they are going through the same rollercoaster of feelings while working together.

Human Connection Requires the Integration of Head, Heart, and Gut

In the age of AI, our ability to engage head, heart, and gut in service of connecting with one another is what gives us a competitive advantage. Human beings are the only creatures to have the capacity to fully engage and respond with our true selves in the moment. To step into that unique experience, we must be willing to open ourselves up to others; step into experiences; and immerse ourselves in emotions and thoughts that are not our own.

When we fail to connect head, heart, and gut, we may cognitively understand someone else's perspective, but we become more likely to filter it though our own logic and judgment. We end up presenting ourselves from a position of agreement or disagreement, whether an opinion is needed or not.

All three aspects—head, heart, and gut—are equally as important, demanding the same amount of effort and attention. If we were to lean too much on our head, we would miss empathizing with others and ignore picking up signals from them that could be beneficial. Too much heart may cause us to over-invest our emotions and make the issues about ourselves, instead of other people. When we rely on our gut alone, we might become so focused on our own intuitive thoughts that we ignore the facts in front of us and the invaluable input of others.

When we master head, heart, and gut in the workplace, we create a safe place for people to contribute at the highest level. Co-workers work harmoniously and seamlessly as they collaborate and build trust. In time, the team feels as if they can read each other's minds and anticipate one another's actions before they occur. This is what true connection is all about.

TAKEAWAYS

- When you experience true human connection, you are leveraging the head, heart, and gut as touchpoints.
- Today's businesses—especially those facilitating remote work—must recognize that loneliness is a pervasive issue.
- It is vital that we are conscious of when we accept or defer emotional bids.
- There are three levels of connection that can counter loneliness: intimate (such as partner or spouse); relational (circle of friends); and collective (community).
- Think of the workplace—virtual or on-site—as a community that can support leaders in holding space for emotional connection in a professional context.
- Connectivity is based on four overarching principles: respect, empathy, integrity, and vulnerability.
- Empathy, which includes respect, integrity, and vulnerability, is the true foundation for having emotional connections with others.
- The ability to engage head, heart, and gut in service of connecting with one another is a competitive advantage.

Chapter Nine

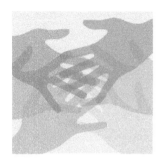

THE POWER OF SELFLESS COLLABORATION

When brilliant minds with big ambitions work toward a common goal, amazing things can happen. You will see employees' complement each other's strengths and weaknesses, eventually forming an unstoppable team. This is why collaboration and teamwork play such a crucial role in any business success. Today, collaboration has taken on much greater significance—especially in the workplace—with about 75 percent of employers rating teamwork and collaboration as "very important." But 86 percent of employees and executives cite lack of collaboration or ineffective communication as causes of workplace failures. *Why is there a disconnect?*

We might not fully understand when or how to use the full power of collaboration in business. We've shifted from working individually to many people functioning across matrices and organizational boundaries to accomplish their goals. Our calendars are overloaded with meetings and interactions—but are we really *collaborating?* As leaders, we might be sending the wrong message to our employees when we say *collaborate,* as this has been misinterpreted to mean *doing it all the time.* We must, therefore, take a step back and understand the distinctions among solo work, cooperative work, and collaborative work.

Contrary to some common usage, *collaboration* is not interchangeable with the word *cooperation*. While both refer to people working together, the similarities end there: *Cooperation* is about doing so while achieving your *individual* goals, whereas *collaboration* involves the accomplishment of *collective* or shared goals with two or more people who believe in the same purpose.

The applications of collaboration are growing deep and wide in today's work environment—regarded as essential for ensuring that an organization is functioning at optimum performance and in sync—but it continues to be conflated with cooperation. In most instances when leaders say *collaborate*, they are referring to cooperation and not *true* collaboration. Leaders must be more intentional and clearer when we offer clues on how we want people to engage with each other. Most organizations are struggling to understand the power of what true collaboration can do to shape a culture that drives results and innovation without confusing people and wasting effort. Here are some rules of thumb in directing resources:

- *Working individually:* When a task is clear, well defined, and requires an employee's deep expertise to achieve a result. Involving others will not bring about a better work product and may even slow progress.

- *Working cooperatively:* When the approach to work or output is not fully defined and may be enhanced by the insights and experiences of others. Or when the work product involves end-to-end processes that traverse organizational boundaries. Involving others may greatly improve outcomes by adding new insights and avoiding operational implementational challenges down the road.

- *Working collaboratively:* When there is a need for transformational impact, innovation, solving complex or ambiguous problems, or addressing opportunities that require a variety of expertise. Here we move beyond gaining input from others to co-creating solutions and new possibilities.

When You Need to Innovate, *Collaborate*

True collaboration requires colleagues to be *interdependent* with each other, which is a shift away from personal ownership and phrases such as "my idea," "my reputation," "my expertise," and "my credibility" to the concept of several people operating as one collective unit. *Positive interdependence* means that, in such a setting, the success of one person is reliant upon the triumph of the entire team. Everyone recognizes the value of working together and believes that the results will be significantly better than if each member were to venture off on their own. Everyone has a piece of the puzzle, but no one person owns it or can complete it alone.

Like any change in behavior, positive interdependence requires several mindset adjustments, including:

- *From control:* We must shift from *We control/secure the outcomes* to *We trust in the team's shared purpose and values.*

- *From consensus:* We must shift from *We all agree on the decision/action* to *Let's immerse ourselves in constructive conflict/debate.*

- *From responsibility:* We must shift from *Let's all commit to doing what we say we will do* to *Let's have shared accountability and do what it takes to empower the team.*

Co-Creation: The Fruits of Collaboration

Recently, *Forbes* cited a survey in which 92 percent of respondents cited that collaboration isn't what happens in formal meetings but rather through *co-creation.* This reveals an effective process that is far more organic, with team members performing various tasks together: drafting documents and slides; tracking a project in shared drives like Google Drive or Microsoft 365; and/or sharing feedback via chat and video. Meanwhile, *asynchronous collaboration*—people sharing feedback or ideas on a project at different times—has proven to be essential not only among distributed teams but also within local ones when the colleagues have varied schedules and work preferences.

This method of working offers myriad business benefits. A recent joint study between the Institute for Corporate Productivity and Professor Rob Cross at Babson College surveying over 1,100 companies revealed that those promoting collaborative working were five times as likely to be high performing. ImageThink, a visual strategy firm, suggests that co-creation may also be applied externally to all stakeholders, including buyers, vendors, customers, and end users. When we engage in co-creation, the following benefits can be realized:

1. It unlocks new perspectives.
2. It provides open participation in which everyone can solve a problem together.
3. It increases idea generation and invites opportunities.
4. It reduces costs, wasted effort, and risk.
5. It builds wider teams and communities.
6. It strengthens transparency, trust, and brand authenticity.
7. It incentivizes the equal division of labor and joint value.

With so many potential upsides, isn't establishing true collaboration as the norm well worth it for your organization?

Strong Collaborators Work with Shared Purpose

The study from the Institute for Corporate Productivity (i4cp) and Professor Rob Cross cited earlier revealed one specific commonality among the organizations that succeeded at collaboration: *purpose*. To be productive in their mutual effort, employees need to feel the work is meaningful and has impact. If the messaging behind *why* they are working together on a project is clear and unified, the whole becomes far greater than the sum of its parts (to paraphrase Aristotle).

An outstanding example of this is Patagonia. The $3 billion clothing brand implements what they refer to as *systematic collaboration* instilled via *collaborative learning experiences* in which employees are encouraged to engage with each other across the spectrum of the organization to share ideas, skills, and knowledge; problem-solve; and innovate. One of their primary principles provides the framework for making this happen and delivering on their organizational purpose: "We show respect and ensure that all voices are heard, and ideas are valued throughout the company…"

The results are staggering: 78 percent of Patagonia workers feel that their ideas and suggestions are recognized and valued; 88 percent freely share ideas and concerns directly with their immediate supervisor; and 91 percent believe their supervisors care about them. By stark contrast, according to a recent Gallup poll, less than 25 percent of employees from the workplace at large believe their organizations care about their well-being.

Collaboration Roadblocks

With so many upsides to collaboration, one wonders why every company doesn't pull out all stops to ensure that the concept becomes ingrained in employees' minds and hearts and embedded in their workflows and processes. The unfortunate reality is that there are a few roadblocks that sometimes get in the way of implementing collaboration. This shouldn't be the case, however, as all four of the roadblocks cited in the sections that follow are easily surmountable and well worth any additional effort.

- *Roadblock #1:* The Scarcity Mindset
- *Roadblock #2:* How Individual Rewards Can Backfire
- *Roadblock #3:* Team Overload
- *Roadblock #4:* Letting Go and Trusting Others

Roadblock #1: The Scarcity Mindset

On a general level, a *scarcity mindset* is when a person feels that there are limited resources and they focus on how best to fulfill their needs to secure them. Remember the COVID-19 pandemic shutdowns when people panicked that there wouldn't be enough toilet paper? When we feel scarcity, we start hoarding; it drastically changes our perspective, and we move into a state of fear and anxiety. When this surfaces in business, the circumstance becomes contagious and leads to a culture of *competition* rather than one of *cooperation* or *collaboration*. We come to believe that, if we help someone else out, they will "look too good" or "perform better" than us, which might lead to that person being assigned more important work or perhaps even getting promoted ahead of us and receiving greater financial rewards.

This also can impact a company's sales. If our salespeople believe they are competing against each other or even with other companies, they miss the opportunity for mutual beneficial partnerships. It is truly just a matter of shifting perspectives from "there are limited clients" to "there is enough business for everyone." Think about it: Can one company possibly serve everyone in the world?

When we see others as competitors, we become mistrustful and suspicious, refusing to be generous with our time or ideas. The caring element that is needed for cohesion wanes as well. We then end up "doing things ourselves" to reap the rewards. Margaret Heffernan, author of *Willful Blindness* and *Beyond Measure,* suggests that when people become too "task-oriented" on their individual assignments and don't build human connections with each other, they assume the worst about others' motivations and become rivals. If the culture breeds this mentality, people don't even know each other well enough to understand what others do and provide help with the challenges they face.

If we want to shift this, we need to develop an *abundance* mindset and learn how to balance giving and taking. When this understanding is accepted across an organizational culture, an employee will gladly assist a colleague because she knows it will be returned at some later date, albeit not necessarily from the same person.

Extreme disagreements—meaning, those that lead to arguments and shutting down—may also contribute to the scarcity mindset and must be approached from a different perspective. Digging in on a position such as "I am right, and she is wrong" sends a message that expressing an opinion is a threat to someone's ego and potentially even her status in the organization. To move beyond this, we must *focus on solving the problem* rather than pushing acceptance of our proposed solutions with the intent of being singled out as a hero. The abundant mindset requires that everyone is *all in* when it comes to problem-solving. When this occurs, it becomes impossible to determine whose idea started the process of co-creation and innovation that ultimately led to success.

Roadblock #2: How Individual Rewards Can Backfire

Everyone loves to receive praise and rewards for their accomplishments, right? We admire those who display their work-related awards and trophies around their offices. When we are rewarded, we become pumped up with confidence and feel inspired to continue to perform at the highest level possible. A raise or bonus doesn't hurt, either.

So, what could possibly be wrong with individual rewards? While individual rewards serve as a perfectly fine motivator on an individual level, they demotivate people from cooperation or collaborating because they want to keep the tangible recognition all to themselves and be set up for long-term career progression. With this in place, why throw yourself out there only to share the spotlight with someone else or give it away entirely? Kevin Martin, chief research officer at i4cp, put it this way: "The lack of incentives and rewards is the most common and powerful barrier to effective collaboration. Yet, most talent management systems are designed to reward individual achievement, not team accomplishments."

In the i4cp study, only 25 percent of participating organizations encouraged collaboration through team rewards. The most successful companies involved in the survey were those that incentivized collaboration by linking team goals and accomplishments with team rewards.

Roadblock #3: Team Overload

According to *Harvard Business Review (HBR)*, "The time spent by managers and employees working together has ballooned by 50 percent or more." While this seems to be a wonderful and exciting development, there is also some pain and suffering occurring under the surface. Most of the added value of true collaboration is generated by only 3–5 percent of the workforce. There is an opportunity to more fully leverage collaboration to solve complex challenges that are abundant in organizations. Nevertheless, what is really going on is an excessive amount of working together with little output on shared and individual goals. Employees are involved in so many things that they end up burning out and feel little sense of accomplishment. Additionally, the *HBR* researchers found that bottlenecks happen because people are waiting too long for everyone to weigh in on decisions. This occurs when workers don't have enough desk time to get back to people promptly.

With lack of clarity on how to allocate resources properly, excessively—or, perhaps more accurately, *unnecessarily*—working together sometimes yields unintended deleterious effects. Sometimes organizations become so gung-ho about people working together that they feel they need to gather and deliberate about everything under the sun. This leads to numerous lengthy meeting sessions that prevent people from executing the jobs they were paid to do. We know of at least one company in which the entire workforce was invited to attend every meeting, whether the subject involved them or not. This ended up creating meetings of wall-to-wall people—sometimes twenty or more—when a half dozen with the right expertise would have sufficed. It also dramatically lengthened the meetings because extra details had to be explained to newcomers and their questions answered. If we want to have the greatest impact, we need to be more deliberate about how to set up teams and meetings and then work together to best leverage collaboration.

When meetings become too large, too frequent, or too long, overload sets in. Time gets wasted arriving at decisions and employees need to put in extra hours to get their work done. The voices of the workers responsible for obtaining the meeting results—and, theoretically, with the most knowledge regarding the agenda—end up getting drowned out amidst the deluge of opinions and questions, which takes us to Roadblock #4…

Roadblock #4: Letting Go and Trusting Others

Many people have a burning desire to be involved in everything and be in the know about whatever happens to be going on—even if it has nothing to do with their role. This is fine and dandy occasionally, as it's good for people to learn how other departments operate and engage with people they don't normally see. It can serve as a good learning opportunity and perhaps even open up the option to have workers rotate positions around the organization. But we must dig beneath the surface and ask where the burning desire comes from to be involved in everything. It's helpful as a leader to uncover the motivations of your direct reports, which may include:

- I want to learn/discover more about how the business works.
- I want to defend myself and/or exert some kind of control.

- I don't trust others to do the work on my behalf.
- I gain knowledge—which equates to power—when I am at the table.
- I'm more interested in other positions than my own.

Some people misinterpret collaboration to mean they have *the right* to know everything, be involved in everything, and contribute to everything—including decision-making. This suggests that we don't trust others to perform their roles and represent our best interests. Ironically, this conceit fosters the notion that "I must be part of every interaction because I am so good at everything, and things can't be done without me" or "My colleagues can't represent my part of the business."

The message: It's acceptable to hold others accountable for their work. We must also trust that our colleagues will represent our needs and points of view, so we don't need to be present for every meeting. If we want to avoid overload, attendees should consist primarily of the individuals with the deepest expertise on the subject under discussion, as well as the key stakeholders impacted.

Moreover, while working in the space of true collaboration, we want to shift from a state of holding each other responsible for what was agreed upon to stepping into a place of shared accountability, where we hold space for everyone to bring their diverse strengths to the table. The goal is to create a co-creative space in which we are willing to be interdependent with one another's strengths to achieve more than we otherwise would alone. Interdependency sometimes means that we must take a step back and take the risk that the outcome may not be achieved as we would like if we were to work on our own. In the end, we must make a choice to be in collaboration rather than in control.

When I was employed at Novartis, I was asked to head a taskforce to redesign the company's performance management system. We were allotted six months to complete the project, which included evaluating the latest research and benchmarks and soliciting input from employees and leaders. We also had to partner with our key stakeholders, which included half of the executive committee and the entire human resources leadership team.

Our team proved highly effective because all six members had expertise in business and performance management. Senior leaders trusted us to do the work while still representing the organization. The project was such a success that many of the recommendations are still being used seven years later.

Our team may not have agreed on everything, but we listened to each other deeply and built off findings gleaned from research, company benchmarks, and employees' wants and needs. For example, at the time there was a building trend among companies to cease internal performance rating processes. The team conducted extensive research and consulted with employees and senior leaders to determine the right path. As it turned out, most people were unsupportive of the idea, and we ended up sticking with performance ratings.

ACTION FRAMEWORK

On a blank sheet of paper, write down the important projects that you are involved in. Pick the most important one and determine whether you are cooperating or collaborating. Then identify contributors or stakeholders, as well as its purpose, goals, and achievements. On the last line, write down if you believe the team (a) consists of the right members (as well as too many or too few) with the right mindsets, (b) has a shared common purpose, (c) is making progress toward its goals, (d) collaborates effectively, and (e) suffers from work overload. What would you change, if anything, on each team?

Once you have a list of action items for the teams, write down initiatives that are being handled by individuals (including yourself) but would benefit from the formation of teams. Then identify potential team members who would best contribute to that team but wouldn't be overburdened by the extra work.

Think Holistically

To prevent and counter potential collaboration roadblocks, you must look at the entire system from a holistic viewpoint. If your organization's mission, purpose, and values are clear and easy for everyone to see, comprehend, and follow, you are already halfway there.

Company culture—typically originated by the founders and then fine-tuned by the senior leaders—plays a key role in ensuring that collaboration is part of everyone's mindset and embedded in the workflow without anyone burning out. The precepts of a collaborative culture must be effectively communicated at the recruiting and onboarding stages, where the message of team performance over individual performance can be instilled while candidates and new hires have a blank slate. New employees immediately pick up the social cues of how they will be rewarded and accepted in the organization.

Leaders play a key role in determining and shaping their team's climate. Employees are always searching for cues from them on what behaviors lead to success in the organization. If the leaders lavish praise and rewards on teams for their collaborative successes, other workers will catch on and strive to follow the same path. Strong individual performance may be simultaneously rewarded, if the accomplishments didn't occur at the cost of potential collaborative efforts that could have led to even better results and a stronger sense of camaraderie.

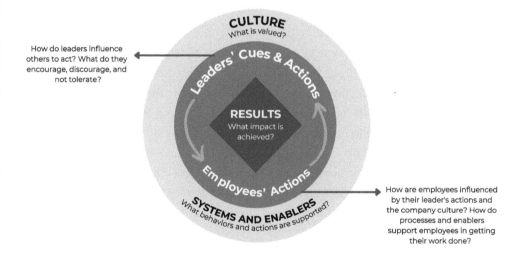

When most companies are recruiting, the tendency is always to search for the crème de la crème—the top talent or "superstars." The question they should be asking themselves: *Does this really work in the long term?* Heffernan argues that it does not. As an example, she cites the auditions at the Royal Academy of Dramatic Arts, where performers are selected based on their *collaborative* abilities rather than their individual dramatic star power. They look for actors who connect with others on stage and support one another behind the scenes. The result is grooming actors who bring out the best in others, as well as themselves. Similarly, when Heffernan studied the organizations with the most creativity and ingenuity, she discovered teams of collaborators; not a single "star" was to be found.

The secret to building a holistic collaborative culture is to search for talented, qualified employees who demonstrate a generous and empathic team mindset during the first interview. It may seem difficult to assess collaborative skills in this setting, but it isn't. In the interview process you can gauge responses to the following two questions:

1. Tell me about a time when you helped a colleague in need without being asked.
2. Tell me about a time when you co-created a project with a team or another individual.

The first thing to track is the candidate's usage of the pronoun "I" versus "we." If she uses first person ("*I* did this" and "*I* did that") 80 percent or more of the time, you already have indications that she is more about what she can accomplish as an individual contributor than as a team player. If the applicant struggles to provide compelling stories in response to the above, she is likely not the right person to fill your company's needs. Sometimes a candidate—especially someone in sales—might be good at "winging it" with their answers, so you need to pay close attention to the level of detail provided, as well as their enthusiasm for collaboration. If you have any doubt, follow up with these questions:

- Tell me about a time you had a conflict with another team member? How did you resolve it?

- What do you think is the right balance of time spent between individual work and team work?

Manage Collective Creativity

John Cleese, comedian, actor, business coach, and author of *Creativity: A Short and Cheerful Guide,* once said, "If you want creative workers, give them enough time to play."

The importance of creativity in the workplace cannot be under estimated. Without creativity, we wouldn't have the iPhone (Apple) or Optimum Prime (Amazon). In both cases, the company leaders were important—especially Steve Jobs with the iPhone—but the creative execution and problem-solving wouldn't have transpired without creative team collaboration. When a workforce receives sufficient inspiration to work together, unexpected and remarkable things organically arise from their efforts.

Linda Hill, co-author of *Collective Genius,* espouses the idea that "innovation genius isn't about solo genius, it's about *collective* genius." As a case in point, she cites how Pixar Animation Studios creates successful feature films one after another, each involving 250 people over a four- to five-year span, and yet most people couldn't even name or recognize the company's CEO (Jim Morris). When Hill and her team studied several innovative companies around the world—including Pixar and Google—she discovered that they all leverage three things:

1. *Creative abrasion:* The state of creating an environment in which ideas are discussed and debated. Polite and respectful disagreements are encouraged to produce a range of alternatives for consideration.

2. *Creative agility:* The process of initiating experiments intended to learn and adjust. Mistakes are expected, so improvements may be made. In this way, there is no right or wrong ideas.

3. *Creative resolution:* This component involves inclusive decision-making. The leaders form conclusions by connecting contrasting ideas from the team to form something new. In doing so, everyone feels as if their contributions are part of the final product.

Many people in organizations fear engaging in heated discussions because they feel uncomfortable or lack the courage to expose the truth. Egos are known to be fragile, and people often believe they must defend their position or be polite. This is when the leader sets the tone and makes it clear that even her ideas require deliberation and may end up nixed or will evolve into something else. Professional, healthy friction—well short of raised voices, of course—means that the idea or solution will be massaged until it becomes something better, bolder, and bigger.

Becoming a selfless collaborator requires a new way of thinking, speaking, and behaving. It means developing a level of self-awareness about what we say and how we say it. To present ourselves as strong collaborators, we must be generous with our time, emotional energy, and mental horsepower.

FROM	TO
Cooperation: Everybody works together to achieve their goals.	**Collaboration:** Everybody works together to achieve collective/shared goals.
Mission and Vision: Everyone is clear on what we're doing and where we're going.	**Values and Purpose:** Everyone is clear on why we're going in a certain direction and the principles that will guide our way.
Diversity: Everyone is invited to contribute their perspective and strenths.	**Equity and Inclusion:** Everyone is offered what they need to deliver their best.
Capability: Everyone has the capability and expertise to take the actions required. Confidence and strength are conveyed and rewarded.	**Vulnerability:** People are free to ask questions, seek support, and invite feedback with a view to grow their expertise. Authenticity and openness are conveyed and rewarded.

(Continued)

FROM	TO
Independence: People rely on their own resources, insight, and decisions to generate success.	**Interdependence:** People rely on each other and depend on shared resources, insight, and decisions to generate success.
Control: People rely on process and direction to secure reliability.	**Creative Disagreement and Shared Accountability:** We discuss together until we reach a place where we collectively own a decision and action—even if we may not fully agree.

When creative collaboration is handled with the right care and everyone becomes aware of themselves and the interests of others, the concept becomes embedded in your company's ecosystem, and everyone wins. Ultimately, you will achieve your desired results in terms of both employee engagement and the bottom line.

TAKEAWAYS

- Always be clear on when it is best to work individually, cooperatively, or collaboratively and leverage organizational resources accordingly.
- Collaboration involves the accomplishment of shared goals with two or more people who believe in the same purpose, whereas cooperation is about doing so while achieving your individual goals.
- To establish a collaborative culture, the organization must create a team rewards system, in addition to one that is offered to individuals.
- Be aware of and guard against collaboration roadblocks, such as the scarcity mindset and team overload.

- A collaborative work culture has a holistic view of how employees work together that involves vetting candidates for this trait and communicating this philosophy during the onboarding process.
- Our mindset, language we speak, and view of relationships determine if we are able and willing to collaborate.

Chapter Ten

EMBRACING OUR DIFFERENCES

Every day at work, we attempt to bring this concept to life to maximize resources and have greater impact. The only way to accomplish this and achieve true synergy is by embracing our differences. Imagine the unbridled energy that is unleashed when this occurs. It leads to substantial progress and breakthrough successes that otherwise would not have been possible.

In good faith, employees go to work each day with a desire to contribute as best as they can. Unfortunately, this isn't possible if they don't feel that they belong or are accepted as they are. Brené Brown states, "True belonging doesn't require that we change who we are; it requires us to be who we are." With the right effort, strategies, tools, and programs in place, organizations can overcome these circumstances and establish work cultures that accept differences and reward teams for their synergy.

Invite Them to the Party *and* Ask Them to Dance

Over the past two decades, organizations around the world have taken a much greater interest in diversity and inclusion programs. Initiatives have been established to address the systemic biases and injustices toward minority and underrepresented groups that have been embedded in society. While strides have been made to improve diversity, inclusion has been a bit late to the party.

Inclusivity depends on value and respect. This means doing more than just acknowledging or allowing differences; it involves actively valuing the perspectives, experiences, ideas, and approaches of all parties—no matter how varied. It doesn't require us to adopt the same perspective or agree with everyone's ideas. It means we must establish an environment in which all perspectives are welcome and people feel valued and respected.

Diversity without inclusion leads to frustration, disengagement, and hurt feelings. We've all been in situations where we've felt ignored, isolated, or even invisible; we're in the room, but we may as well not be. Offering everyone a seat at the table isn't enough to embrace differences; we also must help them feel as if they belong. As diversity advocate Vernā Myers brilliantly put it: "Diversity is being invited to the party, inclusion is being asked to dance."

Diversity and inclusion are not just the right thing to do from a humanistic perspective; they can also have measurable business impact. Research has proven time and again that a diverse team will outperform a homogenous one. In 2020, McKinsey & Company reported findings from their study revealing that organizations with gender diversity outperform others by a margin of 15–25 percent; for those with ethnic diversity, the number is around 35 percent higher. These numbers tilt even more when leadership is diverse from gender and ethnic perspectives. With such overwhelming evidence proving the efficacy of diverse work cultures, why not do whatever it takes to make it a reality?

We Are Better Together

Diversity and inclusion are important in today's world because they help us learn from each other and understand that everyone is unique and has their own level of genius. They also lead to better outcomes in various aspects of life, fostering creativity, innovation, empathy, and social cohesion. In addition, they help build a more just and inclusive society in which everyone has an opportunity to contribute, succeed, and shine. Diverse work cultures have greater collective wisdom and superior tools to drive business impact and innovation.

Collective Wisdom

When an organization embraces diversity and inclusion, the level of internal experience and knowledge deepens and widens. Products, services, and programs may be developed or adapted to appeal to entirely new populations of people because deep familiarity about them has been embedded in the culture. With such innate intelligence, a company can identify trends while avoiding blind spots in marketing and advertising campaigns that could otherwise create a backlash. The collective wisdom is most valuable if the company has such representation in leadership; builds diverse teams; listens to all groups while collaborating; and learns how to extract information at the right moment to solve a problem or take advantage of an opportunity.

Deep Impact

Many studies have shown that diversity drives stronger business impact. In 2017, *HBR* concluded that cognitively diverse teams—those bearing different perspectives and processing styles—solve problems faster than those of teams with members who are alike. *HBR* also noted that, while many organizations might already be cognitively diverse, "people like to fit in, so they are cautious about sticking their necks out. When we have a strong, homogeneous culture, we stifle the natural cognitive diversity in groups through the pressure to conform."

Decision-making speed is another distinct advantage diverse teams have over non-diverse ones, to the tune of 60 percent. Unfortunately, in most organizations, male leaders continue to make about 38 percent of decisions—a statistic that is far worse among Silicon Valley tech companies. Scott E. Page, author of *The Diversity Bonus*, presents the case that, when problems are solved from predominantly one perspective, the error rate increases by about 30 percent.

Coca-Cola, together with Georgia State University, formed a supplier-development institute several years ago to provide education on how to start businesses for small and disadvantaged groups. Coca-Cola also has the

STEP initiative to support women entrepreneurs through training, education, and mentorship.

Coca-Cola's philosophy of diversity and inclusive supply chain has benefited the company in terms of greater responsiveness and agility. A study by Hootology demonstrated that it also boosted their brand. Individuals surveyed who were aware of Coca-Cola's supplier initiatives were 45 percent more likely to perceive the brand as valuing diversity, 25 percent more likely to think favorably about it, and 49 percent more likely to buy their products. Hootology estimated that these favorable perceptions would lead to an additional 670,000 consumers using the company's products more frequently.

Diversity—The Mother of Innovation

Innovation—creating revolutionary new ideas, processes, products, or methods of service—benefits greatly from diversity. In 2013, Deloitte reported that "when employees 'think their organization is committed to and supportive of diversity, and they feel included,' their ability to innovate increases by 83 percent."

Not only does a homogenous workforce comprised of people with different backgrounds, experiences, and skills lead to innovation, it also can yield an extraordinary payoff on the bottom line. According to McKinsey & Company, diverse executive boards have a 95 percent higher return on equity than those with non-diverse boards.

When it comes down to it, the individual, the team, and the organization all benefit when diversity becomes part of a company's culture. Better together is, quite simply, *better.*

We Belong

Whether at home or at work, we volunteer to join teams for two reasons: we want to contribute, and we need to feel that we belong. Regarding the latter, our compulsion to connect and become part of a larger community is hardwired in our brains. The Center for Talent and Innovation conducted a research study, "The Power of Belonging," which analyzed why belonging has become so critical in today's workplace. The research identified the following four components of belonging:

- *Seen*: When you are seen at work, you are recognized, rewarded, and respected by your colleagues. They acknowledge your unique genius and the value you bring.

- *Connected*: When you are connected at work, you have positive, authentic social interactions with peers, managers, and senior leaders.

- *Supported:* When you are supported at work, those around you—from your peers to senior leaders—provide the tools, resources, and training needed to get your work done.

- *Proud:* When you are proud of your work and your organization, you feel aligned with its purpose, vision, and values.

 REFLECTION: HOW DO YOU RATE BELONGING IN YOUR ORGANIZATION?

On a scale of 1 to 10 with 10 being the highest, rate each dimension of belonging for each of your team members—seen, connected, supported, and proud—in your work environment.

- What did you discover about your team?
- What risks might have surfaced?
- How does this impact their energy and happiness factor?
- How does this enable or not enable them to fully contribute?

Leaders play a critical role in setting the tone for creating a company culture in which the concept of belonging is encouraged, accepted, and put into practice. One way to accomplish this is to honor individual and organizational values. Another is to thoughtfully assign stimulating tasks that entail greater responsibility and give people a chance to show what they can do.

Letting go of some decision-making can also be empowering and help employees feel they belong. We can't put all this responsibility on leaders, who have more than enough responsibilities and often add delays while everyone awaits their signoffs. By delegating some decision-making to team members, they feel trusted and gain confidence. Once the decisions have been made, leaders must thank the employees, offer support and encouragement, and provide timely, honest feedback.

Progress May Be Limited

Many leaders undergo hours of training to study and improve their shadow selves. This often includes intense diversity and inclusion programs and workshops, sometimes facilitated by external expert coaches and consultants. There is no doubt that such leaders—which may include you—work hard to improve their hiring metrics pertaining to diversity, as well as inclusion and engagement numbers revealed in surveys. When there is tangible progress—even if marginal—it is important to celebrate the results. Keep in mind that transforming your organization into an entity that is a picture-perfect model of diversity and inclusion isn't easy and doesn't happen overnight.

A colleague of mine once shared the following story with me on measuring inclusion.

Years ago, she was facilitating several inclusion workshops at a large financial services company. These forums included employees from all levels of the organization. Inevitably, as always seems to happen, the seats in the middle and the back were filled first, leaving the ones in the front row free. Several members of the C-suite had been in an executive leadership meeting just before the session started and arrived late, so they filled the empty seats toward the front. During the workshop, the facilitator asked everyone to hold up their fingers and rate the organization's diversity score on a scale of 1-10 with 10 being the highest. Hands flew up in the air. Nearly everyone present held up seven fingers or more. The executives scanned the room and smiled, understandably pleased with the response and the fact that they had successfully attracted diverse talent.

The facilitator next asked everyone to hold up their fingers again, this time to rate the level of *inclusion* within the organization. A radical shift occurred in the tenor of the room. While all the executives in the front held up eight fingers or more, the employees behind them displayed five or less.

When the leaders craned their necks to gauge the responses behind them, they were stunned by what they saw. They had believed the organization was inclusive through and through, but it wasn't. The barriers to people feeling as if they belonged were invisible to them because they personally felt valued and included. The leadership team had good intentions and desired an inclusive organization. Without participating in this exercise, they would have remained in the dark about the reality of their non-inclusive culture.

The leaders at this session discovered that people experience the same working environments, roles, and conversations differently. The key to embracing differences is recognizing and acknowledging this fact and then having the willingness to talk about it, even though it can often feel uncomfortable.

The Road to a Diverse Utopia

If we want to truly embrace our differences and achieve superior business results, we must begin our journey at the self-level, in four areas:

1. Recognize our own genius.
2. Be secure in yourself.
3. Address unconscious bias.
4. Leverage empathy and curiosity.

Recognize Our Own Genius

Each person has a superpower, so to speak, uniquely their own. When developed and strengthened, it becomes an even more specialized and valuable capability. By identifying and cultivating our own genius, we become able to recognize it and leverage it in others. A good example of this is a senior leader with whom I worked in a global pharmaceutical company. He demonstrated strong business insight and vision, so the company gave him the oncology business to run. He built it from virtually nothing to a value of $10 billion, making it the second largest such oncology business in the world. He had a remarkable ability to see the future and know which products to invest in. He didn't simply keep his genius to himself, either. In meetings, he would ask powerful questions that allowed others to explore various business scenarios and grow their insight. He hired the right people and trusted and empowered them to accomplish goals that had the greatest impact on the organization.

 REFLECTION: WHAT IS YOUR GENIUS?

To uncover your genius, ask yourself the following questions:

- What things come naturally to me?
- What things interest me and draw me in?
- What am I most passionate about?

Be Secure in Yourself

It's only when we fully step into our personal power and know who we are and what we stand for—including our strengths and our weaknesses—that we become confident enough to recognize when others have more knowledge, skill, or talent than we do and invite them in. There is a misconception that all of us must develop in every single area. This is not the case; there are many opportunities to bring collaborators onto a team or project to boost capability and proficiency. We can also recruit people outside the organization to fill in any gaps. Being secure in ourselves means getting past the feeling that someone is going to outshine or replace us. True

 REFLECTION: HOW SECURE ARE YOU?

Assess how secure you are in yourself by answering the following questions:

- On a scale of 1-10 with 10 being the highest, how secure do you feel in yourself?
- Have you ever hired people who have more talent or experience than you?
- How have you supplemented your talent in your organization?
- Do you ever expect your new hires or direct reports to demonstrate behaviors like you?

visionaries stay out of the nitty-gritty, recognizing that qualified people are tasked with overseeing execution and maintaining operational excellence.

Address Unconscious Bias

Stereotypical perceptions or assumptions about people based on ethnicity, race, religion, gender, sexual preference, and other areas continue to exist—both above and beneath the surface. *Unconscious bias* is when we make judgments or decisions based on our prior experience, personal deepseated thought patterns, and assumptions or interpretations, but we aren't even aware that we are doing it. Many of us believe we aren't prejudiced, so we take our assumptions at face value. While we can't eradicate our unconscious bias in full, we can acknowledge that it exists, open ourselves up to it, and ask others to challenge us when it occurs, so we can recognize and tackle it in the moment. In a TED Talk, Vernā Myers offers two ways we can change our lens: get out of denial and move toward discomfort.

Get Out of Denial

Bias is a natural function of the human brain; we all have it to some degree. It is only through self-awareness that we can view ourselves more honestly, expose it, and shift accordingly. To accomplish this, we must look at:

- *Who do you go to as a default?*
- *Who do you trust?*
- *Who are you afraid of?*
- *Who do you avoid or run away from?*

In my prior company, we ran assessment centers to determine who should and would be effective as a general manager (GM). After analyzing the data of participants' ratings and their respective placements as a GM, we found something unusual: People who scored high weren't being placed in that role. We scratched our heads in bewilderment. We then conducted a study to find out why. Lo and behold, the organizations placed the people they were *most comfortable with*—the ones they trusted—versus the unknown factors of those who scored high in the assessments.

Move Toward Discomfort

Our natural tendency is to choose what is most familiar or comfortable. If we want to embrace each other's differences, we must expand our social circles and engage with those who aren't like us. We might feel disoriented and uneasy at first, but this is to be expected. If you approach the situation with curiosity and an open heart, you might say the wrong thing, but, in the end, you'll learn and broaden your humanity.

Everyone has blind spots, but they are especially damaging when it's the leader who demonstrates bias. If a leader categorizes, compares, or assumes things that reinforce their favoritisms, preconceptions, or stereotypes, individual and company reputations can be ruined and lawsuits potentially filed—even if the statement or behavior is unintentional.

Here are three additional ways to become more mindful of any unconscious biases and obliterate them:

a. *Actively engage:* When we make the effort to be aware of and address our biases, we actively behave in ways that make people feel valued, included, and respected.. This will mean we need to challenge our assumptions and beliefs and address those times when we unintentionally act in ways that limit others' contributions and sense of belonging. This may make us feel vulnerable or uncomfortable staying curious and open will support us to bring our bias to the surface so we can clear our lens and embrace new perspectives, connections, and the strengths of everyone we work with.

b. *Ignore:* When we don't address our biases, we allow them to limit the contribution of others. This impacts their sense of belonging and, ultimately, diminishes their engagement level and potential for success. On a personal note, this happened to me when I served in a large organization. A male senior leader joined the company to head a significant part of a business. I noticed that, when we met, he didn't make eye contact with me or listen to what I had to say. While he paid attention to my male direct reports, he never demonstrated any interest in a discussion with me. I felt frustrated, slighted, and undervalued. I observed that he behaved the same way to all women I saw him engage within the organization, not registering what they had to say. One can only imagine the opportunity cost to the company caused by this executive's feeling more comfortable with men—ignoring a substantial portion of the workforce based on their gender.

c. *Avoid disrespectfulness:* When we intentionally or unintentionally exhibit verbal or nonverbal behavior that communicates negative, hostile, or derogatory messages, we can affect people's emotional, mental, and physical well-being. These behaviors may vary from microaggressions (everyday slights, snubs, or insults); to harassment; and even abuse.

Leverage Empathy and Curiosity

We previously addressed leveraging empathy to understand others. To embrace differences, we must also activate our interest in learning more about people. Empathy and curiosity reinforce each other and fuel connection. These skills help us raise, address, and manage our biases, become more open-minded and less judgmental, and improve our decision-making ability.

ACTION FRAMEWORK

Think of a colleague with whom you've had past friction. Recollect a situation in which tension or conflict existed. Now, see it through a new lens.

- Place your hand on your heart, take a few breaths, and then answer questions to explore empathy:
  - What might the other person's needs have been in the situation?
  - What were her or his hopes and fears?
- Write down any new insights gleaned.
- Now, explore curiosity by answering the following questions:
  - Where could you have been more curious?
  - Where did you get stuck in your own point of view?
  - How did you test the other person's thinking to learn more?
  - What did your colleague bring to the table that you overlooked?

The Leader's Role: Serve as a Role Model

We all know that children need positive role models to help them become strong, capable, confident, and upright citizens. Employees and teams need role models as well, to provide examples of behaviors that are desirable and encouraged in the organization.

Be Brave and Bold

One such attribute is courage, which we explored in Chapter One. This trait fosters a sense of inclusion and belonging. Leaders who are willing to have others challenge them, identify blind spots, apologize for their missteps, and acknowledge the privilege of their position and use it to champion others set the tone for the whole culture that fosters genuine belonging.

Always show courage and lead into the unknown. If you do, colleagues will turn to you to feel safe and assured that it's okay to not always have the right answer. When you display courage, the workforce will join you wherever you lead them.

Set the Right Climate

Leaders must create an environment in which people feel valued and respected, so they can build confidence and thrive. There are seven key areas a leader must focus on to establish a positive, encouraging climate:

1. Be a multiplier not a diminisher.
2. Cultivate psychological safety.
3. Value different styles.
4. Encourage a Multicultural Paradox Mindset (see page 172).
5. Leverage the wisdom of the group.
6. Address and manage conflict.
7. Slow down to speed up.

Multiplier Effect

Some leaders can bring out the best in us and make us smarter. Liz Wiseman, a best-selling author of leadership books, refers to such individuals as *multipliers*—those who create collective, viral intelligence in organizations. Other leaders, who discourage and therefore deplete the organization of talent and acumen, are known as *diminishers*. What do multipliers do differently than diminishers to elicit more from their people? They look beyond their own ability and focus their energy on extracting and bolstering the genius of others.

Cultivate Psychological Safety

Amy C. Edmonson, the Novartis Professor of Leadership and Management at the Harvard Business School, coined the term *psychological safety*, which means that everyone in the organization is allowed to speak up about anything—including questions, concerns, ideas, and mistakes—without risk of repercussions, such as criticism, threats, ostracism, revenge, or humiliation. There must exist a shared expectation among team members that they will not embarrass, reject, or punish each other for expressing ideas, taking risks, or soliciting feedback. Psychological safety at work doesn't mean that everyone agrees with each other all the time; rather, it provides an atmosphere in which people feel comfortable to brainstorm together and provide healthy discussion and deliberation.

Value Different Styles

If we seek to embrace differences, we must respect and appreciate individual work styles and discover the multitude of benefits that may be gleaned from them. To accomplish this, leaders must establish enough time for team members to get to know each other, understand respective processes, and determine how to leverage the best of all individual methods. For example, a team with five big thinkers and one member who is process-minded should consciously take the time to ask the latter individual questions such as: "Is there anything we missed or failed to consider?" There is rarely just one way of doing things or a process that couldn't be improved with input from those who work differently, so, while this approach may occasionally add a bit more discussion time, ultimately it will lead to increased respect, teamwork, and camaraderie; better ways of doing things; and stronger results.

Encourage a Multicultural Paradox Mindset

The multicultural paradox mindset (MPM) is defined by Christine Shalley and other researchers at Georgia Tech Scheller College of Business as "the degree to which one is accepting of and energized by intercultural tensions, both emphasizing cultural differences and finding common ground." Team members who demonstrate high MPM can positively accept and embrace conflicting ideas to influence team behavior. "A diverse team has the potential to be better at information elaboration, and, thus, creativity, than a non-diverse team," Shalley said. "However, this potential needs to be unlocked. The presence of a member with high MPM is one way to achieve this within multicultural teams." Such individuals take "the cultural-blind approach," embrace differences, and encourage other team members to express themselves and their perspectives, bringing more value to the creative process.

Leverage the Wisdom of the Group

It never fails to surprise me how little we know about team members' past experiences when we join a group. I've been on hundreds of teams in my professional life and have found it rare for people to take the time to get to know each other on more than just a superficial level. When we jump right into the task at hand, we miss the opportunity to leverage others' experience and wisdom. The following questions can prove immensely beneficial to identifying those who have prior experience and wisdom:

- Who has seen this problem before?
- How did you go about solving the problem?
- Is there anyone we know outside this room who encountered this issue before?
- Are there any other companies that tackled this challenge before us?
- What can we learn from the successes and failures of other companies?

Deal with Conflict

Disagreements are not a bad thing and shouldn't be feared or avoided if the discussions are respectful and productive. It's alright for healthy tension to exist, especially if it means ensuring that all team members' opinions are heard and considered. There's no need to force consensus, but before decisions are made, all perspectives should be considered. If there is lingering conflict in the room after the discussion, it must be addressed and amicably resolved as soon as possible.

Slow Down to Speed Up

This sounds like a paradox, but it isn't. In many situations, leaders feel they are under so much pressure to move things along that they consult with the same select "go to" people every time. This prevents the opportunity for a robust discussion to occur and other points of view to emerge. By taking the time to pause and involve other parties—aka, "slowing down"—leaders can discover more available options. When we march too quickly to solve a problem, we often create three more down the road.

The Path to Diversity and Inclusion

Denise Campbell, the former president and chief executive officer of Campbell Soup Company, once said: "The path to diversity begins with supporting, mentoring, and sponsoring diverse women and men to become leaders and entrepreneurs."

What steps are you taking in your organization to embrace diversity and mine its myriad benefits?

Of course, diversity and inclusion alone won't connect everyone in your business or secure the high level of performance possible. There is one key ingredient remaining: *trusting other people.*

TAKEAWAYS

- Businesses that embrace diversity perform significantly better than those that do not.
- Diverse work cultures have greater collective wisdom and superior tools to drive business impact and innovation.
- Leaders have a responsibility to create a company culture in which belonging is encouraged, accepted, and practiced.

- If we want to truly embrace our differences and achieve superior business results, we must begin our journey at the self-level, in four areas: recognize our own genius, be secure in yourself, address unconscious bias, and leverage empathy and curiosity.
- Leaders must be brave and bold and establish the right climate in an organization.

Chapter Eleven

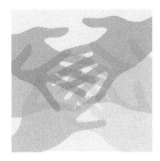

THE WILLINGNESS TO TRUST OTHER PEOPLE

Trust is the glue that holds our society together. We put trust in our leaders to do the right thing and our institutions to keep everything humming and moving forward. We sometimes don't notice the importance of this concept until it breaks or erodes. When trust breaks, we feel it profoundly, as if someone has pulled the rug out from under our feet. Trust is a value enhancer for corporate valuation; conversely, a lack of it can destroy market value in an instant.

According to the American Psychological Association (APA), *trust* is "the reliance on or confidence in the dependability of someone or something." Trust is an intangible thing that exists, and it forms the basis of all our relationships, including among groups of people. Like air, we don't see it, but, without it, we would cease to exist. For it to take hold in our professional as well as our personal lives, trustworthy behaviors must be demonstrated with frequency and consistency—which, in turn, reveals the level of emotional investment or commitment we have in each other.

It's impossible for us to function without being able to trust others. It's indispensable in every aspect of a relationship and may be broken at any time with just a single written or spoken word; a physical response, no matter how subtle or obvious; or an action. Sometimes even *inaction* can cause a loss of trust.

Building trust—whether with a colleague, friend, or partner—requires us to be vulnerable and step into being authentic, especially when we are willing to share pieces of ourselves with another person. It's one of the conundrums we face in life: We are afraid of trusting and getting hurt, but if we don't trust others, we can't have fulfilling relationships or deliver the impact we want in our professional lives. It's no coincidence that the verb that most commonly signals the beginning of a trusting relationship is *to* dare (give) or enter the relationship with an open heart and mind. When trust has been broken and the relationship is beyond repair, the one word that marks the end of a relationship is *perdere* (to lose). When a personal or business relationship ends, both parties lose something they once cherished, and it leaves an indelible mark that can impact future relationships.

Trust yields myriad benefits that are important for forming healthy relationships and maintaining strong emotional well-being. Trust allows us to feel safe, secure, and positive; experience intimacy and closeness with others; and reduce conflict. When you trust someone else, you have an opportunity to relax, be yourself, and depend on them for comfort, reassurance, assistance, and affection.

In Family We Trust

Erik Erikson, a well-known twentieth-century development psychologist, established that, if we can trust others and the world we live in, we give birth to the virtue of *hope*. Trust begins during our childhoods when we look to others to fill our basic needs. Assuming this occurs, we learn how to ask people for support whenever needed and depend upon them for survival, affection, and security. We build self-esteem, form relationships and attachments, and express ourselves emotionally.

We begin learning to trust other people from birth through approximately eighteen months of age. During this stage, an infant is uncertain about the world around her and looks toward her primary caregiver for stability and consistency of care. If the baby's care is predictable and reliable, she learns to trust other people and carry that sense of security to other relationships—even when threatened. If the care has been unpredictable and unreliable, however, the child may become mistrustful, suspicious, and anxious. As a result of this circumstance, the infant may lack confidence in the world, doubt other people, and feel uncertain about her ability to influence situations.

Learning trust in our first phase of life leads to *secure attachment*. British psychologist John Bowlby described this as the ability to confidently build relationships with others while also being able to act independently when appropriate. Children who are securely attached feel safe and supported by their caregivers.

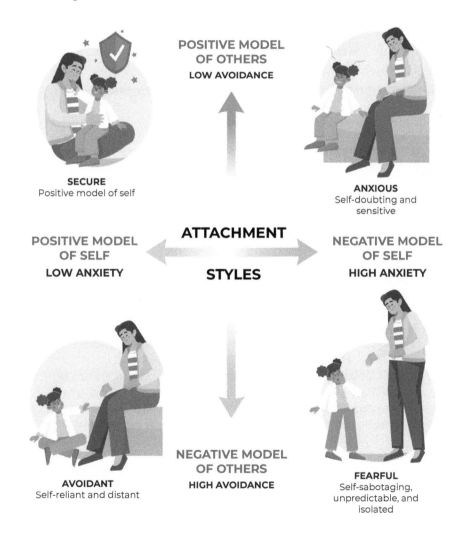

POSITIVE MODEL OF OTHERS
LOW AVOIDANCE

SECURE
Positive model of self

ANXIOUS
Self-doubting and sensitive

POSITIVE MODEL OF SELF
LOW ANXIETY

ATTACHMENT STYLES

NEGATIVE MODEL OF SELF
HIGH ANXIETY

AVOIDANT
Self-reliant and distant

NEGATIVE MODEL OF OTHERS
HIGH AVOIDANCE

FEARFUL
Self-sabotaging, unpredictable, and isolated

An adult with a secure attachment style behaves in a consistent, inter-dependent, and confident manner while forming relationships that tend to last and maintaining a healthy balance between relying on a partner and meeting her own needs. Having achieved this balance, she can create deeper intimacy through vulnerability while retaining her individuality.

About half of the population has a secure attachment style, while the rest fall into one of the insecure categories (anxious, avoidant, or fearful). It's no wonder relationships are challenging in the workplace when so many people seem to be grown-ups on the outside but are wounded children on the inside. Sometimes, when we see people clamoring to get their way at work or trying to control outcomes, it indicates that they are experiencing their own trust issues from childhood. In the past, you've probably gotten annoyed or even frustrated, but today you may see these past situations in a new light and have more compassion for your colleagues.

 REFLECTION: ARE YOU TRUSTING?

Even with our childhood patterns, we can still learn to trust others later in life. To ac-complish this, we must become more self-aware of our issues and create an intention to be more open and willing to earn the trust of others. Can you relate to any of these behaviors?

- *Always assuming the worst*: Do you believe people will treat you badly, even when they have proven themselves trustworthy in the past? For example, when someone offers to assist you, do you wonder if she is expecting something from you later?
- *Suspiciousness:* Do you doubt the good intentions of others, even if there is little to indicate that their actions are dubious? For example, you might assume without any evidence that others are trying to harm or deceive you.
- *Self-sabotage:* Do you do things that hurt your chances of obtaining what you want? For example, you might intentionally damage a positive relationship be-cause you assume it's better to end things early rather than be disappointed later.
- *Unhealthy relationships:* Do you find yourself flitting from one relationship to the next? If you've been avoiding healthy, long-lasting relationships, it's likely because you lack trust.
- *Lack of forgiveness:* Do you drop people from your circle when they make a mistake? The inability to forgive and forget can cause you to lose friends and suffer from loneliness.

(Continued)

- **Distancing yourself:** Do you build walls between yourself and other people? You may even avoid relationships altogether because you fear betrayal or disappointment.
- **Focusing on the negative:** Does your mind always head straight to what can go wrong rather than what can go right? If this is the case, you probably focus on others' flaws, weaknesses, and mistakes rather than their positive attributes.

A Company You Can Trust

We already defined trust in the general sense, but in the workplace, the word takes on a different flavor. In most cases, there is an element of perceived risk and the vulnerability associated with it. Trust is essential in organizations because it's rarely possible to have 100 percent certainty on everything. Decisions must be made—even when ambiguity exists due to a lack of data or due to a time sensitivity. Charles Feltman, author of *The Thin Book of Trust*, defines trust as "choosing to risk making something you value vulnerable to another person's actions." We might ask ourselves, "Can I rely on another to help me get my work done or do I really need to reveal my personal life to others to build trust?" He cites four factors for trust to exist in the workplace:

1. *Sincerity:* "I mean what I say, say what I mean, and act accordingly."
2. *Reliability:* "You can count on me to deliver what I promise."
3. *Competence:* "I know I can do this. I don't know if I can do that."
4. *Care:* "We're in this together."

It's important to note that when it comes to your organization, trustworthiness is not defined by you but how others view your behaviors and interactions based on the above criteria. The explanation for why trust breaks down in an organization can be complicated. For example, I once worked with a senior finance leader who was hell bent on transforming the organization. She had a clear mandate from senior leadership, and she felt she was doing her job. There was one major thing she overlooked: Her peers didn't know her well on a personal level. The thought of being vulnerable with her peers was a step too far, so she put up emotional boundaries. When she pushed the initiative forward, her peers didn't see it as a company mandate but rather as *her* agenda. The more she pressed, the more they resisted her efforts. In the end, she felt others didn't have her back, which reinforced her mistrust. To earn the trust of a team, people must know enough about us, see our vulnerable side, and feel that we care about them, as well as their needs, fears, and hopes.

Trust Comes in Many Forms

Earning trust at work isn't simple and straightforward or one-dimensional. We typically think of trust between two people, but it goes well beyond that in organizations, creating a level of complexity for leaders. To complicate things further, it's likely that relationships falling into the groupings below may be occurring simultaneously and yet are in different stages, which means varied approaches are required. A leader must develop an awareness of where each relationship stands, as trust may be high for one type and low for another.

- *Interpersonal:* Individual to individual. Do I trust another?
- *Institutional:* Individual to organization. Do I trust my organization to do the right thing?
- *Team trust (or psychological safety):* The belief that the environment is safe to express oneself without fear of retribution. Do we trust each other in a group setting?
- *Enterprise trust:* This is when trust expands past internal boundaries and relationships are built outside the immediate team. Do we work as one company?
- *Interorganizational:* Organization to organization, such as with a client or vendor. Are we seen as trustworthy outside our company?

As leaders move up and take on greater leadership scope, they become more accountable for ensuring that there is a culture of trust. They must constantly think about setting the tone and transmitting messages that support trustworthy behaviors. Leaders sometimes don't realize that people are watching their every move and using it to calibrate their own behaviors. Just imagine for a moment what happens if enterprise trust isn't fully embedded. Infighting and silos emerge, and, if interorganizational trust is broken, this can have a severe impact on bottom line results. As a leader, therefore, it is of paramount importance that you cultivate trust for every type.

Giving or Withholding Trust

It can be risky to trust other people, something many of us learn the hard way as children. When we are young and trust people too soon, we leave ourselves open to betrayal, disappointment, and hurt. When this occurs at an extreme level or with too much frequency, we put up walls, become mistrustful, and don't reinvest ourselves in others. Sometimes our standards become so high that we expect people to prove themselves to us first before they can earn our trust. A "wait and see" attitude may cause us to miss opportunities.

Our goal shouldn't be to teeter back and forth, but rather to ask ourselves what is the level of investment that is required for the situation and context. In business, acts of trust tend to grow and can go a long way toward earning mutual trust. Once you instill trust in someone else, that individual develops a sense of confidence because you believe in him. This increases the likelihood that he will take the responsibility seriously and do everything in his power to prove that your faith is justified. Similarly, the positive benefits derived from your willingness to believe in others will inspire them to be more willing to trust people as well.

A Story of Trust

John, a newly appointed senior leader to drive business transformation, wanted to show everyone that he deserved his promotion. His role required working with an existing team. He'd heard unfavorable things about the employees from the team's previous leader and concluded that they lacked the capability to successfully accomplish their goals. Rather than getting to know them and hear their ideas, he recruited two former colleagues he knew and trusted to join the team. Unfortunately, the pair lacked the specific knowledge required to lead the transformation as it impacted a key customer and nearly lost a key account. When John received the angry call from the customer, he realized that by not trusting the existing team members, he put the company's reputation at risk and damaged the inter-organizational trust. The original team had to step in and repair the relationship with the customer. John had been so preoccupied with his desire to secure an outcome that reflected well on him that he neglected to realize the impact of not trusting and leveraging his full team. This was a leadership lesson that he would never forget.

 REFLECTION: HOW DO YOU APPROACH TRUST?

Think about how you approach trust:

- Do you trust people but pull trust from them the moment they disappoint you?
- Do you believe people must earn trust before they are considered trustworthy?
- Do you intentionally withhold trust for any reason?
- Are you self-aware enough to have the right level of trust given any context?

As you reflect on your answers, consider the impact of how you give or withhold trust.

You Can Bank on Trust

Our everyday actions and behaviors have the potential to build or break trust. In *The Speed of Trust*, Stephen M.R. Covey suggests that we all have a metaphorical "emotional bank account" in which we balance our deposits and withdrawals of trust that add up to a fluctuating statement. The withdrawals carry much greater weight than the deposits; it may take only one misstep—whether intentional or not—to overdraw on an account. We can perform many positive actions to fill up the account, but then botch one major interaction and end up in the red.

Every individual's trust bank is different, both in terms of how much we deposit and withdraw and the amounts we invest in the accounts of others. It goes without saying that a leader's trust bank is generally the most visible, vulnerable, and volatile. You must assume that everything you say and do as a leader will be witnessed or heard by *someone* and then perceived by others in the organization—and perhaps externally—as trustworthy or not. For this reason, you should regard your trust bank as that of a public company; everyone has access to your shareholder's report and will gawk if your name appears in the news.

You've probably heard the old expression, "Trust takes years to build, seconds to break, and forever to repair." Suffice it to say, when trust is broken—or sometimes even just nicked—it can take a long time to get the bank account back in the black. It requires significant effort to repair a damaged reputation and reestablish oneself as sincere, credible, reliable, and caring. One must acknowledge the behaviors, apologize to those impacted, and maintain a clean slate thereafter.

I once led an exercise with a group of 250 senior leaders at a large multinational company. Each attendee was handed twenty-five chips and a cup. To begin, they were instructed to drop ten chips into the cup. I then told them to add a chip for each trust-building act I read aloud that they exhibited. For example, when I read inquiries about an employee's recent personal event, the leaders sat up taller in their chairs as they beamed with pride and filled their cups. Intermixed were the trust-breaking behaviors. When each one was announced—such as failing to admit when you're wrong, even when it's apparent to others—the leaders were directed to remove *three* chips from the cup. They groaned and slumped in their chairs with each callout. Not only did they suddenly recognize their own untrustworthy actions, but they also began shouting out at others in the room they identified as guilty of the misdeeds.

During this exercise, there was a collective understanding of the damage that gets done any time trust is broken. Everyone admitted to having been guilty of several indiscretions; many cups emptied even before all the untrustworthy behaviors were mentioned. By tipping the scales three to one, the leaders became keenly aware of the fact that negative behaviors impact the bank account far more severely than positive ones.

Try the Trust Bank Exercise yourself using the accompanying chart. Start with ten points in your bank. For every item where you have built trust, give yourself a point. For every behavior where you have broken trust, subtract three points. When you are done, count how much you have left in your trust bank (if anything).

Scoring +1	Builds Trust	Scoring -3	Breaks Trust
	Enquires about an employee's recent personal event.		Negatively talks about an associate to another associate.
	Expresses both positive and negative feelings to others.		Interrupts others and doesn't allow others to share their thoughts and ideas.
	Follows through on commitments.		Tells people what to do without asking for their input.
	Honors values.		Has difficulty admitting when wrong even when it's apparent to others.
	Regularly gives positive feedback that reinforces positive behavior.		Is not aware of what others' value.
	Sets clear expectations in work assignments.		Focuses on getting the work done and ignores the interest and needs of others.
	Regularly rewards others for work well done.		Makes continual changes to work assignments.
	Communicates information readily to others that impacts their work.		Blames others for work not getting done without looking at one's own role in the process.
	Gives timely constructive feedback in for others to course correct.		Does not like being vulnerable in front of others at work.
	Gives associates challenging assignments that allow them to grow.		Agrees to one thing but does another.
	Coaches others to develop new skills.		Gives constructive feedback in front of others.
	Is positive and upbeat with others.		Believes mistakes are not acceptable.
	Asks for others' side of the story before assuming somebody made a mistake.		Avoids conflict and confronting others as issues arise.
	Celebrates others' success.		Takes credit for others' work.
	Collaborates with others in getting work done.		Gives indirect feedback to another manager or staff member instead of directly talking to the person you have an issue with.
	Actively seeks out other's point of view even if it opposes yours .		Relies on your "go to people" rather than giving someone else a chance.

Ask yourself:

- What can I do to build greater trust?
- What behaviors do I need to stop doing that break trust?

How to Master Trust

As you can see, trust is dynamic through our everyday actions and inter-actions, as well as through words that we say aloud or write. Some consider trust as binary—either you trust someone, or you don't—but I don't believe this to be true because your bank account fluctuates with every ticking second. I take stock in what a former manager of mine once said to me: "If you want to build a partnership with strong trust, you must work side by side with this person."

Life is too short to carry around baggage and be judgmental. For every-one to succeed, we must give people the benefit of the doubt. We are all fallible as humans. Every one of us makes mistakes, overlooks something, or drops the ball at one time or another. Sometimes our actions do not match our best intentions. This becomes exacerbated by the ever-increasing speed of business and the rate of technological advancement. Leaders are deluged with constant communication and must make instant decisions amidst per-petual change. They are faced with ambiguity, shifting priorities, and con-flicting demands—all of which carry some risk of sacrificing trust. When we see each action and word as an opportunity to build and grow trust, we become proactive stewards of trust within our organizations. Of course, we also need to stay tuned to when trust is negatively impacted, lost, or broken, so we may take steps to address this and strengthen our trust bank.

Don't Hold Back Feedback

Repairing the damage caused by broken trust is never quick or easy. Typically, the culprits are the last to find out there is even an issue, as the injured may be afraid of imagined potential repercussions or don't want to cause problems or be part of any kind of drama. Telling someone that they broke our trust can feel like we're accusing the person of being unscrupu-lous. We associate trust with integrity and, for some, it doesn't feel right to make this personal callout. But, when we hold back giving feedback, we do more damage to the relationship than if we were to courageously share our own disappointments that someone did not live up to what they had agreed upon, whether on purpose or unintentionally. The fracture goes well beyond the relationship and leaves a negative impact on progress being made throughout the company. Just imagine if you could see a number ticker counting all the occasions when people in your organization withhold feedback. You might be astonished by the revelation. As leaders, we need to encourage our staff to have honest conversations with each other, so we can repair and rebuild trust and make our organizations stronger and more vibrant.

Often, we only find out about a break in trust when we notice someone is behaving differently around us or a manager brings it to our attention during a one-on-one meeting or a performance review. Sometimes, the recipient of the broken trust shares her story with one or more colleagues "in confidence." If this information is passed along, it can impact people's reputations and career opportunities. We must remember that we are all fallible and will never get everything right every time. Just recently, I overcommitted myself and found I had to do work at the last minute for an upcoming project. The client was upset and questioned whether I could deliver on time. At first, I was angry because I never let my clients down. After careful reflection, I realized that *I* was the one who had overcommitted and had to be held accountable for not having completed the work done earlier. It wasn't easy, but I admitted my error and repaired the relationship.

The obstacles mount when we're at fault yet remain in the dark. Some people assume that, because you are a leader, you should automatically recognize when you've said, written, or done something wrong. But we're all guilty of blind spots. How can we be expected to stop doing something or make amends for crossing a line when we're unaware we've slipped up in the first place?

The objective is to establish a culture early on that not only encourages people to comfortably express themselves without facing any repercussions but also makes it an understood expectation to speak up. In this environment, the leader must invite others to provide feedback on her style and impact. She must then accept it without seeming irritated, defensive, or argumentative. Trust flourishes when the leader shows a deep understanding of the feedback and indicates that she'll take steps to improve. We need to act as role models by demonstrating vulnerability when we've made a mistake and accidentally broken trust.

It requires courage to inform others—especially those in more senior-level leadership positions—when they've broken trust, not lived up to an agreement, or otherwise missed the mark. We need to recognize and reward those who display such courage, as this will demonstrate to everyone across the organization that trust is valued. Open communication improves integrity and enhances authenticity, which are key components of a trusting culture. At one time or another, all of us have been afraid of providing feedback, and we rely on the "up and over process" where, instead of providing direct feedback to a colleague, the individual first makes a beeline to her manager, after which it crosses to another manager who communicates the issue to the person. This type of behavior leads to a giant game of telephone in which the message becomes diluted among many parties and then mushrooms into hurt feelings that could have been averted if the offended party had just been transparent and direct in the first place.

Don't Make Assumptions

It's all too easy to misinterpret the intentions and behaviors of other people and assume the worst about them. There is a significant difference between trust and control, and yet the two tend to become conflated, because those who have trust issues also often feel a need for control. If you are wired to act controlling in work situations, you must be mindful that this can be interpreted to mean you are mistrustful of others' abilities, which may be considered insulting. Having compassion for others, acknowledging their needs, and forgiving their mistakes are natural parts of growth and development that can help overcome this issue.

It's most difficult to build trust with someone we are meeting for the first time, such as a new employee. According to Dr. Anne Böckler-Raettig, a professor who studies trust at the University of Wurzburg in Germany, we often decide who to trust within a few hundredths of a millisecond. She asserts that we look at two key areas to determine trustworthiness in a person:

1. *Facial features*: This is not an accurate or fair measure, and yet it's human nature for people to form impressions based on certain characteristics. We typically rely on the shape of the eyes and

mouth to presume if someone is trustworthy; however, there is no evidence indicating that parts of the face (such as mouth formation) have anything to do with whether a person is trustworthy or not. This means it's all too easy for false assumptions to be made. Realizing this, try to avoid forming an opinion about someone based on a feature that has no bearing on their behavior.

2. *Authority or competence:* When we meet people for the first time, we look for signals of authority and competence. Sometimes a person's gait—whether she stands up tall or walks with a slight bend—presents what might be a false clue about her trustworthiness. Even more commonly, we judge people based on their clothes to determine stature and ability, which can be even more misleading. As the cliche goes, "Clothes don't make the man"— or woman.

Be aware of the principles on which you are basing your trust. Challenging ourselves to be specific about why we are investing trust (or not) will help to avoid instinctive judgments and unconscious bias.

Don't Poison the Well

The phrase "poison the well" has been around for centuries, originating from a time when invading armies would literally add poison to the enemy's fresh drinking water in advance of an attack. In modern times, it has since come to mean casting aspersions about a person before he's had a chance to say or do anything. When a new person joins an organization, the natural inclination is for employees who knew him elsewhere to share their opinions and prior experiences with colleagues, which can be negative. These individuals are automatically claiming leverage and power over the newcomers, even if they believe they are warning others and protecting the company. This poses a bigger risk than we think. When we meet others for the first time, we tend to listen a lot to what others have to say about them—that is, their reputations. In fact, prior information we have about somebody else can have such a strong influence on our expectations that we entirely ignore how this person behaves. So, we ignore somebody's trustworthy behavior toward us because we already expect them to be untrustworthy.

The crux of the message is that we must allow people to form their own opinions of others. If someone shares dirt with you about a new employee, delete it from your brain or you risk misconstruing everything she says and does because you already expect she will exhibit certain behaviors.

Don't Limit Relationships to Transactions

Trust is an investment. If two people are invested in a relationship, it is more likely to become reciprocal and both parties will benefit from it. We need to think differently about trust. It's not one plus one equals two. If both people invest in the relationship and make the proper investment, the returns become exponential. We build trust by finding the right balance between giving and receiving, and this only happens by engaging with others authentically, working side by side, and revealing who we are at our core. We need to be mindful of our interactions with others—especially when we are under pressure—because it's too easy to focus on tasks and avoid the proper level of affiliation that is needed to nurture relationships. When we focus more on receiving than giving, we become imbalanced, and others experience our relationships as transactional. With proper reflection, we can keep our balance in check.

Don't Hold a Grudge

In her research, Dr. Anne Böckler-Raettig identified why trust declines so rapidly in some interactions yet strengthens in others. A common ingredient among thriving relationships is that both parties have a *willingness to forgive*. There are going to be times when people let us down and others when we are the ones who mess up. When someone is at fault, that person already carries with her some guilt or embarrassment about the situation and is insecure about her standing. The best way to reduce this uncertainty and get the person back on track is to forgive her and reinvest in the relationship. Why not give her another chance when you both work for the same team?

ACTION FRAMEWORK

Part I: Think of people you work with who let you down, causing trust to suffer.

- Write down how you feel they let you down.
- Did you share your disappointment?
- If you haven't shared your disappointment, do so now.
- Think about what actions you can take to reinvest in the relationships.

Part II: Think of people you work with who you let down, causing trust to suffer.

- Write down how that person might have felt when you let them down. *How might they have viewed the situation differently?*
- Reflect whether you took accountability for the interaction. *What tendencies do I have that might have gotten in the way?*
- Share with them how you let them down, and try to see things from their perspective. You can even go one step further and invite them to disclose things from their own perspective.
- Think about what actions you can take to reinvest in the relationship and earn back trust.

Since we're hardwired for human connection, we genuinely enjoy being trusted by others. It helps us feel good about ourselves, valued, and important. Bestowing and receiving trust are sacred gifts and the foundation of all our relationships. When they are present in organizations, employees become more engaged in the work and invested in each other, and positive results follow. However, as mentioned, it only takes one crack to form to cause a breakdown, forcing leaders to step in and repair things. Our role as leaders is to ensure we create the right environment for trust to take root and flourish, reducing and repairing the impact when trust is broken in some way. This is hard work but well worth the effort. As Stephen Covey said, "Contrary to what most people believe, trust is not some soft, illusive quality that you either have or you don't; rather, trust is a pragmatic, tangible, actionable asset that you can create."

- Trust forms the basis for all our relationships, including among groups of people.
- The ability to trust other people starts at birth and continues to approximately eighteen months of age.
- An adult with a secure attachment style behaves in a consistent, interdependent, and confident manner, but only half of the population have it.
- Four things are required for trust to exist in a work environment: sincerity, reliability, competence, and care.
- Trust banks have two accounts: our actions add to or detract from the level of trust that others place in us. We can all become stewards of our own trust banks.
- To master trust, don't make assumptions, hold a grudge, or "poison the well." Rather than limiting relationships to transactions, invest in relationships and communicate about any breaches of trust.

Part IV

CO-CREATING POSSIBILITIES

Leader (Andrea) SAYS: Violet, we just received $3 million in funding for embedding AI into our digital transformation work. It's so exciting! I'm going to ask each team member to give some thought to the topic and come up with their best ideas, and then we'll all meet and share our ideas.

Leader (Andrea) THINKS: I'm doing such a great job of involving everyone in the process, igniting curiosity, and getting everyone to contribute to this fantastic opportunity.

Direct Report (Violet) SAYS: That's a great idea. I'll start to look at some research and see what applications we can use for our current agenda. I just read a research article about some work going on at MIT that might be relevant.

Direct Report (Violet) THINKS: This sounds like a wonderful opportunity. I know I'll learn and grow from the process, but I don't like this dog and pony show. As usual, Sam will present his brilliant ideas during the team meeting. All the other ideas will fall by the wayside, and we'll concentrate on implementing his suggestions. There has to be a better way of managing this so that everyone on the team can contribute in a more meaningful way.

Leader (Andrea) SAYS: That sounds great, Violet. When you have a chance, send the article to the team and me, so we can all read it before our session next week.

Direct Report (Violet) SAYS: Sure—I'll share it the second I find it.

Chapter Twelve

ESTABLISHING SHARED CLARITY OF PURPOSE

Leaders are constantly grappling with the question: *How do we get our staff to fully commit and go above and beyond what is being asked of them?* In 2010, Simon Sinek launched his famous YouTube video "How Great Leaders Inspire Action" that addresses this topic. It comes down to everyone connecting to the *why* or *purpose* of an organization. This transcends well beyond making a profit, touching employees on an emotional or even "soul" level. It taps into what employees care about and intermeshes with their own value systems.

The tides toward purposeful leadership have swelled. If you want your employees to co-create and innovate, they must care about why the company was started, what it stands for, and what it hopes to give back to society. Organizations are now tasked with being socially responsible, meaning that, besides maximizing shareholder value, they must also operate in a way that benefits society.

Getting People to Truly Care

I recently viewed a rerun of *Shark Tank* TV reality show (Season Twelve, Episode Six) in which two entrepreneurs, Riki and Oron Franco, were seeking an investment in their product, Prime 6 Charcoal. Their pitch seemed like a no-brainer: an invention for charcoal that was sustainable and didn't involve toxic smoke or chemical additives. Even the process of producing Prime 6 was environmentally friendly, as it was created from recycled sawdust as opposed to the traditional method of chopping down trees. The financials also looked good: The couple already had orders from Walmart and Lowes. Even with all of this going for it, one of the show's Sharks, Blake Mycoskie—founder of TOMS' Shoes and the Social Entrepreneurship Fund—passed by saying, "You have a great product, but I don't care about it enough to get behind it and invest; I am out."

Riki and Orion didn't go home empty-handed, however. Another Shark, Kevin O'Leary (aka "Mr. Wonderful"), invested in the company. The business continues to exist three years later and has since grown to $2 million.

While the story has a happy ending, it still leaves open the following question: Why did Blake Mycoskie—well known as a philanthropist—drop out of the running to invest in a viable company that added social value? What did he mean by "I don't care about it enough to get behind it and invest"? If it's this challenging to lure someone like Mycoskie into supporting Prime 6 Charcoal, how could organizations possibly be expected to entice their employees to care about their products?

Firms of Endearment Is an Organization's Best Friend

Not long ago, caring words such as *affection, love, joy, authenticity, empathy, compassion,* and *soulfulness* didn't have any place in business. That has completely changed. Today, a growing number of companies comfortably embrace these terms, which is why authors Raj Sisodia, David Wolfe, and Jag Sheth coined the phrase "firms of endearment" (FoE). In their book *Firms of Endearment,* they examine how world-class businesses, such as Harley-Davidson, BMW, and Costco, profit from passion and purpose.

The key distinguishing factor of an FoE is that the company endears itself to stakeholders by bringing all groups into strategic alignment. One stakeholder doesn't benefit at the expense of another. When one prospers, all of them succeed. These companies meet the functional and psychological needs of their stakeholders in ways that engender affection for and loyalty to the company. FoEs have significantly outperformed the market in timeframes ranging from three to fifteen years.

Your Mission

The first step in establishing clarity and purpose involves identifying the *why*—or purpose—as well as the vision and mission statements. These crucial messages help employees: develop a sense of belonging and identity, form a personal connection to the company, motivate people to work harder, and foster the right mindset that will lead to business growth. People define purpose, mission, vision, and goals differently, so let's clarify them before moving on:

- *Purpose:* Defines the reason your company exists, above simply making a profit. Also illustrates how your product or service positively impacts the people you serve. Provides a sense of why you do what you do that engages and sustains you and your people, making them feel proud to be part of the organization. For example, Google's original purpose was to "organize the world's information and make it universally accepted and useful." Netflix's purpose is "to entertain the world."

- *Values:* The core beliefs, philosophies, and principles that guide the way your employees act and conduct business. Values shape and influence organizational culture and drive how employees do things, particularly regarding standards of conduct and ethical practices. While business plans and strategies may change, the core values of a business will usually remain the same.

- *Vision:* This statement expresses your organization's aspirations for its best possible future. A powerful vision inspires employees to progress the company toward its idyllic state. This is an excellent way to motivate and excite people to create, achieve, and deliver unified results.

- *Mission:* This is the approach you will take to achieve your purpose and vision and communicate how you define success.

- *Strategy:* This is how a company seeks to create value for the organization and its stakeholders and gain a competitive advantage in the market. A strategic plan must be in place before any goods or services are produced and delivered.

- *Goals (Objectives):* Itemizes specific measurable actions that must be taken in the short term to support the strategic plan.

What Is the Purpose of a Purpose Statement?

A purpose statement defines a company's journey; it applies both internally (for leadership and employees) and externally (for customers and investors). It serves as a blueprint for the future and helps guide all the decisions you make—from how you produce your products to how customers experience your marketing campaigns.

Your purpose influences your customers. According to recent research from Accenture, 63 percent of global consumers prefer to purchase products and services from companies that stand for something—in other words, have purpose. Consumers today have greater influence than ever before, as they can support and love your products or buy something else if your values do not resonate with theirs. That's why it is critical to continually engage consumers as part of your company's journey, stand in your integrity, and remain aligned to your company's purpose. The Accenture study also found that companies standing for something bigger than what they sell are more likely to attract consumers and influence purchasing decisions.

Leaders around the world are taking note of the rise of purpose-driven companies. Lise Kingo, CEO and executive director of the UN Global Compact, stated, "The idea of business as an agent of change and a purveyor of positive values is gaining traction and legitimacy around the world. With a growing number of companies taking steps to be more responsible in how they treat employees, communities, and the planet, we are seeing business emerge as a real player and solution-provider in the quest to put our world on a better course."

Beyond attracting customers and increasing your bottom line, clarifying your company's purpose is important for the following three reasons:

1. *Stand out from the crowd:* Purpose defines what makes your company special and unique. Your products or services might be able to be duplicated on some level, but it's difficult for anyone to copy your company's purpose.

   Customers and employees can be genuinely inspired by your company and want to get behind what it stands for. For example, the purpose of Life is Good—a designer of t-shirts and apparel—is to spread the power of optimism. When I first came across this brand, I jumped right onto their bandwagon and bought their products because I was impressed by their messaging, which resonated with my life outlook.

2. *Help meet goals:* Purpose guides you along your company's journey as you move forward, informing you on how your strategies and goals should be developed beyond financial performance. A strong purpose should ignite passion and serve as an indicator of how well you are progressing in terms of impact.

3. *Informs company culture:* A recent employee survey by the *HBR* found that only 28 percent of employees felt connected to their company's purpose and only 34 percent thought they were contributing to their company's success. According to *HBR*, a lack of purpose among employees can create a negative company culture in which employees feel unmotivated and misaligned.

We Sometimes Start in the Wrong Place

There are some senior leaders who continue to believe that it's their responsibility to define the vision and mission on their own and then cascade them down to the organization. Though mission statements may have been crafted this way in the past, this rarely works in today's collaborative business environment. Employees want to take part in shaping the companies where they work.

Leaders who are inclusive and engage a team to develop the company's vision and mission statements see improved results because those involved are invested in the process. The collective wisdom of the organization is assembled as a mighty force, which represents more diversity of thought and brings greater unity and cohesion to the effort.

While vision and mission statements play a significant role in setting direction and motivating and inspiring others, they aren't enough on their own to provide meaning and facilitate genuine connection. This is where establishing purpose becomes all important. Author and leadership guru Linda Hill states, "Leading innovation and leading change are different. When you lead change, you have a vision, and you are trying to inspire people to follow you to the future. When you're trying to innovate, you don't have a vision. You can't inspire people to get there because you don't know where you're going. What you have is a purpose, and a purpose is *why* you're going and what you're trying to do versus *where*."

Microsoft, under Satya Nadella's leadership, went on a five-month journey to better define and embed the company's purpose in the organization. During this process they encapsulated their purpose in this statement: *To empower every person and every organization on the planet to achieve more.* Guided by such clear purpose, the company has ended up focusing on and innovating around accessibility. Chief Marketing Officer Chris Capossela said, "There wasn't a single day where the senior leadership team said, 'We now shall care a lot about accessibility and all product teams need to figure out what that means.' Frankly, it came much more bottom-up inside the company." This has now become embedded in company events and led to such revolutionary ideas as the Microsoft Seeing AI app, which was invented by a visually impaired Microsoft engineer named Saqib Shaikh.

To create meaning on a more tangible level, the business needs to provide values that each person can connect to on a personal level. This helps individuals become enriched on each step of the journey toward achieving the vision. When people find value and meaning rather than just trying to achieve a result, they become more present to opportunities that connect them with their team members, expand their thinking, and offer fresh insights and discoveries. When provided with the right context and a safe place to contribute, employees gain confidence with each new initiative. They also become fully engaged because they enjoy the experience of investing their collective effort in something with shared meaning. This process establishes a mutual investment between leadership and the team in which everyone feels a sense of ownership, pride, and responsibility toward the same commitment and intended result.

State Your Purpose

A 2020 report by Edelman found that 80 percent of respondents expect brands to "solve society's problems." This puts greater pressure on companies because most people don't believe governments are able to solve major

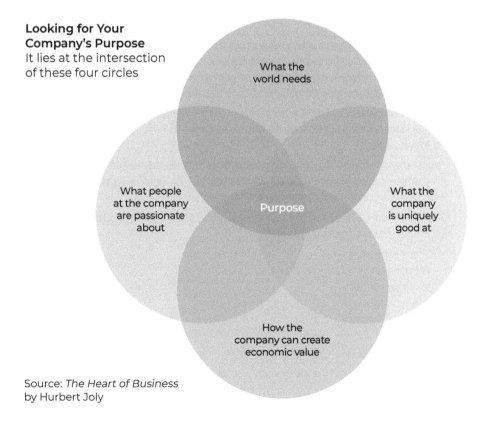

Looking for Your Company's Purpose
It lies at the intersection of these four circles

What the world needs

What people at the company are passionate about

Purpose

What the company is uniquely good at

How the company can create economic value

Source: *The Heart of Business* by Hurbert Joly

global challenges, such as climate change. According to Hubert Joly, the former chairman and CEO of Best Buy, companies need to root themselves in purpose to drive engagement and profitability, which he doesn't believe are mutually exclusive.

ACTION FRAMEWORK

The following six steps have been inspired by Hubert Joly's four circles that surround purpose (see chart on the following page), as he detailed in *HBR*.

Step 1 (first circle): Explore what your company is uniquely good at doing. Identify the products or services you offer that fulfill certain consumer needs in a way other companies don't.

Step 2 (second circle): Explore what the world needs. Identify the problems that no one else is solving and see how filling this need fits your company's mission and vision.

Step 3 (third circle): Explore what your workers are passionate about. Consider how you are going to solicit information about what is in the hearts and minds of employees. This might include focus groups, one-on-one interviews, or pulse surveys. Your objective is to determine what motivates and excites people.

Step 4 (fourth circle): Explore how the company can create economic value. Now you want to identify opportunities from the prior three circles that might be monetized or could add profit.

Step 5: Integrate the findings and write your purpose statement. Now that you have filled all four circles, you can zoom out and see how they tie together. Write down a concise purpose statement that connects all four circles.

Step 6: Pressure test your purpose statement. Joly offers the following questions to assess the quality of your purpose statement:

- Is it *authentic?*
- Is it *credible?*
- Is it *powerful?*
- Is it *compelling?*
- Is it *meaningful?*

Activate Your Purpose

It's not enough to have a compelling purpose; it must become part of the ecosystem and drive business decisions and actions. Below are some effective ways to activate the company's purpose:

- *Ensure the company's purpose is aligned:* Every decision and action must connect in some way to the purpose. Leaders need to ensure that it flows into the company's vision, mission, values, and goals. While it's good to display the purpose on a wall where it's visible to everyone (such as in the lobby), it must also be embedded in discussions and activities during off-site meetings, everyday meetings, and one-on-one sessions. The leader's role is to preface every decision and action with how they link to the purpose. Constant reminders are helpful to everyone so that the messaging is never lost or confused.

  Sometimes companies must make certain trade-offs that test the company values. Employees must understand the how and why behind how such determinations are made. For example, when I worked at Chase Manhattan Bank, leadership was committed to equal opportunity for all employees. In an office based in the Middle East, a potential customer with high net worth refused to interact with a female banker. Chase could easily have substituted a male worker for the female to please the wealthy customer. Instead, the bank stuck with its values, turning away the client and declining millions of dollars in revenue. This costly decision yielded positive results, however, as employees felt proud to work for a company that put people ahead of profit.

- *Engage employees in the purpose journey.* Once workers have expressed what is meaningful to them, they should connect their personal purpose with that of the company. Leaders must devote time to review this with each team member to cement the concept.

- *Embed purpose in your customers' experiences.* Of course, purpose isn't just for the employees. The messaging must also extend outward to serve customers. Canva, an online design and communication platform, aspires to "empower everyone in the world to design anything and publish anywhere." The company practices what it preaches, scoring high in terms of engagement and favorable Glassdoor ratings (referrals from former employees). According to their website, their "teams operate a bit like mini start-ups within Canva, setting and driving crazy big goals. We want our people to thrive at Canva by focusing on goals, collaboration, and impact, not titles and level."

 REFLECTION: HOW DO YOU ACTIVATE YOUR PURPOSE?

Answer the following questions to assess how you activate purpose as an individual:

- What actions do I take that link daily activities to purpose?
- How do I tap into what personally matters to others?
- What actions can I engage in that will ignite people's passion?

Purpose and caring must be embodied in every aspect of our business—from how we treat our customers and employees to how we make big and small decisions. When the purpose is well defined, it creates clarity while helping people stay emotionally connected and engaged.

Sometimes, especially when we are trying to achieve mundane day-to-day tasks or accomplish specific annual goals, we lose sight of why we're doing the work and what the company stands for. The need for achievement and driving profitability becomes our driving force, which impacts our ability to motivate our teams and please our customers. The short-term benefit of checking something off a to-do list sacrifices the long-term benefits of purpose for yourself, as well as internal and external stakeholders. Simply by having read and absorbed this chapter, you've already taken the first important step toward establishing shared clarity of purpose in your organization.

Chapter Thirteen

OPTIMISM AND HOPE

In our personal and professional lives, it's inevitable that challenges will emerge or things will go wrong. We may, for example, find ourselves concerned with quarterly numbers that didn't meet expectations while dealing with an emotional issue at home, such as with a teenager. During a regular workday, a host of things can go sideways: there could be a setback in product development; a customer might be disappointed with service; a key team member might resign, taking a role with a competitor; and so forth. We may even be presented with an exceptional business opportunity but realize there is little available bandwidth to realize it. This may leave us feeling bewildered with the wind taken out of our sails. We can either drift in despair or grab the rudder and redirect.

When these situations occur, where do we go for support or inspiration to bounce back or move through emotions that feel insurmountable? We need an infusion of energy or a change in perspective to help us move forward.

Optimistically Hopeful

The words *optimism* and *hope* might at first sound synonymous, but they have distinct connotations. *Optimism* is a state of mind and one's belief that a favorable outcome is *likely* to occur. When someone is optimistic, she has a level of confidence that her favorable perspective will win out. Meanwhile, *to hope* as a verb is defined by Merriam-Webster's as "wanting or expecting something to happen or be true." Whereas optimism is a state of being or a positive world outlook, hope is more rooted in action or process driven.

Irish poet Seamus Heaney distinguishes the two states of mind this way: "Hope is not optimism, which expects things to turn out well, but something rooted in the conviction that there is good worth working for." A 2004 study concluded: "Optimism focuses more broadly on the expected quality of future outcomes in *general* where hope focuses more directly on expectations about the personal attainment of *specific* goals."

To illustrate the difference, let's look at the example of a particular Human Edge client. This private equity–owned healthcare company was a spinoff of a large, well-resourced multinational. Once it split off as a separate company, the processes, technology, and resources that provided results vanished overnight. The firm found itself in turmoil because it needed to deliver on expected growth targets. This was daunting, especially since it only had 2,500 employees to handle 100 projects, which wasn't nearly enough. Leaders and staff alike felt overwhelmed and disenchanted, as their current processes didn't work with everyone stretched so thin.

While the senior leaders focused on strategy to improve profitability, employees and lower-level leaders jumped ship. At first, the executive committee attributed the spike in turnover to the employees being "a bad fit." However, the bleeding continued even after departing employees were replaced. The CEO—a strong and well-respected strategic leader—had a hard time emotionally connecting with his staff. He did little to improve morale, uplift people, give them a reason to stay, or even offer something positive to help them get through this turbulent time.

Optimism and hope are essential tools to help leaders deal with setbacks and bring about a better future. This frame of mind can counter setbacks and frustration and guide leaders and teams alike to keep plowing ahead, despite seemingly insurmountable circumstances. When used in tandem, hope and optimism can instill enough confidence to help a business shift from survival mode to thriving. Let's take a closer look at each one individually.

Optimize Your Optimism—with a Healthy Dose of Reality

Optimism is a desirable personality trait for an employee to have. Optimists see things in the most positive light, and this gives them a high degree of energy to propel them through life's challenges. Optimism is associated with a wide variety of favorable outcomes, including better mental and physical health, and improved motivation, performance, and personal relationships.

On the opposite end of the spectrum are pessimists, who automatically decide—with or without supportive data—that an outcome will be a worst-case scenario. Optimists have a greater amount of resilience than pessimists, as they respond better to disappointment and don't have as much stress. Even when things are declining, optimists expect things to get better and search for signs ("light at the end of the tunnel") that indicate a turnaround is somewhere on the horizon. Experts claim that the real difference between optimists and pessimists isn't necessarily their level of happiness or how they perceive a situation but rather how they cope when the chips are down.

Optimists search for the bright side of a situation and try to identify the good in people. They want the world to be a feel-good experience for everyone in which "everything is working out." Optimists gaze at a garden and see the flowers, not the weeds. That's not to say you want people to wear rose-colored glasses about the reality of an unfavorable situation. People need to be objective and transparent about what is happening based on the available facts. If an issue has a potential negative outcome, you want to be around leaders and employees who are open about it and confident the team will find a solution.

When people are too optimistic, they may overlook problems and not heed obvious warning signs. For this reason, we must always have one foot firmly rooted in optimism and the other in realism. The latter allows us to recognize issues and address them; if we don't weed our garden, for example, the flowers will eventually be overtaken. Realism also helps us see both sides of a person—both the good and the bad.

Applying the right degree of optimism places us in the driver's seat of life and gives us more freedom to explore options and develop authentic relationships. Optimistic leaders who balance the positive with a touch of reality tend to be engaging communicators. They share positive stories about what the future will look like while helping settle down those who might be feeling anxious.

Mind Your Assets

Dr. Kathryn D. Cramer, founder of The Cramer Institute, and Hank Wasiak, co-founder of the Concept Farm, offer a new way of seeing things called *asset-based thinking*. Put simply, this means focusing on positive strengths. It goes beyond optimism, as they state that it isn't whether the glass is half full or half empty but rather, *the quality of the water*. Focusing on the assets that are available keeps teams inspired and alert, builds enthusiasm, and helps them think in terms of possibilities, as opposed to making the same old assumptions and only seeing problems or opportunities with a limited perspective. Imagine what could be possible if leaders and colleagues devoted their time and attention to:

- Opportunities rather than problems.
- Strengths more than weaknesses.
- What can be done instead of what can't.

What prevents us from being asset-based thinkers? The opposite, or *deficit-based thinking* (DBT), which relies heavily upon:

- Personality gaps and weaknesses.
- The things that bother and irritate others.
- The ideas that aren't working and hold everyone back.

For the glass of water to be simultaneously half full and half empty, we must place our attention on where the most power and value reside. For example, we need to ask what the water in the glass is for and whether there is a tap nearby. To continue the garden analogy, we need to see both the weeds *and* the flowers. We tend to focus on the weeds when making room for flowers and grass, but we might also recognize that certain ones, such as dandelions, have medicinal value. If we're only trained to pay attention to what is wrong, we miss important nuances that provide value.

When we shift to asset-based thinking (ABT), we transition from threat to opportunity and change how we see ourselves, other people, and situations. From the chart below, we can leverage our personal, situational, and relationship assets to create a positive ripple effect that everyone will follow.

The ABT Ripple Affect

Tap your personal assets first, all others will follow

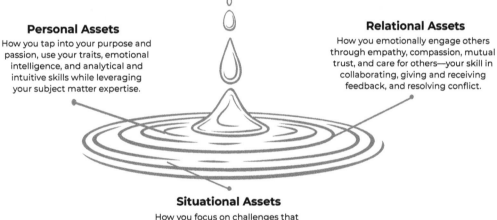

Personal Assets

How you tap into your purpose and passion, use your traits, emotional intelligence, and analytical and intuitive skills while leveraging your subject matter expertise.

Relational Assets

How you emotionally engage others through empathy, compassion, mutual trust, and care for others—your skill in collaborating, giving and receiving feedback, and resolving conflict.

Situational Assets

How you focus on challenges that promote breakthrough solutions, use setbacks to promote new standards of performance, leverage experimentation to offer unique insight and learning, and find opportunities for innovation.

With permission to use from *Change The Way You See Everything Through Asset-Based Thinking* by Kathryn D. Cramer, PhD and Hank Wasiak

Retrain Your Brain

Some people are wired to be optimists; others are innate pessimists. By the same token, whichever way one is leaning—based on brain chemistry and DNA—can be influenced by a person's childhood surroundings and experiences. In other words, an optimist can be converted into a pessimist and vice versa. The good news is that, even if you were a born pessimist, there are effective ways to retrain your brain to focus on the positive.

Of course, this isn't as easy as consciously thinking happy thoughts. Below are a few simple suggestions to retrain your brain to think positively:

- *Turn a negative thought into an uncomfortable physical action:* Wear a rubber band on your wrist throughout the day. Every time you have a negative thought, give it a light snap against your skin. This will cause negativity to be internalized by the subconscious as something unpleasant to be avoided.

- *Hang out with optimists:* Positivity and negativity are both contagious, so make a conscious choice to spend more time with friends, family, and colleagues (when possible) who are grounded and uplifting.

- *Listen to inspirational stories:* Spend less time reading, listening to, and watching the news and social media feeds, as tragic world events and posts can bring you down. Instead, listen to inspirational stories via podcasts and audiobooks.

- *Gratitude:* Devote 5–10 minutes a day writing in a gratitude journal or notebook the things that make you feel grateful. Simply acknowledging them leads your mind to think positive thoughts.

- *Acceptance:* Sometimes we must admit when we've tried out everything to solve a problem, but it is beyond repair—at least for the time being. Accepting the outcome allows us to move on to something else that has potential for success.

If you're continuing to internally struggle in a battle of optimism versus pessimism, consider the following quote from the Dalai Lama: "Choose to be optimistic. It feels better."

Hope Isn't Just Wishful Thinking

Hope enables individuals to draw upon resources in their environments that lead to healthy development and achievement. It can inspire people to imagine a better future and create positive energy to move forward. For this reason, hope has been described as "an integral part of what it is to be human" or "the most human of all mental feelings."

There is a wonderful moment at the end of the first season of the Apple TV series *Ted Lasso* when the AFC Richmond football team faces relegation—demotion to a lower level. Ted, the team's coach, enters the locker room to give the players a pep talk. He begins by taking issue with the British maxim "It's the hope that kills you." He proceeds to champion the vital importance of hope, asking his team: "Do you believe in miracles?" Before they can reply, he intervenes: "I don't need you all to answer the question for me. I believe in hope, I believe in belief… I need you all to answer it for yourselves."

Ted's speech is impactful because he doesn't force the athletes to look on the bright side; nor does he deny their pain or misery. He simply holds space for them to explore a small shift of perception—which is the essence of a miracle, not whether they win an important game. The miracle is how the players respond to Ted's presence as their leader. We see the energy shift in each of their faces as Ted reframes the situation. The internal change in perception may be intangible, but its effects are deep and long lasting. (I won't go any further by providing spoilers that would reveal what these effects are.)

Hope isn't about ignoring or dismissing the frustration of setbacks but rather rechanneling our thoughts and emotions to focus on our passion, purpose, and values. When we do so, we can consciously expand our perceptions to allow shifts that empower us to feel hopeful. Leaders who master this skill can coach their team members to anticipate challenges and press on without interference from the negative thoughts and feelings associated with them.

How Do We Build Hope?

In some instances—such as if one were to receive a cancer diagnosis—hope is born out of despair and then becomes a powerful ally throughout the treatment and recovery process. Among cancer patients, hope has been linked to reduced symptoms, decreased fatigue, and lower rates of depression. It is critical for a patient's relationship with her doctor to take hold, so she can find a greater level of hope when new treatments and medications are provided.

The Attributes of Hope

"Hopeful people cannot just wish things into existence," says John Parsi, executive director of the Hope Center. "Hope requires a person to take responsibility for their wants and desires and take action in working toward them." To give rise to hope, researchers have identified the critical attributes of hope as: *affective* (feeling of expectancy); *cognitive* (goal setting/vision); and *affiliative* (relationships/team building). These attributes have direct application to leaders as they engage in developing a feeling of expectancy (possibilities) within their team. It also directly correlates to goal setting based on a shared vision and in terms of building strong and positive relationships among team members.

Hope Theory

Hope is created from within and needs to be nurtured. Charles Snyder developed what has become known as Hope Theory. He identified the three components of hope: goal-oriented thoughts, strategies to achieve goals, and motivation that encourages effort to complete goals. If an

REFLECTION: WHERE IS HOPE BENEFICIAL FOR YOU?

- Look at your life and see if there are places where hope might be beneficial. Think of a current personal or work challenge and reflect on the following questions:
- What outcomes do I expect?
- How can having goal-oriented thoughts move things forward?
- What is my plan of action of working through the challenge and achieving my intended goal?
- How can I anticipate things that will go wrong and overcome them?
- Where can I find the motivation and energy to overcome this challenge and achieve my goals?

individual believes he will accomplish all three of the above, the potential for hope increases. We can guide employees by having them think through what could go wrong and anticipating alternative pathways. This way, when things don't work as planned, they can tap into hope and bounce back more readily.

A Roadmap for Leading with Hope

Leading with hope requires you to activate hope in yourself by having a mindset of abundance, tapping into uplifting memories, clarifying your personal priorities and, most importantly, being in alignment with our values and purpose. When we're individually and collectively connected to *why* we're doing something, we can then step beyond any single outcome and look to the future as an opportunity to do more of what matters, regardless of where we are today. Leading with hope requires you to be goal-oriented but, at the same time, fluid and flexible enough to thrive in an ever-changing environment.

In everyday business, roadblocks and speed bumps—such as a faulty process—will sometimes show up out of nowhere. Leaders need to help minimize the impact as much as possible, since interferences zap people's energy and sometimes cause feelings of hopelessness. In addition, it's important to always leave space for people to express their fears and frustration while keeping the conversation constructive and focused on solving the problem.

In Chapter Eleven, we explored Erik Erikson's stages of human development, which explains that a person's trust level is formed in the first eighteen months of life. Erikson also concluded that, when trust is in place, it gives birth to hope. Leaders who create a conversational space where trust can exist have already planted the seeds of hope to emerge when necessary.

If you look back through history, the most impactful leaders were those who were able to generate hope and help people step forward with courage. Among these are such historic figures as Civil Rights leader Rosa Parks, U.S. President John F. Kennedy, Israeli Prime Minister Golda Meir, South African President Nelson Mandela, and U.S. President Barack Obama, to name a few. Many of these individuals were inspiring, eloquent speakers who captivated audiences. Notably, Nelson Mandela uttered many hopeful pearls of wisdom:

- "Don't judge me by my successes, judge me by how many times I fell down and got back up again."
- "It always seems impossible until it's done."
- "A winner is a dreamer who never gives up."

ACTION FRAMEWORK

Below are seven steps for turning hope into action and igniting possibilities.

Step 1: Identify a specific challenge or obstacle for which hope or optimism would bring out a better outcome.

Step 2: Take a few minutes to craft how the future could look better and what new opportunities might emerge. Answer the question: *How will the future be better than today?*

Step 3: Engage in a team activity in which you are building deeper, more trusting relationships. For example, Human Edge's CORE™ Connect Cards may be used in team settings.

Step 4: Invite your team to dream together and create a vision of the future, including "Mount Everest"-level goals—those that represent the peak, the culmination, the supreme achievement that we can imagine, well beyond ordinary success.

Step 5: Identify the milestones of success and determine how you will celebrate them.

Step 6: Brainstorm the potential obstacles hindering achievement of the milestones and what new paths might need to be forged.

Step 7: Organize regular check-ins and craft your message to maintain hope and optimism. During these sessions, ask these questions:

- What key messages might I communicate to keep the team motivated?
- How do I address hope deflators that zap people's energy?

To inspire this level of hope, leaders must learn how to:

- *Inspire others.* Hope must begin with you. It requires you, as a leader, to fully commit to your calling by placing your mind, body, heart, and soul into the experience. When you fully realize your calling, you become energized and spark others into action. Your deep caring and passion speak volumes to your audiences, and you instill others to care just as deeply.

- *Be emotionally present.* If you want to instill hope, you must be emotionally present and listen intently to others. People will then share their fears and concerns with you. It also gives space for coaching and enabling others to solve their own problems and move forward with self-confidence.

- *Create possibilities.* Hope isn't possible without the option of a better future. Your role as a leader is to bring possibilities to life by communicating your positive picture of what will happen. These hopeful messages touch on a genuine longing and need of others.

- *Be a catalyst of change.* Mastering change is required for you to transform your organization and engage others in the process. By dealing with the emotional side of change, you can help others overcome resistance to it. Remember, you are asking others to step into the unknown, where unanticipated challenges will materialize. You want to ensure that your team has the tools to navigate these choppy waters.

- *Engage in storytelling.* Telling stories of people overcoming obstacles can instill hope in our teams. Stories help team members unlock internal perseverance and move forward, despite setbacks and disappointments.

I n 2006, I attended a leadership conference where I had the privilege of listening to the firsthand story of Nando Parrado, one of the survivors of the plane crash in the Andes mountains that gave rise to the famous book and film *Alive*. He and Roberto Canessa walked for ten days to find salvation. As Nando shared his story with the audience, I felt like I was with him on his journey during moments of despair. I could almost feel his frozen hands as he touched the ice while climbing the mountain. Just as he and Roberto were about to give up, Nando brought into focus how he desperately wanted his sister—who was near death—to survive. Ultimately, they found the strength to carry on and save themselves and thirteen other passengers. To this day, I think about those heroes when I need to summon enough hope and courage to overcome my own challenges.

We must remember that *hope is a process* that is required to bring ideas to life. It starts with describing the future, setting goals, identifying potential setbacks, celebrating success, and learning from failure. When you address setbacks with honest communication, your team members learn to stay the course and materialize the envisioned future.

The Presence of Hope Changes Many Things

Hope is an independent variable, meaning that it can stand alone and impact the outcomes of many other things. Dr. Karen Kirby, a psychologist at Ulster University in Northern Ireland, proved this theory. As each level of hope increased, the prediction model for the nine factors became statistically significant. This means hope can improve resiliency, self-care, and social support seeking, along with positive emotions and higher emotional control. When hope is present, depression, anxiety, and negative emotions tend to diminish or disappear.

In the *Journal of Leadership & Organizational Studies*, Martha R. Helland and Bruce E. Winston reviewed the research on hope and concluded that "high hope individuals are better able to cope with ambiguity and uncertainty, and, indeed, are energized by the challenge of journeying into an undefined future without having all the answers yet knowing that in time the answers will be revealed. It is this enlarged capacity to remain open to possibilities, to envision a positive future in the face of uncertainty and to creatively construct pathways that can be embraced as people collectively seek to turn possibilities into reality that links hope with the enactment of leadership." In a work context—where people often feel overwhelmed and burned out—hope can be the fuel that keeps employees at all levels focused, engaged, and inspired.

Operationalizing Hope

Hope isn't something that should be implemented on just the individual level or as something to manifest only when problems surface. A hopeful approach needs to become part of the fabric of your business and tangible for people to grasp, which means operationalizing it. We must tap into the following factors adapted from the latest research in positive psychology:

- *Interpersonal:* Addresses how we can work together and understand our current context. This is known as *WePower.*

- *Intrapersonal:* Taps into the fact that humans are goal-oriented and want to achieve. As leaders, it's important for us to infuse goals with a sense of purpose, which fuels motivation with structure and direction. This is known as *WhyPower.*

- *Motivation to succeed:* This lies deep inside each person, providing the ability to overcome obstacles and stay the course. As leaders, we have an opportunity to link the overall possibilities with what is most meaningful to others individually. This is known as *WillPower.*

- *Planning to meet goals:* This brings possibilities to life by breaking our dreams into smaller action steps that lead to success. Proper planning allows hope to transition into action. This is known as *WayPower.*

TAKEAWAYS

■ Optimism and hope overlap but have different meanings and applications.

■ One can became more of an optimist in a variety of ways, including spending more time with positive people, listening to inspirational stories, limiting consumption of news, and practicing gratitude.

■ Consciously identify and leverage all the resources around us—personal, relational, and situational—and available in the moment.

■ Being hopeful doesn't mean that you are ignoring problems.

■ There are many ways to increase hope in your life and inspire others, including setting high goals, being emotionally present, refusing to give up, and celebrating key milestones.

■ Employees look to their leaders to establish a hopeful culture.

■ The following factors can help operationalize hope in an organization: WePower, WhyPower, WillPower, and WayPower.

Chapter Fourteen

GENERATING AND CATCHING INSIGHT

I n today's environment, businesses can't survive without a significant amount of creativity and innovation. These elements are essential for developing new and exciting products and/or services; problem-solving; competing in a constantly changing global, technology-driven marketplace; and building frameworks that will survive and thrive into the future.

The capacity to generate and capture insight is a vital ingredient for co-creation and driving innovation. Leaders have a vital role to play in facilitating the insight power—the collective genius of their teams to unlock greater possibility. When we talk about insight, we are referring to those powerful moments of realization, ideation, and instinct that drive us forward. Research into this area shows that those all-important *a-ha* moments aren't born from the analytical part of the brain. While analysis is a crucial aspect of our working lives and can be done through logic, insight requires generating or creating something new.

Research by John Kounios of Drexel University and Mark Beeman of Northwestern University reveals that insight is generated in the deeper, more emotional part of our brains. "Although all problem solving relies on a largely shared cortical network, the sudden flash of insight occurs when problem solvers engage distinct neural and cognitive processes that allow them to see connections that previously eluded them." In short, insight is born from making new connections—among ideas, concepts, and perspectives—among things that never existed. This is why organizations often bring people together for ideation; when we engage with others, we unlock a collective, co-creative power that is greater than our own.

Whether you're running a small startup or are part of a large corporation, creative insight requires the formation of internal incubators to nurture and develop breakthrough ideas. Right before insight occurs, the brain goes into the gamma brain wave state, which is extremely focused, fast, and of a high frequency that ranges between 30 and 80 hertz (Hz). Gamma waves are so powerful they can promote improved states of awareness and brain function during meditation.

To summarize, gamma waves provide the following benefits:

- Improve your cognition and problem-solving ability
- Help you with information processing
- Improve your memory
- Increase your attention span
- Enhance your level of awareness and mindfulness
- Boost your brain's immunity and function

To stimulate this state of brain activity, we need a different approach from the deliberate problem-solving strategies that we normally employ in the workplace. Insight requires a reorganization of data that results in a novel, non-obvious interpretation that can spark innovation. In group settings, as you prepare to facilitate the collective insight of the group and initiate the co-creation process, you can...

- Tune into compassion and take deep breaths in the heart area.
- Acknowledge what it would be like if the solution or opportunity was fully realized and who would benefit from the result.
- Listen to 40 Hz binaural beats with headphones for five minutes (Google it).

Once the right environment has been established, co-creation is an effective method to apply. These steps set the stage for co-creation. When we facilitate this process, we unleash the collective creativity, tap into strengths, create new opportunities, and cultivate a flexible, human-centric culture. Effective co-creation regards every stakeholder as a creative contributor without any hierarchical limits to ideas and input. Anyone—from a junior employee to the most senior executive—can provide key insights to a successful project or initiative. Imagine their perspective of feeling heard and being heard; these are powerful tools. Greater engagement equals a greater sense of ownership and personal investment while reducing resistance to change.

Employees who participate in the co-creation process and generate insight show greater engagement and satisfaction in response to their employer's trust in their judgment. Why do companies have so much untapped potential? Many employees' skills go unnoticed or underutilized, leaving employees not fully engaged. Your role as a leader is to find and unleash potential by setting the table for collective insight.

Setting the Table for Collective Insight

In today's business environment, it's up to the leader to "set the frame" that gives employees the freedom to co-create with one another and use the power of collective insight to bring the purpose to life. *Framing* refers to establishing the perimeter in which an organization plays—that is, clarifying what the organization will and will not do. For example, a car company doesn't make watches and Google doesn't produce food. At the business unit or team level, framing creates a space in which the teams can function individually or as a whole; it ensures that the doors of creativity are wide open to explore new ideas and opportunities while also defining clear boundaries to indicate what team members should and shouldn't consider. The frame makes it clear to everyone the limits and responsibilities associated with such freedom, to avoid heading down rabbit holes that would lead to wasted time and effort. Framing gives everyone's genius a place in which to play.

As one example, my team happened to be exploring how to incorporate AI into our work with clients. At the beginning of the initiative, I said,

"When we look at AI, it must be aligned to our purpose: *bringing human potential to life*. We're not interested in creating solutions that in any way dehumanize people, such as how some major companies are using this technology to fire people." This simple statement provided direction and a boundary for the team without offering a specific solution. It also gave me peace of mind knowing that company time wouldn't be spent investigating areas that are counter to our core business values.

When the framing is clear and consistent, people naturally follow it, creating a powerful feeling of team unity. Employees feel entrusted and empowered to accomplish the goals with minimal interference and judgment. However, when the framing is vague and inconsistent, people stick to their own frames and/or compete over whose interpretation should be followed. This causes confusion and limits leveraging the brainstorming power within an organization.

Here are six steps to proper framing:

Step 1: Establish the business opportunity or the problem that needs to be solved. Be sure to identify the benefits of success in either circumstance.

Step 2: Determine how the opportunity aligns with the company's purpose. At times, the opportunity may cause things to shift or even lead to a major disruption. One documented example of shifting purpose occurred when Philip Morris International pivoted to offer smoke-free products, which are less harmful than traditional cigarettes (but aren't completely risk-free, as they still contain nicotine). Netflix is an example of a company that stayed true to its purpose while transitioning from physical entertainment rentals (such as DVDs) to online streaming and creation of their own original content.

Step 3: Establishing boundaries determines what should be included or excluded from the context and answers the question: "What should we explore and what should be left alone?" If we don't create boundaries, people tend to waste time and effort and feel demoralized in the end. A few examples to consider: product portfolio, geography, technology enablement, customer group, and merging sectors.

Step 4: Identify the organizational and team capabilities. This instills all members with a sense of what they can build on or a sense of needs to be augmented, depending upon the level of disruption involved in the change.

Step 5: Allow the team to get to work by granting them enough freedom and safety to fill in the frame. To give everyone an opportunity to contribute, empower team members to tap into their knowledge, experiences, curiosity, and networking contacts to bring forth new kernels of ideas.

Step 6: Share with team members that you want them to each "bring a brick, not a cathedral." This is a lesson gleaned from the art of improvisational comedy. When you're in the audience of an improv performance, it's easy to be blown away by how well the players on stage spontaneously create a complete and (almost) flawless story. The concept is that each member of the troupe is contributing a piece of the sketch (the brick) and not the entirety of the scene (the cathedral). If a comic were to try to bring a whole idea into a scene by himself, he would minimize the potential for miraculous co-creation. While one hilarious gag may get a big laugh from the audience, that's not enough to sustain an entire show. However, if each performer contributes a nugget, the sum of all the bricks forms an impregnable structure. The true magic of improv is watching the actors build on each other's ideas. Imagine if we brought this concept to board rooms. Meetings would be something to be excited about!

In business, there are times when an individual will present her perspective as if it's the only way to accomplish a goal. If we want to co-create, we must be willing to bring a seed of an idea to the table and allow others to build on it. Soon people forget who originated the idea because, in the end, it's only the team's performance as a unit that matters.

Don't Fixate on Fixing Things

If we want to co-create and create new insights, we need to focus on transformation and creating long-term value for our companies. Our tendency in business is to spend much of our time putting out fires and fixing problems. We often focus on what is right in front of us or what is being presented in the moment. It's easy to fall into this pattern because the challenges are almost always labeled "urgent" or "important." If our focus is continually on emergencies, we're not moving our organization forward. We forgo progress. Co-creation, on the other hand, is about looking to the future and generating something new. Although it feels like daily challenges use a lot of our energy reserves, taking a step back and thinking longer-term can take more effort and require us to navigate the unknown. We seek clarity in organizations, which is healthy in terms of implementing key initiatives. However, the unknown is like a newborn child that requires a great deal of love, care, and attention for development to flourish.

While sometimes there is no avoiding getting sucked into squelching certain blazes, most of the time those "fires" could have been avoided or anticipated with continuous improvement and proper feedback loops. When you free up everyone's time for more creativity, ideation, and innovation, the organization is able to leap forward. It's also a prime opportunity for you to challenge your teams and think of ways to allow space for co-creation in all areas of the business.

It's only when we push ourselves beyond our boundaries that we can discover new avenues of exploration and creativity for our teams and ourselves. If our minds are free and clear, we can think about *what is* possible, rather than *what isn't*. For example, Ray Kurzwell, a Google scientist-turned-futurist, predicts that one day humans will attain immortality by using nano technology; nanobots will be injected into our veins and fend off aging and illness by repairing human bodies. How's that for human ingenuity?

Bask in the Glow

According to research by Lynda Gratton, a professor at London Business

School, less than 20 percent of workers feel engaged and energized by their work. To counter the worsening pattern, she developed a concept, *glow*, which she defines as the ability/decision "to radiate positive energy that fosters a great working experience that excites and ignites others through our own inspiration and delivers superior value through our work."

It isn't easy to build an organization beaming with glowing team members. First, as a leader, you must dig deep and channel the latent energy in yourself. If you aren't exuding positive vibes, you can't expect to become a catalyst for others. The objective is to identify your passion—something in your daily work that excites and ignites you—that you can translate outward. Once you've done so, you can ask igniting questions of team members in areas of topical interest that spark curiosity and encourage open dialogue. They might include questions such as "How can we quickly clean up our planet?," "How might we make a real difference in our community?," "How might our current project do something to help eliminate world hunger?," or "How might we build an electric car for less than $10,000 that low-income people can afford?" When we ask these igniting questions and slow down to hear the answers, we become connected with insights that we might not have otherwise noticed.

ACTION FRAMEWORK

Another technique for reclaiming your passion and inspiring others to glow involves storytelling, which is a powerful way of cultivating hope. Think about when you were starting out in business and what drove you to enter your industry or join your organization. Sometimes, these emotional drivers fade over the years in the wake of making revenue and profit targets, keeping up with competition, and dealing with everyday issues. Spend an one hour in a quiet place undisturbed and see if the reason behind why you initially followed your path returns to you. Write it down, read it, and then share it with your team.

Phil Knight, co-founder of Nike and author of *Shoe Dog*, has one of the great business origins stories. An avid runner from his youth, he went on to become a competitive athlete at the University of Oregon. During this time and thereafter, he became dissatisfied by the running sneakers that were then available. He consulted with Bill Bowerman, Oregon's track and field coach, who agreed this was a problem

(Continued)

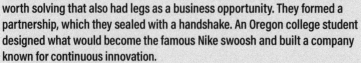
An Innovative Solution for Engaging Customers and Stakeholders

Gaining new insight shouldn't be limited within the organization; customers and other stakeholders (such as end users/consumers, buyers, and vendors) need to be engaged as well. Clayton Christensen—the late renowned Harvard Business School professor and author of such classics as *The Innovator's Dilemma, The Innovator's Solution,* and *The Innovator's Prescription*—once famously said, "There are over 30,000 new products introduced every year, and 95 percent fail." He later walked his statement back to 80 percent, a number that largely continues to be accepted as accurate to this day.

Companies that use design thinking and involve their customers are much more impactful. An example of this is GE Healthcare and their MRI scanning machines. Having an MRI scan is generally not a pleasant experience for adults, let alone children. Children often struggle to remain still during the process and may be fearful. Sometimes the experience even leads to tears. Before taking a traditional MRI, 80 percent of children needed to be sedated.

The chief designer at GE Imaging Machines decided to do something about this. He conducted primary research with children, educators, and physicians and came up with CT Pirate Island Adventure. The frightening tubular MRI scanner was recreated as a pirate ship. A child could enter an engaging fantasy in which he or she had the starring role. With the CT Pirate Island Adventure, the need for sedation dropped to 10 percent. By co-creating with children, the GE designer had transformed a traumatic experience into an engaging one.

This is why it's of the utmost importance to not only ask your customers what they want but also to follow these tenets to generate insight:

1. *Inspire to participate:* Share the challenge, frame it for those not directly involved, and involve them in the purpose.

2. *Invite the genius of others:* Seek out those who bring fresh insight, deep expertise, and diverse perspectives.

3. *Trust the process:* Make it collaborative, fun, and productive.

4. *Raise the bar:* Solicit ideas and solutions, encourage everyone to reflect on what has been discussed, and challenge the group to improve on what they've identified.

5. *Lead the change:* Follow-through is crucial, which means everyone must be held accountable for doing what they agree upon. The leader must roll out implementation of decisions and communicate progress with all stakeholders, even when things aren't going according to plan.

Involving the customer and consumer helps inform you on what should and shouldn't be developed. After initial concepts have been created, it is recommended that you survey individuals outside the organization for detailed feedback. This may include areas of confusion and ideas for making the product even better.

Experiment with Co-creation

Imagine the production of a film or TV show. Each scene usually requires myriad takes, the best of which appear in the final edit. There are many that end up on the cutting room floor. At work, we don't have the luxury of retakes—we simply call it a mistake, suffer the consequences, assign blame, trudge it up at the guilty party's annual review, and move on.

What if we were to instead look upon work as *experimentation*, much like a director shooting a film or TV show or an inventor perfecting her latest innovation? Thomas Edison failed *2,774 times* (not 1,000, as many people believe) to create an operational lightbulb. Sometimes things don't go exactly as planned the first time around—but so what? Rather than getting frustrated, throwing in the towel, and assigning blame, wouldn't it be much more productive to simply chalk it up to experimentation, uncover what went wrong, and try again?

Things rarely work out as originally envisioned. Due to signals given to us during childhood from parents, teachers, and others, we try to be 100 percent correct on the first attempt at an endeavor. The reality is that this doesn't lead to innovative ideas and breakthroughs. When we invest our effort with a sense of purpose, we form a connection with what we are doing and begin to feel that the work *matters*. If we don't get it right the first time, we are inspired to sustain that effort, redirect it, and dig deeper.

Returning to the film analogy, let's imagine an actor reading lines from the script on the set for the first time with the rest of his cast. Upon performing the scene in front of the camera with the entire cast and crew, a whole new world is revealed. The actor may pick up on a character nuance he and others missed; the director may wish to shoot the scene from a different camera angle; or the co-stars may have improvised a reaction to the actor's dialogue that adds more humor or drama to the scene. What is the very next thing they do? Give the new direction a try on the next take!

There are countless examples of spontaneous creative shifts in the world of film and television, but one will suffice. During the production of the first *Shrek* film, actor/comedian Mike Myers initially portrayed the titular character with a Canadian accent. When he heard the recording alongside the snobbish British voice of Lord Farquaad (John Lithgow), Myers realized his vocal needed more contrast and he switched to a Scottish accent. The change captured lightning in a bottle, as Shrek has since become an iconic, beloved character easily recognized by this brilliant accent.

It's a pity that, for the most part, the typical work environment doesn't grant the same space for creativity to evolve organically. With the prevalence of data and metrics, businesses are constantly seeking ways to get things done better, faster, and more economically—without necessarily taking experimentation into account to develop something surprising and innovative. Businesses want safety, stability, and security, which means keeping the pipeline moving.

The fact of the matter is that, while certainty makes us feel safe, it's all an illusion. Predictability is great when it comes to following a process and ensuring the same result over and over, but it won't lead to breakthroughs, new discoveries, and increased business opportunities. Professor Charles A. O'Reilly and Michael L. Tushman at Stanford University looked at companies that do well, versus those that fall behind or fail. They found that companies that lag and collapse practice *exploit*, meaning they tend to focus too much on operational excellence and cost cutting. By contrast, companies that flourish over the long run *explore* by maintaining a variety of innovation efforts. This requires companies to generate new insights and connect the dots in both areas that improve operational effectiveness and create breakthrough ideas. The ideal scenario is for companies to become ambidextrous, which, like being able to lead with either the right or left hand, combines the best of exploit and explore. Statistically, 90 percent of ambidextrous companies are able to achieve their goals and secure their place in the future.

When it comes to generating insights and encouraging creativity, we must become comfortable and patient enough to throw certainty out the

 REFLECTION: WHAT LESSONS CAN YOU GLEAN FROM MISSED OPPORTUNITIES?

Take a few minutes to recall some of your team's suggestions from the past that were shot down for one reason or another. Ask yourself the following questions:

- In retrospect, might any of the suggestions have been worth taking the time to brainstorm?
- What would the best-case scenario have been if one of these ideas had been developed and executed?
- How might we find the kernel of an idea we previously dismissed?
- What new insights can we generate about the past solution presented?

window and allow each team member to experiment and try something different. We must allow room for employees to be bold and shoot for the stars. We need to encourage people to operate in the unknown and be playful, as a crazy idea can lead to a breakthrough. Most people tend to play it safe and don't volunteer ideas because they fear criticism, so it's important to grant everyone the space and security to throw mud against the wall and see what sticks. When we play, it gives us the space to see things in a new way and connect things that we normally wouldn't associate with each other. As innovation pioneer Peter Diamandis once said, "The day before something is a breakthrough, it's a crazy idea."

The creative process or insight generation allows for unexpected and exciting things to be birthed that may take the team in new directions. Once set in motion, the initiative must be treated with care and intent; the point isn't to give lip service but to play the ideas out to explore their fullest potential while demonstrating genuine support to team members. This means steering clear of trying to apply structure and enforce limiting rules. The human imagination benefits from free-form thinking, daydreaming, counterintuitive thinking, and engaging interaction.

As mentioned earlier, failure is to be expected—and, in many cases, it should even be welcomed. We learn from our failures and often don't know whether something will work unless we see it through. One prime example is Rovio, the game company best known for the creation of Angry Birds. Before that game's release in 2009, Rovio had developed fifty-one other products—all of which flopped. In fact, Rovio was near bankruptcy at the time. Rather than giving up, the company continued to work on concepts and develop something that would catch on. Angry Birds sold over a billion downloads between 2009 and 2012 and has since become a franchise phenomenon with tie-in dramatic animated adaptations in television and film.

It's been proven time and again: Teams that are experimental and unafraid of failure succeed in the end. At that point, no one thinks about the company in terms of the past efforts that bombed—only the remarkableness of their persistence and eventual success.

More Lessons from the World of Improv

Improvisational comedy is perhaps the purest form of co-creation in motion. An improv stage performance simultaneously excites the actors and audience and creates an environment of playfulness and wonder. It frees the mind to create new associations. We become intrigued and entertained at the same time. Imagine what it would be like to assimilate that kind of infectious fun into a work environment. Below are some tips from improv that you can apply to your generating insights efforts:

1. *The fun is always on the other side of a Yes:* There is a wonderful message expressed in the two words "Yes, and…" It means you plan to accept and build upon the ideas of your scene partners. When you choose to say *Yes* to someone's prompt on stage or colleague's suggestion in the workplace, great things await you on the other side.

2. *Don't be defensive:* It's okay to admit that we all have lapses and are occasionally guilty of defensiveness. Somebody says something and we instantly choose to take umbrage, rather than pausing, listening, and responding in an appropriate manner. Ideally, we want to create a culture of listeners who think and reflect before reacting.

2. *If this, then what?:* This statement rides on the coattails of "Yes, and…" It relies upon the notion, "If one thing is true, then what else might also be true?" It keeps us in discovery mode and prevents us from getting stuck. By asking ourselves this question, we become able to expand on ideas in a methodical way.

4. *If we treat each other as if we are all geniuses, poets, and artists, we have a better chance of becoming that on stage:* This quote, originated by improv legend Del Close, suggests that, by treating each other as the smartest people we know, we will work together to create something remarkable. It's not often that we get to choose the people we work with. Differences of point of view are inevitable and favorable. When you make space for another's perspective, insight can flow from a different angle. By

presuming all colleagues are on the same brilliant level playing field, you glean the best results out of everyone and consider their statements in the best possible light.

Insight Generators Are Artists with Purpose

To win people's hearts and minds, we must tap into what is meaningful for them and drives their purpose. Guiding teams to channel the power of their intuition and create requires a deep level of commitment to things they truly care about. The world is filled with problems, but how many are you willing to invest your time and energy to try to solve?

We all know technical people in the business world who assert, "I am not an artist." This statement alone diminishes their ability to be creative. The fact of the matter is that *we are all creative*, which means we have the potential to become artists in our own right. Unfortunately, many people leave this aspect behind during childhood, perhaps because they were discouraged in some way. It is our responsibility as leaders to summon that childlike behavior among team members and spark their creative juices.

ACTION FRAMEWORK

Encourage your team members to take a walk together. Stanford University researchers examined creativity levels of people while walking versus sitting and found that walking stimulates imagination to a much greater extent. A person's creative output increases by an average of 60 percent during such an activity. Walking in nature, listening to its sounds, and breathing fresh air boosts free thinking and enables team members to say things they might not within the office walls.

It's been well documented how Walt Disney Studios and Pixar have managed to establish creative work cultures that breed an enormous pool of talent and inspire their teams to produce entertaining screen miracles. Their collaborative environments enable childlike thinking to thrive and produce such animated classics as *The Lion King*, *Beauty and the Beast*, and multiple installments of the *Toy Story* franchise. These and many other blockbusters are beloved by kids while masterfully bringing out the children in adult viewers as well.

Disney has no qualms about inviting fans in on their special secret: *imagination*. At EPCOT Theme Park in Walt Disney World in Florida, the Journey into Imagination attraction—featuring Figment, the purple dragon—reminds us that we all have the ability to dream, create, and generate insight. As Walt Disney himself once said, "Laughter is timeless. Imagination has no age. And dreams are forever."

TAKEAWAYS

- Insights or *a-ha* moments come from tapping into the emotional side of the brain and making new connections.
- Insight generation requires the formation of internal incubators to nurture and develop breakthrough ideas.
- Leaders must spend less time fixing problems and more on driving innovation and creativity.
- Framing—which clarifies what the organization will and will not do—gives employees the freedom to co-create with one other and bring the purpose to life.
- Lynda Gratton, a professor at London Business School, recommends that leaders rediscover their passions to create teams that glow.
- Co-creation must involve external stakeholders—end users/consumers, buyers, vendors, etc.—as well as employees.
- Co-creation requires playful experimentation and an environment that is receptive to occasionally crazy ideas.
- Everyone has the potential to make creative contributions to an organization, especially when there is a shared unified purpose.

Chapter Fifteen

INTEGRATION, SUSTAINABILITY, AND RENEWAL

The pressure at work is on every day, as we are always being asked to do more with less. The bar is raised year after year. We are continually asked to cut our budgets while producing greater revenue. The situation can be likened to trying to wring water out of an already dried towel; it leaves everyone in the organization feeling unfulfilled and knocked down. Somehow, we muster enough strength to continue playing this game and muddle through. Once we finally feel we might be approaching steady ground, we are forced to make sudden choices that challenge our integrity or else suffer the consequences, which are often financial. Over and over we adapt to our environment to meet the needs of stakeholders and profitability targets—but at what cost?

In 2005, novelist and university professor David Foster Wallace addressed the graduating class at Kenyon College with what has since become one of his most read speeches. In the piece, he argues, against "unconsciousness, the default setting, the rat race, the constant gnawing sense of having had, and lost, some infinite thing." He introduces the following parable:

There are these two young fish swimming along, and they hap-
pen to meet an older fish swimming the other way, who nods at
them and says, "Morning, boys. How's the water?" And the two
young fish swim on for a bit, and then eventually one of them
looks over at the other and goes, "What the hell is water?"

We've grown so accustomed to our environment that we don't challenge it or ask: "Is this the best we can do? We're running sprints every day and breathing our own fumes. We really need to figure out how we can pace ourselves to run a marathon without passing out."

If we want our teams to thrive, we must lead in a new way that challenges our preconceptions of everything we think we know about work, including clichés accepted as facts. For example: *Is time really money? Does achievement bring long-lasting happiness?*

For all of us to run the marathon with ease, we need to make significant shifts to help us reorient ourselves and make work more sustainable and rewarding for all concerned. The following six factors—which will be addressed in the following sections—guide us through this integration process:

- Shift from *task orientation* to *purpose-driven work.*
- Understand *the true drivers of happiness.*
- Recognize the aspects of our environment that will *always be uncontrollable and chaotic.*
- Transition from *fixed work hours* to *flexible.*
- Flip from the mindset that you are *managing time* to *regulating energy.*
- *Welcome laughter.*

Be Intentional on Purpose

Recall the first job you ever had. The first thing you were taught is to *successfully complete a task.* I remember working at one of my early jobs, at Whitman Packaging, in Hauppauge, New York, which packaged Estée Lauder makeup. My two friends and I spent our high school summers putting in four-hour shifts on an assembly line. On arrival, we had to clock in and then find our place on the factory floor. Sometimes, we went back to the same line from the day before; other days we were directed to a new location. Once we chose our spots on the assembly line, our supervisor assigned our tasks, which we performed for four hours straight. It was clear to us on every level that our unrewarding work was just a means to an end. The only reasons we stuck around were because the pay was higher than McDonald's and, occasionally, we were handed free makeup (which was designed to discourage stealing). This job set the stage for us to work in an organization. If you effectively complete your tasks, you keep your job and receive a fair wage.

Years later, after having gained two university degrees and worked in some of the best multinationals in the world, I've found that the task-oriented mentality remains prevalent in workplaces. If you search deeper into major companies with powerful strategies, you'll find that often they can't see the forest for the trees. The focus at most levels remains on task completion and driving key performance indicators (KPIs).

Throughout my career, my managers asked me questions like "Where do you see yourself in five years?" and "What are your annual goals?" I can't think of a single leader who ever asked me "What impact do you want to have on the world?" or "How might your work help serve others?"

When I interview candidates for positions at Human Edge, one of my first questions is inevitably: "If we were eighty years old and having coffee or tea together and reflecting on our lives, what legacy would you describe having left behind?" Surprisingly, many people are caught off guard and don't know how to respond.

As leaders we need to encourage others to find their purpose. According to McKinsey & Company, 70 percent of employees state that their sense of purpose is defined by their work, which means that today's employees expect their jobs to bring a significant sense of purpose to their lives. In addition, purpose can be an important contributor to employee experience, which, in turn, is linked to higher levels of employee engagement, stronger organizational commitment, and increased feelings of well-being. Leaders must help fill these needs or be prepared to lose talent to companies that will.

So, like it or not, you play an important part in helping your employees find their purpose, or calling, and live it. This means thinking in terms of the workers' entire journey, not just the outcomes they are required to generate.

To shift from *task* to *purpose*, we must learn to let go of control. We need to step back and trust that, when we have the right employees in place who come from a place of purpose, they become highly committed to achieving results and don't need constant oversight. If you doubt you have the best people, that is a separate challenge to address. Our goal, as outlined in Chapter Fourteen, is to set the frame and provide enough room for the team to fill in the gaps. This empowers them to use their own genius to tap into what matters to them and then align it with the purpose and the tasks at hand.

I realize that it may be difficult for some leaders to undo their mind-set—which may have served them well in the past—and change the way they operate. If you're among these leaders, trust your people and allow them to surprise you with their talents and willingness to go the extra mile. You will be amazed by what they can accomplish on their own, which frees you up to work on bigger picture strategies.

Come on Get Happy

Harvard Professor Arthur C. Brooks has spent years researching happiness and our obsession with money, power, pleasure, and fame and what provides a lasting sense of satisfaction. In *The Atlantic*, he wrote:

> *The insatiable goals to acquire more, succeed conspicuously, and be as attractive as possible lead us to objectify one another, and even ourselves. When people see themselves as little more than their attractive bodies, jobs, or bank accounts, it brings great suffering...You become a heartless taskmaster to yourself, seeing yourself as nothing more than* Homo economicus. *Love and fun are sacrificed for another day of work, in search of a positive internal answer to the question* Am I successful yet? *We become cardboard cutouts of real people.*

We now know from Arthur Brooks's research what doesn't work—but what *does* deliver lasting happiness and how does it tie in with great leadership? Brooks discovered that there are four key drivers of happiness: family, friends, faith, and work. The first two are clear, but the second couple need a bit more unpacking to understand how they are linked to happiness at work and what leaders can do to increase it. He asserts that virtually anyone over the age of fifty had some type of faith—not necessarily a formal religious practice but a sense of transcendence or an ability to zoom out and see the bigger world beyond physical needs and reality. By the last element, he is referring to *meaningful* work, where we move beyond the self and earn success through serving others. It can be described as investing in yourself, so your skills meet your passion.

With this knowledge, how do leaders manage the stress and happiness levels of their workforce while ensuring goals are met? When people—leaders and team members alike—are maxed out, they become addicted to the brain's dopamine (a neurotransmitter that sends pleasure signals) hit and can't stop working. It's like any other craving that can turn addictive, such as sugar in a chocolate bar. Once the sugar races through a person's system and burns up fuel, the individual has a reduced amount of energy and needs even more chocolate. The temporary impact of stress is no different. Driven type-A employees feed off the lightning pace of running on the work treadmill and feel a certain "high," which floods the pleasure centers with dopamine. As soon as the rush ends, these workers are left with an empty longing to repeat those pleasurable circumstances and try to get another "fix."

Leaders who see this cycle in motion tend to see the positive side of things: energized, buzzed workers who thrive on stressful challenges. What they are missing, however, is finding out whether these employees are truly happy and satisfied from working without ever taking a break.

REFLECTION: WHAT IS YOUR HAPPINESS LEVEL?

As a leader, you can determine the level of happiness of yourself and others by asking a few simple questions.

For yourself:
- What is the quality of my relationships with family?
- How am I investing in my most cherished friendships?
- What experiences do I enjoy that bring me a feeling of transcendence?
- How am I giving back to others through my work?

For others:
- Do you have enough work-life balance?
- Are you getting enough time for hobbies and/or exercise?
- If you were to take pauses every now and then to recharge your batteries, do you think you might perform even better?
- What do you like to do with your friends for enjoyment?
- What sustains you from the inside?
- How can your work become more meaningful?

Riding the Roller Coaster

We live in a world of chaos, not knowing what global crisis or disruption will strike next. It's like being on a roller coaster all the time and not knowing how to get off. A brief roller coaster ride can provide fun and excitement, while an unexpected loop de loop can be exhilarating. Once we exit the ride, we need to calm down and rebalance ourselves. What happens, however, if we're constantly on the ride at work and can't find our equilibrium?

In Chapter Four, I referenced Jamais Cascio's theory that the elements of our VUCA (*volatility, uncertainty, complexity*, and *ambiguity*) world have become so entrenched and normal that the term has lost all meaning. His assertion is that we now live in a BANI world: *brittle, anxious, non-linear,* and *incomprehensible.*

An example of this is U.S. retailer Bed, Bath, and Beyond, which went out of business at the end of June 2023. At its height in 2017, it had 1,552 stores across three brands in North America, with $12.3 billon in revenue and approximately 65,000 employees. A series of bad merchandise strategy decisions, a change in consumer preferences, and not being able to keep up with e-commerce and fierce competitors, such as Walmart and Target, toppled this once beloved retail giant.

If the executives at Bed, Bath, and Beyond had approached the situation differently, would they still be with us today? Could the leaders have tapped into the wisdom of their staff members on the floor to reverse course and avoid death?

In my work, I see many leaders and teams that are knee-deep in BANI yet lack the all-important mindset and behavioral skills to counteract the chaos. The results often mean employee burnout, disengagement, reactivity, and a feeling of being overwhelmed. None of the states of BANI are pleasant. A brittle structure, situation, or market may snap at any moment. When we're anxious about a decision, a course of action, or even a conversation, it feels like any move could be counterproductive or even harmful, and we may end up retreating or holding back for fear of the consequences. When something is non-linear, the normal rules don't work, and cause and effect are no longer in a logical sequence. When something is incomprehensible, we feel powerless to understand and impact it.

Resistance within all these states inevitably causes energy depletion. Cascio doesn't suggest surrendering; he recommends other ways to combat these states and move beyond the chaos, fear, and resistance that characterizes them. These involve intentional shifts of energy away from a reactive and resistant state to one that is more yielding, connected, grounded, and strong.

What this means for leaders is that we must acknowledge and validate the environments in which we operate. We can't put our heads down and work longer and harder and think we've found the solution. If we succumb to this, it's all a matter of time before everyone flames out. We need to tap into our resilience, show empathy, provide flexibility, be transparent, and ignite our intuition.

ACTION FRAMEWORK

Organize a team meeting to explore the following:

- Ask the group to find out what drives their individual resilience. Have them share their perspectives, so they can better support each other.
- Engage the team to find out what causes them stress and anxiety. Allow each person to share their individual stresses. Once the information has been collected, use empathy to acknowledge their experiences and associated emotions. Once they feel heard, conduct a brainstorm using igniting questions that spark curiosity and encourage open dialogue to help them tap their intuition and overcome their challenges.

Stop the Clock-Watching

Earlier in the chapter, I referenced my first job and how I "punched in" a timecard to clock my work hours. In today's modern era, things have become a bit higher tech. There are some outlier businesses that monitor employees' hours the moment they turn on their computers and log in on company servers. A few companies take things several steps further, using their technology to track employees' screens and keyboards and ensure their attention is solely focused on getting company work done during paid hours.

While I doubt your organization practices these extreme machinations, you may be guilty of another undercurrent: the expectation that employees are somehow always "on the clock." The lines dividing work-life balance have blurred over the years, largely due to factors such as burgeoning off-site/hybrid employment, the increasing demand for flex hours, and the ability for people to log into the company at all hours from almost anywhere in the world and perform work in real time. This has become the case especially since the pandemic made working at home a far more standard practice. However, the reality is that the division between work and life was never absolute, even in the days before broadband connection. Not every aspect of work is done while you're physically on the job, wherever or whatever that may be. People generate ideas, plans, and strategies in the shower, in line for groceries, or while taking their kids to school. People socialize with colleagues outside of work in a way that strengthens relationships and accelerates the effectiveness of teams and partnerships within working hours. When we care about our work, it's always with us in some way, like reading an article or magazine and seeing a connection to a piece of work that is waiting for us back at the office. Life and work have never really been entirely separate.

The tide of homeworking that was generated by the COVID-19 pandemic challenged the common conception that our work and private lives are separate. When offices closed as "shelter in place" and lockdown guidance was brought in, the divide—which, arguably, was never fully there—disappeared overnight. Like all sudden change, this presented a challenge. Employees burnt out because they felt they were always at work. Conversely, many organizations became anxious that people were not truly "working" and that other aspects of their lives were limiting their effectiveness. This created an opportunity, embraced by many, to shift our perception. Instead of regarding employees' time and expertise as something contracted and owned for set periods of the day, organizations and leaders suddenly had to engage with people in another way. It became necessary for leaders to give people a degree of freedom to integrate their work and other aspects of their lives for business continuity. This opened new ways of working which, for many, continue today. When we create space for people to work in a way that functions best for them, we also open an avenue for people to fully show up for work.

If we expect this level of commitment from our staff, we need to spend more time focusing on how we can enable people to find a healthy level of integration, sustainability, and renewal. According to a survey conducted in late 2022 by Future Forum—a research consortium backed by Salesforce Inc.'s Slack Technologies—employees around the world are, quite simply, exhausted.

More than 40 percent of people with desk jobs feel burned out at work—a pandemic-era high. The pain is particularly acute outside the United States, where the burnout rate has been rising to such an extent it offsets the slight improvements seen by American workers.

Economic uncertainty, the constant fear of job cuts, and rising pressure to return to on-site work have added to workplace malaise. Women and younger workers are especially struggling to get through work overload.

The same Future Forum survey also revealed that pandemic-era workers who have more freedom to choose where and when they work are generally more satisfied, productive, and less likely to quit. It's no coincidence that more than half of the people who felt dissatisfied with their level of flexibility were also burned out. Employees with immovable work schedules are more than twice as likely to admit that they are searching for positions elsewhere.

If we want our team members to be fully energized and engaged both inside and outside of work, we need to approach things from a fresh angle and provide them with the flexibility they need to manage their own lives. A good example of this is how IBM has institutionalized flexible work arrangements (FWAs), which enable employees to have sufficient rest and personal time while still meeting work goals. At IBM, the work philosophy is, "Work is what you do, not where you go."

IBM, which has a workforce consisting of line managers who closely interact with employees and oversee business targets, recognizes that they have a significant impact on the success of their work-life strategy. All new managers are trained through an orientation program that outlines the company's work-life philosophy, programs, and policies. This training includes how to find a best-fit solution that allows a manager to tailor the work for each employee based on their stage of life. After the training, managers are empowered to approve special accommodations for employees, whereas most other companies require signoffs from human resources and perhaps additional people up the chain. To ensure impact, IBM runs biannual employee engagement surveys that provide managers with feedback on their team's engagement levels.

When employees have flexibility and aren't forced to stick to traditional nine-to-five working hours, their engagement levels rise. This also means they are more relaxed and don't mind if their intuitions happen to turn on during their time off, enabling them to solve challenges and come up with fresh ideas that otherwise might not have surfaced. When they officially come back online, they bring a new level of insight that infuses the company with positive energy.

REFLECTION: HOW DO YOU VIEW TIME?

Ask yourself the following questions to probe your view of time:

- What is my belief about how people must work to create output?
- How can I provide more flexibility to my team to drive engagement?
- What examples can I demonstrate during the day to help employees find work-life integration?
- When I email a team member, do I expect an immediate response—no matter what time of day it might be?
- Do I write to employees on weekends, holidays, and during their paid time off or on sick days and expect an answer right away?

Bundles of Energy

One of the common threads I've noticed among my clients is a strong desire to build greater resilience among their teams. They universally recognize that the demands of sustained high performance in today's world are so high they exceed their resources, which generates frustration, anxiety and, ultimately, attrition.

Create Simple Rituals

Time is life's great equalizer. It's the one thing that is finite; it's impossible for anyone to attain more of it. If leaders focus too much on managing the clock, they'll find themselves backed into a corner and will hear complaints that there just isn't enough time in the day to get everything done, which would be a fair and honest statement.

Here is the common misconception: Time is the most valuable resource we have. That simply isn't true. It's neither time nor the budget; *energy* overrides everything else. When leaders communicate their need to build resilience, they're unknowingly asking for guidance on how to balance, sustain, and renew the energy of their people. Time may be a limited resource, but personal energy is renewable. Tony Schwartz, president and CEO of The Energy Project, and Catherine McCarthy tested the notion that simple rituals—such as taking brief breaks and expressing appreciation to others—can help employees regularly replenish their energy while building greater physical, emotional, and mental resilience.

This concept requires that leaders do significant rethinking. When we measure someone's contribution by the minutes they spend at a desk "working," we are assessing that person's value in terms of time rather than the quality of invested energy.

Dr. Brett N. Steenbarger, associate professor of psychiatry and behavioral sciences at State University of New York Upstate Medical University, asserts that effective leaders emotionally energize their teams. They provide enriching, engaging experiences daily, drawing out the visible and hidden strengths among employees.

Give Everyone—Including Yourself—a Break

Ultimately, effective leadership isn't about getting the most out of people but rather understanding how to create an environment that doesn't drain them of their reserves. A good place to start is how we prioritize. It's impossible for anyone to do everything all at once, move the needle, and have a healthy sense of well-being. One senior executive I work with put it this way: "We need to start saying *No* to good things." To accomplish this, trade-offs must be made. This means choosing the initiatives that have the greatest strategic impact and are most closely aligned to the organization's purpose.

It's all too easy to get excited about opportunities and say *Yes* to more than what you and/or your organization can handle. I admit that I often find myself in this boat, overcommitting myself and then having to work on weekends with little time for renewal. We rationalize this in our minds because we enjoy our work and like the idea of getting ahead of things (even if that never quite happens). I need to become more aware of my own limitations and protect my time, so I can spend more of it with friends and family—as well as by myself to relax, collect my thoughts, and recharge my batteries.

Let's look at it another way. Most of us love ice cream. Part of us would be thrilled to have gigantic scoops of our favorite flavor every day with all the toppings. The problem, of course, is that too much of anything—even something delicious—will give a person a stomachache. In addition, regular ice cream is loaded with cholesterol, fat, and calories, which is detrimental to one's health when consumed in excess. A few days after a break from the treat, a reasonable serving of ice cream won't hurt (unless one has a specific health issue), and then it will probably taste even better than before.

Leaders are role models for others, whether we admit it or not. Our teams look at us as a gauge for how much time they think they should devote to work. If employees see us as workaholics 24/7 who slave away while on vacation, they'll think they need to do the same to meet our standards, if not impress us.

When people see that we are properly managing our own energy, we send the unstated message that it's all right for them to devote the right amount of time to rest as well. Not only do we gain greater energy for ourselves, we then have more available in reserve to help employees, as needed.

By the same token, we need to grant space for people to renew, relax, and recharge. We do so by leaving them alone while they are on vacation. In fact, sometimes we must give a little bit of a nudge for employees to take their well-deserved time off and enjoy themselves.

When they do head out of the office, they need to feel as supported as possible, meaning their workload is covered and they can go away with peace of mind and return refreshed without being barraged by unsolved problems and incomplete tasks.

Curve Your Stress

The amount of work on one's plate matters. You want to ensure team members have enough meaningful work to but aren't being overloaded. There is a tendency to overtax the A players by assigning the best stretch tasks to them, since you have a high amount of confidence that they'll get them done properly. What happens next? The A players burn out, while the B players remain at a flat level of performance and don't have sufficient opportunities to prove what they can do. They also have energy to spare that gets wasted, which weakens them in the long run.

Be mindful that everyone's energy level is different. Some thrive under pressure, whereas others might require more space and time to figure things out. I use a simple technique based on the concept of *eustress*—the reasonable amount of beneficial stress for an individual. Eustress is what one feels when a good amount of excitement is present. A person's pulse quickens and her hormones surge, but there isn't any kind of perceived threat or fear. If I happen to notice that a direct report seems anxious, I'll ask her to pinpoint her stress level on a scale of one to ten. If she reports six or seven, I leave it alone and congratulate her, as this is in the ballpark of eustress. If she says eight or higher, however, I work with her to see what can be done to bring it down.

The key for any team to accomplish its goals is to have the right amount of stress with timely opportunities to become renewed and energized. It's alright that we can't innovate all the time or with a mere snap of our fingers. Sometimes we must iterate and operationalize because innovation and implementation require a great deal of heavy lifting and can often be exhausting and energy draining.

This goes for managing a broken process. If a task requires too much manual effort and drains the team, it might be worth investing in a new system to alleviate the burden. Some of these projects require a significant expenditure of time, money, and training, but these factors need to be balanced against the toll that a faulty system takes on the team's emotional—and perhaps even physical—health. Once employees are working with a better system and process, you'll find that they become happier and far more productive.

Lastly, sometimes we have to say *No* to short-term gains—even if it means sacrificing a revenue opportunity—for everyone to have enough in reserve for the future. We need to be responsible stewards of our resources. When we handle this right and focus on managing energy instead of time, we award people the gift of freedom and the room to grow at their own healthy pace.

Laughter Is the Best Medicine

Poet E.E. Cummings once wrote, "The most wasted of all days is one without laughter."

When most people think about their work, their minds immediately go to bearing down, focusing, and becoming deathly serious. They devote their brainpower and emotional energy toward solving whatever issue or crisis is most pressing at the time. The belief is that all other thoughts must be tuned out or they will be distracted and not find the right solution. The sum of all this is that many people dread going to work the next morning, especially if it happens to be a Monday. Is this how we want them to live—spending over forty hours of their week doing something unpleasant and the rest dwelling on the negative aspects of that time? Wouldn't it be so much better if they could look forward to starting work each day?

When I worked at Pfizer—which had its fair share of brainpower—I could hear a pin drop as I walked through the hallway. Everyone was hunkered down at their individual work with the same serious expression. I longed for at least some indication of lightheartedness. It was only later that I discovered the importance of shared laughter in a workplace, as it's the sign of true human connection.

Appropriate humor—not sarcasm or anything negative, derogatory, prejudicial, or disparaging—can be a powerful tool in the workplace. Evidence suggests that it builds trust, forges bonds among colleagues, helps us cope with stress, and inspires creativity and problem-solving. In short, laughter is the secret weapon for building great teams.

You might not think it possible, but great comedy—such as the stand-up work of the late comedian Robin Williams—can help contribute to your bottom line. John Kounios from Drexel University and Mark Beeman from Northwestern University once tried an experiment. Before handing out tricky logic puzzles for a group of volunteers, they played a video of Robin Williams performing on stage. Laughter ensued. The results were impressive: The laughter improved the group's puzzle-solving ability by 20 percent.

Psychologist Robert Provine has taken a keen interest in laughter as humankind's way to synchronize with each other, particularly in the workplace. Humans laugh to connect with one another. When a group laughs together, it means the individuals feel relaxed and safe and can afford to let their guard down. Or, as Professor Sophie Scott from University College states, "It's a sign if people are laughing that they're not in that anxious state. It's a marker that the group is in a good place."

A lot of humor's power is chemical. When we laugh, our brains produce less cortisol (inducing calm and reducing stress) and release more endorphins (which give us something like a runner's high) and oxytocin (often called the "love" hormone). If a brainstorming meeting feels staid and stiff, the takeaways from the discussion are likely to be just as flat. If, however, people are stimulated and laughing, the group will feel inspired and come up with ideas that lead to breakthroughs. Comedian John Cleese best summarizes the benefits of humor in the workplace: "I'm struck by how laughter connects you with people. It's almost impossible to maintain any kind of distance or any sense of social hierarchy when you're just howling with laughter. Laughter is a force for democracy."

TAKEAWAYS

- Providing a purpose is far more effective than assigning tasks.
- The happiness level of an organization often dictates its potential for success.

- Leaders must ensure the right balance of stress in an organization.
- Simple rituals, such as timely breaks and friendly hallway conversations, can help leaders and employees recharge their energy levels.
- Grant your employees and yourself permission to shut down work during vacation—everyone needs and deserves the break!
- Laughter is often the best medicine in the workplace.

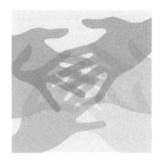

IT'S ABOUT EXPERIMENTING AND EXPANDING—
NOT PERFECTION

I hope you've enjoyed our journey to master the art of bringing everyone in your organization *all in*. It is my sincere hope that you now have a clear path toward achieving greater awareness of the possibilities for connection that exist all around us.

Like all journeys, we need inspiration to propel us forward. Unlike many journeys, however, this doesn't have an official finish line to cross. The place of *all in* is not a fixed destination. When we consciously engage in bringing ourselves and others to a place of deeper connection, we continue to expand. Every connection we establish takes us further, but "completion" is not the goal. The main objective is to be *fully present* with where we are. When we shift our focus to all that is available to us, we fully connect with ourselves, those around us, and the full context of what matters most—our shared purpose—which inspires others to do the same. By integrating head, heart, and gut and fostering a culture that embraces collaboration and co-creation, the possibilities expand exponentially. This is what it means to be *all in*.

There will be some days when everything seems to be humming right along and you see and feel all the possibilities taking shape. Then there will be days when you inadvertently regress and fall back on your old habits. When this occurs, don't throw up your hands in defeat. Instead, recharge by going back to the Reflections, Action Framework boxes, and end-of-chapter Takeaways. You want to dare once again to be fully present in all of life's circumstances, awaken your courage to find your true nature, and love all parts of yourself—even those where you must adapt to survive. Never forget that within each of us there exists a wounded child who begs to feel loved, safe, appreciated, and, most importantly, wanted.

On a deeper level, we recognize that the anxiety and stress we're all feeling isn't right. They are warning signs that we're out of sync with our true nature. Our task is to wake up and realign with our soul's blueprint. We shouldn't fight life's challenges and push them away—labeling them as bad or intolerable—but rather, embrace them as our greatest life lessons. Kuwaiti American author and spiritual teacher A. H. Almaas put it this way:

Your conflicts, all the difficult things, the problematic situations in your life are not chance or haphazard. They are yours. They are specifically yours, designed specifically for you by a part of you that loves you more than anything else. The part of you that loves you more than anything else has created roadblocks to lead you to yourself. You are not going in the right direction unless there is something pricking you in the side, telling you, "Look here! This way!" That part of you loves you so much that it doesn't want you to lose the chance. It will go to extreme measures to wake you up, it will make you suffer greatly if you don't listen. What else can it do? That is its purpose.

We must remember that our view of ourselves is skewed, as we see ourselves through our mental constructs and not our own behaviors. That is why my mom likes to say, "You can see a fly on someone else, but you can't see an elephant on yourself." However, the opposite is true for others; we can only see that their behavior, intent, or what is in their hearts and minds remain hidden. We tend to make sharp inferences as to why we think people do the things they do. We embroil ourselves in judgment of ourselves and others; while we are locked in our critical minds, we close our hearts and stop listening to our intuitive sense.

The greatest gift you can give yourself is to embrace vulnerability as your greatest strength and stand in appreciation of all that is. These open your heart as a gateway to your true self, allowing you to build the deepest connections with others. This self-journey will continue until your last breath. Just think of the magnificence you'll experience when you look back on the tapestry of your life and see all the lessons learned, the people you've touched, and the legacy you've left behind.

As the title of this Conclusion states, uncovering your true nature isn't about getting everything perfect; it's about being willing to experiment and venture outside your comfort zone each day. Your relationship with yourself is dynamic and ever-changing. Today, you may speak to yourself in a loving and compassionate way, whereas tomorrow you might find yourself in self-deprecating mode. Each response is perfect in its way, as it provides an indicator as to where you are on your journey.

If you ever happen to go off-course, self-compassion is the secret that will always lead you back on your journey to reclaim your true self. In this moment, you are a product of your life experiences and ability to honor your values, while your behavior is predicated on your met or unmet needs. If you self-reflect every day for ten minutes, you'll find that you will accelerate your development and expand much more rapidly. The personal insights you glean are the greatest gifts you can give to yourself, prompting greater self-awareness with each passing day and helping you better manage troubling situations as they arise. Moving forward, you can continually build the practice of integrating your head, heart, and gut by asking these five reflective questions:

1. What do I think about this situation or person?
2. What assumptions am I making?
3. How do I feel about this situation?

4. What values do I want to honor or imbue?
5. What does my intuition tell me about the situation and how can I better trust my gut?

When you embrace this process, you become a role model to others and give them permission to be their most authentic selves. The balance between self-acceptance and leaving time for expansion and personal growth requires that you always walk with grace. At the same time, remember that growth doesn't necessarily always involve pain. If you push yourself outside your comfort zone 20 percent of the time, you'll continually expand to a new and improved version of yourself.

Becoming rooted in yourself and your values instills you with the ability to share power, unlock your team's potential, and create possibilities you never dreamed possible. Imagine having a work environment in which high energy is the norm, innovative solutions flow freely, and empathy and caring serve as the new currency. When you invite others to fully integrate their head, heart, and gut, you have more room to work together to maneuver, find creative solutions, and innovate. Instead of a competitive culture, you create a world in which cooperation and co-creation prevail and everyone wins. As Steve Jobs, co-founder of Apple, said in his "You've Got to Find What You Love" commencement speech at Stanford University in 2005: "You can't connect the dots looking forward; you can only connect them looking backward. So, you must trust that the dots will somehow connect in your future. You must trust in something—your gut, destiny, life, karma, whatever. This approach has never let me down, and it has made all the difference in my life."

Appendix

EMOTIONAL STATE WORDS

We can inspire and activate others into action with our words. The next time you are crafting key messages, think about how you want people to feel and then choose words in the list below to help write a sentence. Feel free to use as many words as you believe will enhance your message and integrate the head, heart, and gut.

Emotional Word States			
Curiosity	**Urgency**	**Confusion and Helplessness**	**Safe and Satisfied**
· Secret · Controversial · What no one tells you · Have you heard · Behind the Scenes · Off the record · No one talks about · Unbelievable	· Missing out · Left behind · Magnificent · Remarkable · Startling · Superior · Worthwhile · Immediately · Imminently	· Uncertain · Indecisive · Perplexed · Hesitant · Disillusioned · Uncomfortable · Disoriented · Awkward · Overwhelmed	· Advantage · A cut above · Confident · Delighted · Ecstatic · First ever · Fulfilled · Genuine · Reliable
Happy and Alive	**Inspired**	**Relaxed**	**Peaceful**
· Joyous · Blissful · Delighted · Overjoyed · Gleeful · Thankful · Ecstatic · Satisfied · Cheerful · Optimistic	· Eager · Focused · Keen · Enthusiastic · Bold · Courageous · Upbeat · Clear · Grateful · Uplifted	· Calm · At ease · Relaxed · Balanced · Unburdened · Self-sufficient · Reflective · Grounded · Unhurried · Open-minded	· Content · Appreciative · Serene · Blessed · Glowing · Beaming · Supported · Aware · Still · Graceful

Needs Inventory

The following list of needs is neither exhaustive nor definitive. It is meant as a starting place to support anyone who wishes to engage in a process of deepening self-discovery and to facilitate greater understanding and connection between people.

CONNECTION
acceptance
affection
appreciation
belonging
cooperation
communication
closeness
community
companionship
compassion
consideration
consistency
empathy
inclusion
intimacy
love
mutuality
nurturing
respect/self-respect
safety
security
stability
support
to know and be known
to see and be seen
to understand and be
understood
trust
warmth

PHYSICAL WELL-BEING
air
food
movement/exercise
rest/sleep
sexual expression
safety
shelter
touch
water

HONESTY
authenticity
integrity
presence

PLAY
joy
humor

PEACE
beauty
communion
ease
equality
harmony
inspiration
order

AUTONOMY
choice
freedom
independence
space
spontaneity

MEANING
awareness
celebration of life
challenge
clarify
competence
consciousness
contribution
creativity
discovery
efficacy
effectiveness
growth
hope
learning
mourning
participation
purpose
self-expression
stimulation
to matter
understanding

Feelings Inventory

The following are words we use when we want to express a combination of emotional states and physical sensations. This list is neither exhaustive nor definitive. It is meant as a starting place to support anyone who wishes to engage in a process of deepening self-discovery and to facilitate greater understanding and connection between people.

There are two parts to this list: feelings we may have when our needs are being met and feelings we may have when our needs are not being met.

FEELINGS WHEN YOUR NEEDS ARE SATISIFIED

AFFECTIONATE
compassionate
friendly
loving
open-hearted
sympathetic
tender
warm

ENGAGED
absorbed
alert
curious
engrossed
enchanted
entranced
fascinated
interested
intrigued
involved
spellbound
stimulated

HOPEFUL
expectant
encouraged
optimistic

CONFIDENT
empowered
open
proud
safe
secure

EXCITED
amazed
animated
ardent
aroused
astonished
dazzled
eager
energetic
enthusiastic
giddy
invigorated
lively
passionate
surprised
vibrant

GRATEFUL
appreciative
moved
thankful
touched

INSPIRED
amazed
awed
wonder

JOYFUL
amused
delighted
glad
happy
jubilant
pleased
tickled

EXHILARATED
blissful
ecstatic
elated
enthralled
exuberant
radiant
rapturous
thrilled

PEACEFUL
calm
clear-headed
comfortable
centered
content
equanimous
fulfilled
mellow
quiet
relaxed
relieved
satisfied
serene
still
tranquil
trusting

REFRESHED
enlivened
rejuvenated
renewed
rested
restored
revived

(Feelings Inventory continued on next page)

FEELINGS WHEN YOUR NEEDS ARE NOT SATISIFIED

AFRAID
apprehensive
dread
foreboding
frightened
mistrustful
panicked
petrified
scared
suspicious
terrified
wary
worried

ANNOYED
aggravated
dismayed
disgruntled
displeased
exasperated
frustrated
impatient
irritated
irked

ANGRY
enraged
furious
incensed
indignant
irate
livid
outraged
resentful

AVERSION
animosity
appalled
contempt
disgusted
dislike
hate
horrified
hostile
repulsed

CONFUSED
ambivalent
baffled
bewildered
dazed
hesitant
lost
mystified
perplexed
puzzled
torn

DISCONNECTED
alienated
aloof
apathetic
bored
cold
detached
distant
distracted
indifferent
numb
removed
uninterested
withdrawn

DISQUIET
agitated
alarmed
discombobulated
disconcerted
disturbed
perturbed
rattled
restless
shocked
startled
surprised
troubled
turbulent
turmoil
uncomfortable
uneasy
unnerved
unsettled
upset

EMBARRASSED
ashamed
chagrined
flustered
guilty
mortified
self-conscious

FATIGUE
beat
burnt out
depleted
exhausted
lethargic
listless
sleepy
tired
weary
worn out

PAIN
agony
anguished
bereaved
devastated
grief
heartbroken
hurt
lonely
miserable
regretful
remorseful

SAD
depressed
dejected
despair
despondent
disappointed
discouraged
disheartened
forlorn
gloomy
heavy-hearted
hopeless
melancholy
unhappy
wretched

TENSE
anxious
cranky
distressed
distraught
edgy
fidgety
frazzled
irritable
jittery
nervous
overwhelmed
restless
stressed out

VULNERABLE
fragile
guarded
helpless
insecure
leery
reserved
sensitive
shaky

YEARNING
envious
jealous
longing
nostalgic
pining
wistful

SOURCES

Introduction

Sabine Heim and Andreas Keil. "Too Much Information, Too Little Time: How the Brain Separates Important from Unimportant Things in Our Fast-Paced Media World." *Frontiers,* June 1, 2017.

Tim Porter-O'Grady and Kathy Malloch. *Quantum Leadership: Creating Sustainable Value in Health Care,* fifth edition, Jones & Bartlett Learning, 2017.

Mercer. "Win with Empathy: Global Talent Trends 2020 Report." https://mercer.com/content/dam/mercer/attachments/private/global-talent-trends-2020-report.pdf

Gartner. "Leadership Vision for 2023: Talent Manager Leaders." https://www.gartner.com/en/human-resources/trends/leadership-vision-talent-management

re:Work. "Guide: Understand Team Effectiveness." https://rework.withgoogle.com/print/guides/5721312655835136/

Harvard Business Review (HBR) IdeaCast (podcast). "Work Insights from the World's Longest Happiness Study," January 10, 2023.

https://hbr.org/podcast/2023/01/work-insights-from-the-worlds-longest-happiness-study

Prasarn Sripongplerd and Rungson Chomya. "A Confirmatory Factor Analysis of Moral Courage of Undergraduate Students in Higher Education Institutions in Northeastern Region, Thailand." *Ilkogretim Online—Elementary Education Online,* 20(5), 4419–4426, n.d.

Chapter One

Asım Şen, Kamil Erkan Kabak, and Gözde Yangınlar. "Courageous Leadership for the Twenty-first Century," *Procedia – Social and Behavioral Sciences,* 75, 91–101, April 3, 2013.

Amy C. Edmondson and Olivia Jung. "The Turnaround at Ford Motor Company." Harvard Business School Case 621-101, April 2021 (revised July 2023).

A.J. Hess. "These Are Workers' Biggest Fears About 2023." *Fast Company,* December 14, 2022.

Christian Voegtlin. "What Does It Mean to Be Responsible? Addressing the Missing Responsibility Dimension in Ethical Leadership Research." *Leadership,* 12(5), 581–608, July 31, 2016. https://doi.org/10.1177/1742715015578936

Sean T. Hannah, Bruce J. Avolio, and Fred O. Walumbwa. "Relationships between Authentic Leadership, Moral Courage, and Ethical and Pro-Social Behaviors." *Business Ethics Quarterly,* 21(4) 555–578, October 2011. https://www.jstor.org/stable/41304450

Kyle Swenson. "A Famous French Thinker's Philosophy Was Based on Taking Risks. And That's How She Tragically Died." *The Washington Post,* July 25, 2017.

Eva Chen. "How Overcoming a Childhood Fear Gave Me the Courage to Be a Better Leader at Work." *Fast Company,* April 4, 2023.

Megan Barnett. "IBM's Ginni Rometty: Growth and Comfort Do Not Coexist." *Fortune,* December 5, 2011. https://fortune.com/2011/10/05/ibms-ginni-rometty-growth-and-comfort-do-not-coexist/

Mindset Works. "Decades of Scientific Research That Started a Growth Mindset Revolution." https://www.mindsetworks.com/science/

Second Wind Movement. "How and Why to Develop a Growth Mindset (As an Older Adult)." https://www.secondwindmovement.com

Chapter Two

Andy Greenberg. "How Much Data Fits on a Pin?" *Forbes,* February 19, 2009.

World Population Review. https://worldpopulationreview.com/country-rankings/wheat-production-by-country

"Understanding Unconscious Bias," Short Wave (podcast), NPR, July 15, 2020. https://www.npr.org/2020/07/14/891140598/understanding-unconscious-bias

Amber Murphy. "You Are Not Your Thoughts: What That Means and Why It's True," *Declutter the Mind,* July 16, 2020.

Aksil Rain. "You Are What You Think: Your Thoughts Create Your Reality," Know Thyself, Heal Thyself (blog), November 8, 2021.

"Dr. Bruce Lipton Explains How to Reprogram Your Subconscious Mind." YouTube. https://youtube.com/watch?v=OqLT_CNTNYA

Bruce H. Lipton. "Are You Programmed at Birth?" http://www.healyourlife.com/are-you-programmed-at-birth

Carlos J.F. Candido and Sergio P. Santos. "Strategy Implementation: What Is the Failure Rate?" *Journal of Management & Organization,* 21(2): 237–262, February 2015.

Ali Montag. "Warren Buffett and Mark Cuban Agree This One Habit Is Key to Success—and Anyone Can Do It," CNBC Make It, November 15, 2017.

"Know Your Brain: Ventral Tegmental Area." https://neuroscientificallychallenged.com/posts/know-your-brain-ventral-tegmental-area#:~:text=The%20ventral%20tegmental%20area%2C%20or,the%20VTA%20throughou

Prakhar Verma. "Destroy Negativity from Your Mind with This Simple Exercise." November 27, 2017. https://mission.org

Remez Sasson. "How Many Thoughts Does Your Mind Think in One Hour?" https://www.successconsciousness.com/blog/inner-peace/how-many-thoughts-does-your-mind-think-in-one-hour/#:~:text=Experts%20estimate%20that%20the%20mind,That's%20incredible

Belle Beth Cooper. "Why Getting New Things Makes Us Feel So Good: Novelty and the Brain." May 16, 2013. https://buffer.com/resources/novelty-and-the-brain-how-to-learn-more-and-improve-your-memory/

Center Point Medicine. "How Do You Improve Athletic Performance with Hypnosis?" https://www.centerpointmedicine.com/blog/how-do-you-improve-athletic-performance-with-hypnosis#:~:text=Further%2C%20I%20point%20out%20that,even%20Babe%20Ruth%20(baseball)

Tim Lewis. "A Little Mental Rehearsal Is a Huge Help on Sport's Biggest Stages." *The Guardian,* July 28, 2019. https://www.theguardian.com/sport/blog/2019/jul/28/visualisation-in-sport

Restoric. "What Is Visualization? How Successful Athletes Practice This Proven Technique." November 19, 2020. https://restoic.com/blogs/blog/what-is-visualization-how-successful-access-practice-this-proven-technique#:~:text=Another%20swimmer%2C%20Katie%20Ledecky%2C%20is,me%20achieve%20those%20goals%20...

Daniel Goleman. *Emotional Intelligence: Why It Can Matter More than IQ.* Random House, 2005.

Norman Vincent Peale. *The Power of Positive Thinking.* 1952.

Chris Hedges. "What Every Person Should Know about War." *The New York Times,* July 6, 2003.

Jim Camp. "Decisions Are Largely Emotional, Not Logical." *Big Think,* June 11, 2012.

"Make Your Brain Smarter: It's Not What You Think." Sandra Chapman, Ph.D., at TedxRockCreekPark via YouTube. https://www.youtube.com/watch?v=xh8el8m9mLM

Matt Plummer. "How to Spend Way Less Time on Email Every Day." *Harvard Business Review,* January 22, 2019.

Eckhart Tolle. *A New Earth.* 2006.

Chapter Three

EI Experience. "Top Three Reasons People Don't Show Emotions at Work." https://eiexperience.com/blog/top-three-reasons-people-dont-show-emotions-at-work/

HeartMath Institute. "Energetic Communication." https://www.heartmath.org/research/science-of-the-heart/energetic-communication/

"The Atlas of Emotions with Dr. Paul Ekman and Dr. Eve Ekman." https://www.youtube.com/watch?v=AaDzUFL9CLE

Susan David. "The Gift and Power of Emotional Courage." https://www.youtube.com/watch?v=NDQ1Mi5I4rg&t=14s

Terri Simpkin. "Mixed Feelings: How to Deal with Emotions at Work." https://www.totaljobs.com/advice/emotions-at-work

Ten Percent Happier. "Brené Brown Says You're Doing Feelings Wrong." https://www.tenpercent.com/podcast-episode/brene-brown-436

TED. "The Power of Vulnerability." https://www.youtube.com/watch?v=iCvmsMzlF7o&t=13s

Jocelyn Strange. "Emotions in the Workplace: How to Deal with Emotions at Work." Quantum Workplace, January 21, 2021. https://www.quantumwork-place.com/future-of-work/emotions-in-the-workplace-how-to-deal-with-emotions-at-work

Ideo U. "The Secret Power of Embracing Emotions at Work." https://www.ideou.com/blogs/inspiration/the-secret-power-of-embracing-emotions-at-work

World Economic Forum. "Why Is It Important for Employees to Share Their Emotions at Work?" September 21, 2021. https://www.weforum.org/agenda/2021/09/why-is-it-important-for-employees-to-share-their-emotions-at-work/

Je-Yeon Yun, Geumsook Shim, and Bumseok Jeong. "Verbal Abuse Related to Self-Esteem Damage and Unjust Blame Harms Mental Health and Social Interaction in College Population." *Scientific Reports*, 9, 5655, 2019. https://doi.org/10.1038/s41598-019-42199-6

Christine Liebrecht, Lettica Hustinx, and Margot Van Mulken. "The Relative Power of Negativity: The Influence of Language Intensity on Perceived Strength," 38(2), January 10, 2019, https://doi.org/10.1177/0261927X188085

Johns Hopkins Medicine. "The Brain-Gut Connection." https://www.hopkinsmedicine.org/health/wellness-and-prevention/the-brain-gut-connection

Chapter Four

HeartMath Institute. https://www.heartmath.org/research/science-of-the-heart/intuition-research/

Jeremy Sutton. "What Is Intuition and Why Is It Important? 5 Examples," *Positive Psychology*, August 27, 2020. https://positivepsychology.com/intuition/

Albert Einstein. *On Cosmic Religion and Other Opinions and Aphorisms.*

Eamon McNiff and Harry Phill. "Disaster Predications: People Claim Premonitions of Sept. 11 Attacks, Japanese Tsunami," *ABC News,* October 24, 2012. https://abcnews.go.com/US/sept-11-terrorist-attacks-japanese-tsunami-people-claim/story?id=17553825

Gerard P. Hodgkinson, Eugene Sadler-Smith, Lisa A. Burke, Guy Claxton, and Paul R. Sparrow. "Intuition in Organizations: Implications for Strategic Management." *Long Range Planning*, 42(3), 277–297, June 2009. https://www.sciencedirect.com/science/article/abs/pii/S0024630109000405

Sophia Jacober. "Entanglement Between the Human and Nonhuman." Social Bodies While Distanced, May 14, 2020. https://sites.coloradocollege.edu/social-bodies-distanced/2020/05/14/entanglement-between-the-human-and-nonhuman-during-covid-19/

Gerard P. Hodgkinson, Janice Langan-Fox, and Eugene Sadler-Smith. "Intuition: A Fundamental Bridging Construct in the Behavioural Sciences." *British Journal of Psychology*, December 24, 2010.

David Dellanave. "Intuition: Your Superpower." https://www.dellanave.com/intuition-your-superpower/

A. Bechara, H. Damasio, D. Tranel, and A.R. Damasio. "Deciding Advantageously Before Knowing the Advantageous Strategy." *Science*, 275(5304), 1293–1295, February 28, 1997.

Jeremy Sutton. "What Is Intuition and Why Is It Important? 5 Examples." *Positive Psychology*, August 27, 2020. https://positivepsychology.com/intuition/

R. Brian Tracz. "Imagination and the Distinction between Image and Intuition in Kant." Ergo, 6(38), 2019–2020. https://doi.org/10.3998/ergo.12405314.0006.038

Bonnie Marcus. "Intuition Is an Essential Leadership Tool." Forbes, September 1, 2015. https://www.forbes.com/sites/bonniemarcus/2015/09/01/intuiton-is-an-essential-leadership-tool/?sh=2fbd5d5a1c18

Jamais Cascio. "Facing the Age of Chaos." *Medium,* April 29, 2020. https://medium.com/@cascio/facing-the-age-of-chaos-b00687b1f51d

Alexandra Jones. "The Neuroscience of Intuition and Why It's Time to Hack Yours…" *Stack World,* March 3, 2021. https://thestack.world/news/wellness/self/the-neuroscience-of-intuition-and-why-it-s-time-to-hack-yours-1615539839323

Modesto A. Maidique. "Decoding Intuition for More Effective Decision-Making." *Harvard Business Review,* August 15, 2011.

David Robson. "Intuition: When Is It Right to Trust Your Gut Instincts?" *BBC,* April 4, 2022. https://www.bbc.com/worklife/article/20220401-intuition-when-is-it-right-to-trust-your-gut-instincts

"Steven Spielberg Speech: Follow Your Intuition." Harvard, 2016. https://www.englishspeecheschannel.com/english-speeches/steven-spielberg-speech/

"Tesla on Inspiration." *Big Think,* April 28, 2014. https://bigthink.com/words-of-wisdom/tesla-on-inspiration/#:~:text=%E2%80%9CMy%20brain%20is%20only%20a,I%20know%20that%20it%20exists.%E2%80%9D

Chapter Five

Starhawk. *Truth or Dare: Encounters with Power, Authority, and Mystery.* HarperOne, 1989.

Graeme Stuart. "4 Types of Power: What Are Power Over; Power With: Power to and Power Within?" *Sustaining Community,* February 1, 2019. https://sustainingcommunity.wordpress.com/2019/02/01/4-types-of-power/

Nick Craig and Scott A. Snook. "From Purpose to Impact." *Harvard Business Review,* May 2014. https://hbr.org/2014/05/from-purpose-to-impact

Patsy Rodenburg. "The Second Circle." https://www.youtube.com/watch?v=Ub27yeXKUTY

Patsy Rodenberg. *Presence: How to Use Positive Energy for Success in Every Situation.* Penguin, 2009.

Chapter Six

David Hamilton. "Does Your Brain Distinguish Real from Imaginary?" October 30, 2014.

https://drdavidhamilton.com/does-your-brain-distinguish-real-from-imaginary/

Jeff Kauflin. "Only 15% of People Are Self-Aware—Here's How to Change." *Forbes,* May 10, 2017.

https://www.forbes.com/sites/jeffkauflin/2017/05/10/only-15-of-people-are-self-aware-heres-how-to-change/?sh=48dda9b52b8c

Tasha Eurich. "3 Strategies for Becoming More Self-Aware." https://www.youtube.com/watch?v=uyQIx2p7Qe8

Naina Dhingra and Bill Schaninger. "The Search for Purpose at Work." McKinsey & Company, June 3, 2021. https://www.mckinsey.com/capabilities/people-and-organizational-performance/our-insights/the-search-for-purpose-at-work

Marisa Peer. "To Reach Beyond Your Limits by Training Your Mind." TEDx Talk. https://www.youtube.com/watch?v=zCv-ZBy6_yU

Peter Pruyn. "An Overview of Constructive Development Theory (CDT)." *Medium,* June 8, 2010. https://peterpruyn.medium.com/an-overview-of-constructive-developmental-theory-cdt-667f3e015cc1#:~:text=Kegan's%20theory%20describes%20five%20developmental,to%20and%20making%20it%20object

Chapter Seven

"Kegan's Levels (or Constructive Development Theory)." https://azatris.github.io/levels

Tony Daloisio. "Understanding the 5 Stages of Adult Development." *Psychology Today,* September 30, 2022. https://www.psychologytoday.com/us/blog/the-journey-your-life/202209/understanding-the-5-stages-adult-development

Bhagavan Sri Ramana Maharshi. *Who Am I? (Nan Yar?)* https://www.sriramanamaharshi.org/wp-content/uploads/2012/12/who_am_I.pdf

Cornelius Chang and Robin Groeneveld. "Slowing Down to Speed Up." McKinsey & Company, March 23, 2018. https://www.mckinsey.com/capabilities/people-and-organizational-performance/our-insights/the-organization-blog/slowing-down-to-speed-up

Viktor E. Frankl. *Man's Search for Meaning*. Beacon Press, 2006.

Joaquin Selva. "What Is Self-Actualization? Meaning, Theory + Examples." *PositivePsychology.com*, May 5, 2017. https://positivepsychology.com/self-actualization/#:~:text=Although%20self%2Dactualization%20is%20most,first%20coined%20by%20Kurt%20Goldstein.

Crystal Raypole. "A (Realistic) Guide to Becoming Self-Actualized." *Healthline*. https://www.healthline.com/health/self-actualization#definition

"Burnout: Emily Nagoski Reveals the Secret to a Happier Life." *Flo,* October 27, 2020. https://flo.health/health-articles/mental-health/stress-and-anxiety/burnout-emily-nagoski

Serdar Aydin, Hasan Huseyin Ceylan, and Erhan Aydin. "A Research on Reference Behavior Trend According to Horney's Personality Types." *Procedia–Social and Behavioral Sciences,* 148, 680–685, August 25, 2014.

Kendra Cherry. "Horney's Theory of Neurotic Needs." VeryWellMind.com, March 15, 2023. https://www.verywellmind.com/horneys-list-of-neurotic-needs-2795949

Hogan Assessment Systems. https://cdn2.hubspot.net/hubfs/153377/Research/Derailers%20and%20Leadership%20Level%20QA_Final.pdf

Chapter Eight

"How Often Do You Feel Lonely?" Statistica, 2021. https://www.statista.com/statistics/1222815/loneliness-among-adults-by-country/

Shonna Waters. "Here's How to Build a Sense of Belonging in the Workplace." *BetterUp*, May 11, 2021. https://www.betterup.com/blog/belonging

Jill Suttie. "How Loneliness Hurts Us and What to Do about It." *Greater Good,* May 14, 2020. https://greatergood.berkeley.edu/article/item/how_loneliness_hurts_us_and_what_to_do_about_it

Brené Brown on Empathy (video). https://www.youtube.com/watch?v=1Evwgu369Jw

Ashley Abramson. "Cultivating Empathy." *Monitor on Psychology*, 52(8), November 1, 2021. https://www.apa.org/monitor/2021/11/feature-cultivating-empathy

Ann C. Rumble, Paul A. M. Van Lange, and Craig D. Parks. "The Benefits of Empathy: When Empathy May Sustain Cooperation in Social Dilemmas." *European Journal of Social Psychology,* June 23, 2009. https://doi.org/10.1002/ejsp.659

Tina Dou. "What Is Empathy? Learn About 3 Types of Empathy." *Acuity Insights,* June 24, 2020. https://acuityinsights.app/2020/06/empathy-1/#:~:text=Renowned%20psychologists%20Daniel%20Goleman%20and,%3A%20Cognitive%2C%20Emotional%20and%20Compassionate

"Book Recommendation: Dare to Lead by Brené Brown." Living As a Leader. https://www.livingasaleader.com/Resources/Book-Recommendations/book-recommendations-dare-to-lead.htm#:~:text=Vulnerability%20is%20de-fined%20in%20the,uncertainty%2C%20risk%20and%20emotional%20exposure

"21 Collaboration Statistics That Show the Power of Teamwork!" BitAIBlog. https://blog.bit.ai/collaboration-statistics/

Chapter Nine

Heather M. Caruso and Anita Williams Woolley. "Harnessing the Power of Emergent Interdependence to Promote Diverse Team Collaboration." Emerald Insight. https://www.emerald.com/insight/content/doi/10.1016/S1534-0856(08)11011-8/full/html

Marjan Laal. "Positive Interdependence in Collaborative Learning." *Procedia—Social and Behavioral Sciences,* 93, 1433–1437, October 21, 2013.

Diane Chaleff. "4 Ways Collaboration Has Fundamentally Changed." *Forbes,* May 18, 2021.

https://www.forbes.com/sites/googlecloud/2021/05/18/4-ways-collaboration-has-fundamentally-changed/?sh=66a9191c76b6\

Adi Gaskell. "New Study Finds That Collaboration Drives Workplace Performance." *Forbes,* June 22, 2017.

https://www.forbes.com/sites/adigaskell/2017/06/22/new-study-finds-that-collaboration-drives-workplace-performance/?sh=5292aca83d02

David Lynch. "7 Benefits of Co-Creation." ImageThink, August 10, 2022.

https://www.imagethink.net/7-benefits-of-co-creation/

Patagonia. "Why Patagonia Is a Most Loved Workplace." https://mostloved workplace.com/companies/patagonia/

David Gelles. "Billionaire No More: Patagonia Founder Gives Away the Company." *New York Times,* September 14, 2022.

https://www.nytimes.com/2022/09/14/climate/patagonia-climate-philanthropy-chouinard.html#:~:text=Rather%20than%20selling%20the%20company,trust%20and%20a%20nonprofit%20organization

Jim Harter. "Percent Who Feel Employer Cares about Their Wellbeing Plummets." Gallup, March 18, 2022. https://www.gallup.com/workplace/390776/percent-feel-employer-cares-wellbeing-plummets.aspx

"Margaret Heffernan: Collaboration and Competition." The Knowledge Project podcast, episode 30. https://fs.blog/knowledge-project-podcast/ margaret-heffernan/

Erik Samdahl. "Top Employers Are 5.5x More Likely to Reward Collaboration." i4cp blog, June 22, 2017. https://www.i4cp.com/productivity-blog/top-employers-are-5-5x-more-likely-to-reward-collaboration

Rob Cross, Reb Rebele, and Adam Grant. "Collaboration Overload." *Harvard Business Review,* January–February 2016. https://hbr.org/2016/01/collaborative-overload

Margaret Heffernan "Super Chickens" (video). https://www.youtube.com/watch?v=baHr-8kTbws

"16 Stories of Intrapreneurship and Employee Ideas in Action." Sideways6. com. https://ideas.sideways6.com/article/inspiring-examples-of-intrapreneurship-and-employee-ideas-in-action

"Linda Hill: Innovation Is Not About Solo Genius" (video). https://www.youtube.com/watch?v=HMZcKa7Pul4

Chapter Ten

Laura Sherbin and Ripa Rashid. "Diversity Doesn't Stick Without Inclusion." *Harvard Business Review,* February 1, 2017. https://www.vernamyers.com/2017/02/04/diversity-doesnt-stick-without-inclusion/

McKinsey & Company. "Diversity Wins: How Inclusion Matters." May 29, 2020. https://www.mckinsey.com/featured-insights/diversity-and-inclusion/diversity-wins-how-inclusion-matters

Alison Reynolds and David Lewis. "Teams Solve Problems Faster When They're More Cognitively Diverse." *Harvard Business Review,* March 30, 2017. https://hbr.org/2017/03/teams-solve-problems-faster-when-theyre-more-cognitively-diverse

"Diversity Drives Better Decisions." PeopleManagement.co.UK. https://www.peoplemanagement.co.uk/article/1742040/diversity-drives-better-decisions

Scott E. Page. *The Diversity Bonus: How Great Teams Pay Off in the Knowledge Economy.* Princeton University Press, 2019.

Deloitte. "Waiter, Is That Inclusion in My Soup? A New Recipe to Improve Business Performance." Research report, May 2013. https://www2.deloitte.com/content/dam/Deloitte/au/Documents/human-capital/deloitte-au-hc-diversity-inclusion-soup-0513.pdf

Thomas Barta, Markus Kleiner, and Tilo Neumann. "Is There a Payoff from Top-Team Diversity?" McKinsey & Company blog, April 1, 2012. https://www.mckinsey.com/capabilities/people-and-organizational-performance/our-insights/is-there-a-payoff-from-top-team-diversity

CoQual. "The Power of Belonging: What It Is and Why It Matters in Today's Workplace." https://coqual.org/wp-content/uploads/2020/09/CoqualPower OfBelongingKeyFindings090720.pdf

Vernā Myers. "How to Overcome Our Biases? Walk Boldly Toward Them." TEDx Talk. https://www.ted.com/talks/verna_myers_how_to_overcome_our_ biases_walk_boldly_toward_them

Liz Wiseman. *Multipliers: How the Best Leaders Make Everyone Smarter*. Harper Business, 2017.

Center for Creative Leadership. "What Is Psychological Safety at Work? How Leaders Can Build Psychologically Safe Workplaces." https://www.ccl.org/articles/ leading-effectively-articles/what-is-psychological-safety-at-work/#:~:text=Psy-chological%20safety%20is%20the%20belief,taking%20risks%2C%20or%20 soliciting%20feedback.

Amy Edmondson. "Building a Psychologically Safe Workplace." TEDx Talk video. https://www.youtube.com/watch?v=LhoLuui9gX8

Pier Vittorio Mannucci and Christina E. Shalley. "Embracing Multicultural Tensions: How Team Members' Multicultural Paradox Mindsets Foster Team Information Elaboration and Creativity." *Organizational Behavior and Human Decision Processes*, 173(2), October 2022. https://doi.org/10.1016/j.obh-dp.2022.104191

Georgia Tech News Center. "Researchers Find Understanding and Embracing Intercultural Tensions and Differences in Teams Increases Information Elaboration and Creativity." February 2, 2022. https://news.gatech.edu/news/2023/02/02/ researchers-find-understanding-and-embracing-intercultural-tensions-and-differences

Teambuilding.com. "70 Powerful Diversity and Inclusion Quotes for the Workplace." November 30, 2022. https://teambuilding.com/blog/ diversity-and-inclusion-quotes

Chapter Eleven

"Trust." *American Psychological Association Dictionary.* https://dictionary.apa.org/ trust

Kendra Cherry. "Why You May Have Trust Issues and How to Overcome Them." VeryWellMind.com. June 10, 2023. https://www.verywellmind.com/why-you-may-have-trust-issues-and-how-to-overcome-them-5215390

Saul Mcleod. "Erik Erikson's Stages of Psychosocial Development." Simply Psychology, August 2, 2023. https://www.simplypsychology.org/erik-erikson.html

John Bowlby. *A Secure Base*. Basic Books, 1988.

Charles Feltman. *The Thin Book of Trust*. Thin Book Publishing, 2008.

Amy C. Edmondson. "Psychological Safety, Trust, and Learning in Organizations: A Group-Level Lens." October 2011. https://www.researchgate.net/publication/268328210_Psychological_Safety_Trust_and_Learning_in_Organizations_A_Group-level_Lens

Stephen M. R. Covey with Rebecca R. Merrill. *The Speed of Trust*. Free Press, 2008.

"The Psychology of Trust: Anne Raettig." TEDx Talk transcript. November 13, 2018. https://singjupost.com/the-psychology-of-trust-anne-bockler-raettig-full-transcript/

Chapter Twelve

Simon Sinek. "How Great Leaders Inspire Action." TEDx Talk, 2010. https://www.youtube.com/watch?v=qp0HIF3SfI4

Slack. "How Shared Purpose Drives Collaboration." September 12, 2021. https://slack.com/blog/collaboration/shared-purpose-drives-collaboration

Martha Hurwitz. "Prime 6 Charcoal." November 18, 2020. https://allsharktankproducts.com/shark-tank-products-home/prime-6-charcoal/

Sharktank. "What Happened to Prime 6 After the Shark Tank?" April 23, 2023. https://sharktanktalks.com/prime-6-shark-tank-update/

Rajendra Sisodia, David Wolfe, and Jagdish N. Sheth. *Firms of Endearment: How World-Class Companies Profit from Passion and Purpose*, second edition. Pearson FT Press, 2014.

Google. "Our Approach to Search." https://www.google.com/search/howsearchworks/our-approach/#:~:text=Google's%20mission%20is%20to%20organize,it%20universally%20accessible%20and%20useful.

Netflix. "The Story of Netflix." https://about.netflix.com/en

Michael Boyles. "How Do Businesses Create Value for Stakeholders?" Harvard Business School Online, April 26, 2022. https://online.hbs.edu/blog/post/how-do-businesses-create-value

Western Governors University. "How to Develop Your Company's Purpose Statement." August 9, 2021. https://www.wgu.edu/blog/how-develop-company-purpose-statement2108.html#close

Business Wire. "Majority of Consumers Buying from Companies That Take a Stand on Issues They Care about and Ditching Those That Don't, Accenture Study Finds." December 5, 2018. https://www.businesswire.com/news/home/20181205005061/en/Majority-Consumers-Buying-Companies-Stand-Issues-Care

Bruce Stetar. "Business as a Force for Good." Western Governors University, August 14, 2020. https://www.wgu.edu/blog/business-force-for-good2008.html

Sally Blount and Paul Leinwand. "Why Are We Here?" *Harvard Business Review*, November–December 2019. https://hbr.org/2019/11/why-are-we-here

Brené Brown. "Brené with Dr. Linda Hill on Leading with Purpose in the Digital Age." Dare to Lead podcast. April 2022. https://brenebrown.com/podcast/leading-with-purpose-in-the-digital-age/#transcript

Afdhel Aziz. "The Power of Purpose: How Microsoft Unlocked Inclusivity to Drive Growth and Innovation." *Forbes,* April 29, 2019. https://www.forbes.com/sites/afdhelaziz/2019/04/29/the-power-of-purpose-how-microsoft-unlocked-inclusivity-to-drive-growth-and-innovation/?sh=326acd24e800

Edelman. "Trust Barometer Special Report: Brand Trust in 2020." https://www.edelman.com/research/brand-trust-2020

Hubert Joly and Amram Migdal. "Deciding When to Engage on Societal Issues." *Harvard Business Review,* September 12, 2022. https://store.hbr.org/product/deciding-when-to-engage-on-societal-issues/523045?-sku=523045-PDF-ENG

Hubert Joly. "Creating a Meaningful Corporate Purpose." *Harvard Business Review,* October 28, 2021. https://hbr.org/2021/10/creating-a-meaningful-corporate-purpose

Canva. "Empowering the World to Design." https://www.canva.com/about/

Chapter Thirteen

Fred B. Bryant and Jamie A. Cvengros. "Distinguishing Hope and Optimism: Two Sides of A Coin, Or Two Separate Coins?" Journal of Social and Clinical Psychology, 23(2), 273–302, 2004. https://doi.org/10.1521/jscp.23.2.273.31018

Kathryn Cramer. "Change the Way You See Everything: Asset-Based Thinking." (video) https://www.youtube.com/watch?v=9ZzHOkQYeRU&t=2735s

Jessa Pangilinan. "33 Famous Optimism Quotes to Brighten Your 2023." *Happier Human, June 13, 2023.* https://www.happierhuman.com/optimism-quotes/

Maya Shrikant. "The Science of Hope: More Than Wishful Thinking." Arizona State University Knowledge Enterprise, June 14, 2021. https://research.asu.edu/science-hope-more-wishful-thinking#:~:text=%E2%80%9CHopeful%20people%20cannot%20just%20wish,can%20fill%20the%20glass%20full.%E2%80%9D

Harriet Lerner. "Unwanted Thoughts? Snap the Rubber Band." *Psychology Today,* October 20, 2010.

Charles R. Snyder. "Hope Theory: Rainbows in the Mind." *Psychological Inquiry, 13(4), 249–275, 2002.* https://www.jstor.org/stable/1448867

Kelsey Pelzer. "Get Inspired to Make an Impact with These 75 Famous Nelson Mandela Quotes." *Parade,* July 18, 2023. https://parade.com/1074913/kelsey-pelzer/nelson-mandela-quotes/

Martha R. Helland and Bruce Winston. "Towards a Deeper Understanding of Hope and Leadership." *Journal of Leadership & Organizational Studies*, 12(2), December 2005. https://doi.org/10.1177/107179190501200204

Chapter Fourteen

John Holcombe. "The Science Behind Insight. And Why It Matters." LinkedIn Insights, May 27, 2016. https://www.linkedin.com/pulse/science-behind-insight-why-matters-john-holcombe/

John Kounios and Mark Beeman. "The Cognitive Neuroscience of Insight." *Annual Review of Psychology*, 65(1), 71–93. https://doi.org/10.1146/annurev-psych-010213-115154

WebMD. "What to Know about Gamma Brain Waves." May 25, 2021. https://www.webmd.com/brain/what-to-know-about-gamma-brain-waves

Philip Morris International. "Our Smoke-Free Products." https://www.pmi.com/smoke-free-products

Omerisms. "Bring a Brick, Not a Cathedral." August 27, 2021. https://www.omer-isms.com/blog/2021/8/27/bring-a-brick-not-a-cathedral

NDTV. "Ex Google Engineer Claims Immortality Is Attainable by 2030 With Help Of…" April 3, 2023. https://www.ndtv.com/feature/ex-google-engineer-predicts-nanobots-will-make-humans-immortal-by-2030-3914511

Lynda Gratton. "The Spark of Innovation." *HR Magazine*, June 9, 2009. https://www.hrmagazine.co.uk/content/features/the-spark-of-innovation/

Georgina Guthrie. "95% of New Products Fail—Here's How to Succeed." Nulab, March 21, 2021. https://nulab.com/learn/project-management/95-new-products-fail-heres-succeed/#:~:text=And%20if%20you're%20a,year%2C%20and%2095%25%20fail.

Shay Namdarian. "6 Companies That Have Successfully Applied Design Thinking." Collective Campus. https://www.collectivecampus.io/blog/6-companies-that-have-successfully-applied-design-thinking

This Is Design Thinking. "Changing Experiences Through Empathy—The Adventure Series." GE Healthcare. https://thisisdesignthinking.net/2014/12/changing-experiences-through-empathy-ge-healthcares-adventure-series/

Uncommon Content (blog). "How Many Times Did Edison Fail in Attempting to Invent the Lightbulb?" May 13, 2015. http://uncommoncontent.blogspot.com/2015/05/how-many-times-did-edison-fail-in.html

Kristen Harris. "16 Actors Who Read Their Scripts and Then Said, 'I Have a Better Idea.'" November 8, 2021. https://www.buzzfeed.com/kristenharris1/actors-demanded-character-changes

Charles A. O'Reilly III and Michael L. Tushman. "The Ambidextrous Organization." *Harvard Business Review,* April 2004. https://hbr.org/2004/04/the-ambidextrous-organization

Michael Grothaus. "4 Famous Failures that Became Massive Successes." *Fast Company*, August 20, 2018. https://www.fastcompany.com/90217870/4-famous-failures-that-became-massive-successes

Frank McDade. "5 Improv Comedy Quotes That Also Apply to Business." Googly Moogly Play at Work. https://www.googlymoogly.com/applied-improvisation/5-improv-comedy-quotes-that-also-apply-to-business/#:~:text="Bring%20a%20Brick%2C%20Not%20a%20Cathedral"&text=If%20you%20try%20and%20bring,of%20an%20idea%2C%20a%20brick

World Leader Summit. "You Are the Artist of Your Life." https://worldleadersummit.com/you-are-the-artist-of-your-life/

MPowered Project. "10 Activities to Boost Your Imagination." January 12, 2021. https://www.m-powered.eu/10-simple-activities-to-boost-your-imagination/

Chapter Fifteen

Jenna Krajeski. "This Is Water." *The New Yorker*, September 19, 2008. https://www.newyorker.com/books/page-turner/this-is-water

McKinsey & Company. "Help Your Employees Find Purpose—Or Watch Them Leave." April 5, 2021. https://www.mckinsey.com/capabilities/people-and-organizational-performance/our-insights/help-your-employees-find-purpose-or-watch-them-leave

Ron Carucci. "Why Success Doesn't Lead to Satisfaction." *Harvard Business Review,* January 25, 2023. https://hbr.org/2023/01/why-success-doesnt-lead-to-satisfaction#:~:text=He%20writes%3A, accounts%2C%20it%20brings%20great%20suffering%E2%80%A6

Arthur C. Brooks. "How to Want Less." *The Atlantic, February 8, 2022.* https://www.theatlantic.com/magazine/archive/2022/03/why-we-are-never-satisfied-happiness/621304/

Arthur C. Brooks. "'Success Addicts' Choose Being Special Over Being Happy." *The Atlantic,* July 30, 2020. https://www.theatlantic.com/family/archive/2020/07/why-success-wont-make-you-happy/614731/

Jamais Cascio. "Facing the Age of Chaos." *Medium,* April 29, 2020. https://medium.com/@cascio/facing-the-age-of-chaos-b00687b1f51d

Business Insider. "The Rise and Fall of Bed Bath & Beyond…" May 8, 2023. https://www.businessinsider.com/bed-bath-and-beyond-rise-and-fall-photos-2020-1?r=US&IR=T

Statistica. "Net Sales of Bed Bath & Beyond Worldwide." https://www.statista.com/statistics/1074085/net-sales-of-bed-bath-and-beyond-worldwide/

Matthew Boyle and Bloomberg. "The Global White-Collar Burnout Picture: Americans Are Less Burned Out at Work but Pencil Pushers Abroad Are More Miserable." *Fortune,* February 15, 2023. https://fortune.com/2023/02/15/worker-burnout-high-return-to-office-mandates-layoff-economy-fears/#

Tripartite Alliance for Fair & Progressive Employment Practices. "IBM's Winning Formula: A Flexible Working Culture." June 26, 2019. https://www.tal.sg/tafep/resources/case-studies/2019/ibm#

Tony Schartz and Catherine McCarthy. "Manage Your Energy, Not Your Time." *Harvard Business Review,* October 2007. https://hbr.org/2007/10/manage-your-energy-not-your-time

Brett Steenbarger. "Cultivating the Essential Ingredient in Leadership: Energy." *Forbes,* January 21, 2018. https://www.forbes.com/sites/brettsteenbarger/2018/01/21/cultivating-the-essential-ingredient-in-leadership-energy/?sh=1c9fde4bde1e

Kevin Dickinson. "The Yerkes-Dodson Law: This Graph Will Change Your Relationship with Stress." *Big Think,* September 8, 2022. https://bigthink.com/the-learning-curve/eustress/

Bruce Daisley. "Laughter Is the Sign of a Strong Team—and a Trustworthy Leader." *Business Insider,* February 25, 2020. https://www.businessinsider.com/former-twitter-vp-laughter-sign-strong-team-trustworthy-leader-2020-2?r=US&IR=T

Conclusion

"Diamond Approach: Glossary of Spiritual Wisdom." https://www.diamondapproach.org/glossary/refinery_phrases/struggle

Steve Jobs. "You've Got to Find What You Love." Commencement speech at Stamford University, June 12, 2005. https://www.youtube.com/watch?v=k8rHbV5s8Jk

FURTHER READINGS

Allen, David. *Getting Things Done*. Penguin, 2015.

Bolman, Lee G., and Terrence E. Deal. *Leading with Soul*. Jossey-Bass, 2001.

Bowlby, John. *A Secure Base*. Basic Books, 1988.

Brown, Brené. *Atlas of the Heart*. Random House, 2021.

Brown, Brené. *Dare to Lead*. Random House, 2018.

Brown, Brené. *Daring Greatly*. Random House, 2015.

Chapman, Sara Bond, with Shelly Kirkland. *Make Your Brain Smarter*. Simon & Schuster, 2014.

Christensen, Clayton M. *The Innovator's Dilemma*. Harvard Business Review Press, 2016.

Christensen, Clayton M. *The Innovator's Prescription*. McGraw-Hill, 2016.

Christensen, Clayton M. *The Innovator's Solution*. Harvard Business Review Press, 2013.

Cleese, John. *Creativity*. Crown, 2020.

Cohen, Alan. *Dare to Be Yourself: How to Quit Being an Extra in Other People's Movies and Become the Star of Your Own*. Random House, 1994.

Coelho, Paolo. *The Alchemist*. HarperOne, 2014.

Covey, Stephen M.R., with Rebecca R. Merrill. *The Speed of Trust*. Free Press, 2008.

Cramer, Kathryn D., and Hank Wasiak. *Change the Way You See Everything through Asset-Based Thinking*. Running Press, 2006.

Dweck, Carol S. *Mindset: The New Psychology of Success*. Random House, 2007.

Dyer, Wayne. *Change Your Thoughts, Change Your Life*. Hay House, 2007.

Dyer, Wayne. *The Power of Intention*. Hay House, 2005.

Edmonson, Amy C. *The Fearless Organization*. Wiley, 2018.

Eurich, Tasha. *Insight*. Currency, 2018.

Epstein, Seymour. *Cognitive-Experiential Theory*. Oxford University Press, 2015.

Feltman, Charles. *The Thin Book of Trust*. Thin Book Publishing, 2008.

Frankl, Viktor E. *Man's Search for Meaning*. Beacon Press, 2006.

Gawain, Shakti. *Creative Visualization*. New World Library, 2016.

Gladwell, Malcolm. *Blink.* Back Bay Books, 2007.

Goleman, Daniel. *Emotional Intelligence.* Random House, 2005.

Gratton, Lynda. *Glow.* Berrett-Koehler Publishers, 2009.

Heffernan, Margaret. *Beyond Measure.* Simon & Schuster/TED, 2015.

Heffernan, Margaret. *Willful Blindness.* Bloomsbury USA, 2012.

Hicks, Esther, and Jerry Hicks. *Ask and It Is Given.* Hay House, 2004.

Hill, Linda. *Collective Genius.* Harvard Business Review Press, 2014.

Hill, Linda, and Kent Lineback. *Being the Boss.* Harvard Business Review Press, 2019.

Horney, Karen. *Neurosis and Human Growth.* W.W. Norton & Company, 1991.

Huber, Cheri. *There Is Nothing Wrong with You.* Keep It Simple Books, 2001.

Kabat-Zinn, Jon. *Meditation for Pain Relief.* Sounds True, 2023.

Kabat-Zinn, Jon. *Mindfulness for Beginners.* Sounds True, 2016.

Kabat-Zinn, Jon. *Wherever You Go, There You Are.* Hachette, 2005.

Kahneman, Daniel. *Thinking, Fast and Slow.* Farrar, Straus and Giroux, 2013.

Kant, Immanuel. *The Critique of Pure Reason.* Cambridge University Press, 1999.

Katie, Byron, with Stephen Mitchell. *Loving What Is.* Rider, 2022.

Kegan, Robert. *Immunity to Change.* Harvard Business Review Press, 2009.

Knight, Phil. *Shoe Dog.* Simon & Schuster, 2018.

Lama, Dalai. *The Art of Happiness.* Riverhead Books, 2020.

Lama, Dalai. *The Book of Joy.* Avery, 2016.

Maslow, Abraham H. *Toward a Psychology of Being.* Sublime Books, 2014.

Murthy, Dr. Vivek. *Together: The Healing Power of Human Connection in a Sometimes Lonely World.* Harper Wave, 2023.

Myers, Vernā. *Moving Diversity Forward.* American Bar Association, 2012.

Nagoski, Emily, and Amelia Nagoski. *Burnout: The Secret to Unlocking the Stress Cycle.* Random House, 2020.

Page, Scott E. *The Diversity Bonus: How Great Teams Pay Off in the Knowledge Economy.* Princeton University Press, 2019.

Peale, Norman Vincent. *The Power of Positive Thinking.* Touchstone, 2003.

Peck, MD, M. Scott. *The Road Less Traveled.* Touchstone, 2003.

Porter O'Grady, Tim, and Kathy Malloch. *Quantum Leadership: Creating Sustainable Value in Health Care 5th Edition.* Jones & Bartlett Learning, 2017.

Rodenberg, Patsy. *Presence: How to Use Positive Energy for Success in Every Situation.* Penguin, 2009.

Rodenberg, Patsy. *The Second Circle.* W.W. Norton & Company, 2017.

Roth, Gabrielle. *Maps to Ecstasy.* New World Library, 1998.

Ruiz, Don Miguel. *The Four Agreements.* Amber-Allen, 1997.

Rosenberg, Marshall. *Nonviolent Communication, third edition.* Puddledancer Press, 2015.

Sinek, Simon. *Find Your Why.* Portfolio, 2017

Sinek, Simon. *Leaders Eat Last.* Portfolio, 2017.

Sinek, Simon. *Start with Why.* Portfolio, 2011.

Sisodia, Raj, David Wolfe, and Jagdish Sheth. *Firms of Endearment, second edition.* Pearson FT Press, 2014.

Starhawk. *Truth or Dare: Encounters with Power, Authority, and Mystery.* HarperOne, 1989.

Tolle, Eckhardt. *The Power of Now.* New World Library, 2004.

Walsh, Neal Donald. *Conversations with God.* Hampton Roads Publishing, 1995.

Williamson, Marianne. *A Return to Love.* HarperOne, 1996.

Williamson, Marianne. *A Year of Miracles.* HarperOne, 2013.

Wiseman, Liz. *Multipliers: How the Best Leaders Make Everyone Smarter.* Harper Business, 2017.

INDEX

LISA DANELS

Lisa Danels, Founder and Executive Director of Human Edge, is a senior executive, talent, and leadership consultant and coach. Lisa focuses on developing mindful and purpose-driven leaders, unlocking their full leadership potential. Lisa holds a master's degree in Organization Development and Human Resource Management from New York University and a bachelor's degree in Interdisciplinary Public Policy and Administration with a concentration in International Relations from the University of New York at Buffalo. She is a certified executive coach and a pioneer in the field of leadership and organizational development. She resides in Basel, Switzerland.

ABOUT HUMAN EDGE

Unlocking human potential to help people and organizations adapt and thrive is core to everything Human Edge believes and does. One by one, Human Edge is creating a movement to fuel transformational change with deeper insights and superior solutions to elevate individuals, teams, and leaders at every level. Thomson Reuters, AstraZeneca, VISA, Novartis, Lonza, Roche, Vorwerk, Allianz, and Takeda are among their many prestigious international clients.

Human Edge's work centers on cultivating greater self-awareness in individuals and leaders to create authentic connection. With a research backbone, global business experience, and a holistic, human-centric view, Human Edge delivers innovative talent and leadership solutions that build robust talent pipelines and leverage analytical solutions with measurable impact. Their assessments reveal meaningful insights that identify the root cause of development challenges and enable better talent decisions. They provide clear action plans to empower success with a goal toward building agile, resilient, high-performing teams and unstoppable organizations.

Human Edge is based in Basel, Switzerland.

Applying The Human Edge Advantage

Human Edge company offers leaders and teams additional products and services to improve leadership effectiveness and drive co-creative innovation.

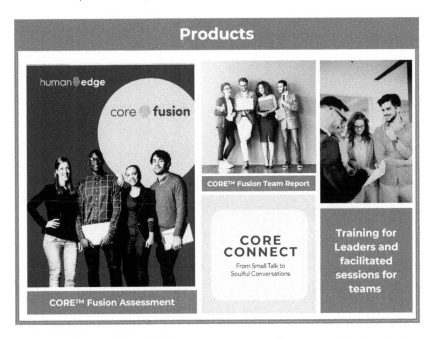

Products

CORE™ Fusion Team Report

CORE™ Fusion Assessment

CORE CONNECT
From Small Talk to Soulful Conversations

Training for Leaders and facilitated sessions for teams

Consulting

human edge

LEADERS

Human Edge provides experiential learning journeys that create self-aware leaders integrated into their heads, hearts, and guts, giving them more capacity to lead. Leaders will go through a personal quest to learn self-mastery and personal agency, learn to better connect to others, and create an inclusive environment where co-creation is possible.

TEAMS

Human Edge provides interactive, practical, and compelling consulting sessions to leaders and their teams. Consultants work with teams across various company sizes and industries, providing concrete tools and concepts that immediately apply to organizations. Ultimately, your team will feel more empowered, connected, engaged, and co-create new possibilities.

For more information, please visit
human-edge.com

Milton Keynes UK
Ingram Content Group UK Ltd.
UKHW042200031123
431935UK00012B/168/J